BUILD YOUR FIRST
WEB APP

Learn to Build Web Applications from Scratch

Deborah Levinson
and Todd Belton

STERLING
New York

STERLING
New York

An Imprint of Sterling Publishing Co., Inc.
1166 Avenue of the Americas
New York, NY 10036

ISBN 978-1-4549-2566-8

Distributed in Canada by Sterling Publishing Co., Inc.
c/o Canadian Manda Group, 664 Annette Street
Toronto, Ontario, Canada M6S 2C8
Distributed in the United Kingdom by GMC Distribution Services
Castle Place, 166 High Street, Lewes, East Sussex, England BN7 1XU
Distributed in Australia by NewSouth Books
45 Beach Street, Coogee, NSW 2034, Australia

For information about custom editions, special sales, and premium and corporate purchases,
please contact Sterling Special Sales at 800-805-5489 or specialsales@sterlingpublishing.com.

Manufactured in Canada

2 4 6 8 10 9 7 5 3 1

sterlingpublishing.com

Interior design by Gavin Motnyk
Icon grid throughout © mikiekwoods/Shutterstock

(CONTENTS)

(INTRODUCTION)

W hen it comes to acquiring new skills, we're big believers in picking things up on our own.

Debby, now a user experience designer, learned HTML in 1995 to code Suffolk University's first website and bootstrapped her way into CSS, bits of Perl, a responsive web framework or two, and enough jQuery® to be dangerous. Todd, a programmer specializing in making disparate systems talk to each other, took a computer science class here and there but eventually realized he'd be better off figuring things out for himself.

There's nothing special about us. We're just people who like to learn.

That's why we wanted to write this book: because there are lots of people out there who are curious about programming but aren't sure whether they're smart enough to do it. *You are.* Learning to program *sounds* complicated because computer code uses so much specialized jargon. But programming languages are just that—languages—and like all languages, they have categorized parts of speech and grammatical rules. And the best part of learning a programming language is that, when you've learned its grammar, you can often apply that knowledge to learn other languages more quickly, much as someone who knows Spanish will find it easier to understand French.

We're not going to teach you to be full-fledged engineers—you're not going to get a job at Google on the strength of your work from this book—but we're going to help you build an actual, functional, responsive web application, and we're going to give you a sense of what the process looks like at a professional level. You'll get to sample all the different stages of modern application design: user research, user experience design, front-end development, and back-end development. By the end of this book, you'll have a better idea of whether web application work—any part of it—is something you want to explore further, either on your own, or with formal training.

But before we begin, let's define some terminology.

WHAT'S A RESPONSIVE WEB APPLICATION?

A *website* is one or more pages written in HTML, usually also including CSS to style type, layout, and page elements consistently. For the purposes of this book, we assume that you already know at least some HTML and CSS, even if you've only ever written them using software with a graphical user interface and never by hand.

If a website is just a set of pages written in HTML and CSS, what makes it responsive? *Responsive* means that the web page's layout and other design elements change depending on screen size and/or the type of device being used to view the page. Responsive design allows coders to use one HTML page to display the right content and features depending on the viewer's situation of use. For example, if you're at home using your laptop to see the #39 bus schedule, you've got a very different situation of use than if you were waiting at the bus stop in the rain. In the first case, you've got plenty of screen real estate, so the website should display a large map and lots of info. In the second case, you've got a much smaller screen, so the map will have to be smaller as well, and information might be overlaid instead of in a sidebar. Responsive design makes those different screen layouts and element sizes possible on a single web page so programmers can minimize their work and so you don't have to search for the public transportation system's mobile-friendly page to get basic information.

So we've covered the *responsive web* part of *responsive web application*. What's the difference between a site and an application?

sched.org is a responsive web app that allows conference attendees to easily build a dynamic schedule of the sessions they'd like to attend. Because Sched's purpose is to be a tool that helps people accomplish a task—locating and flagging conference sessions to attend—we think of it as an *application* instead of just a website.

All web applications are websites, but not all websites are web applications. *Websites* are one or more pages that focus primarily on nonfunctional content, such as text you're there to read or images you're there to look at. A *web application,* on the other hand, is a site whose purpose is primarily functional: the site enables you to perform one or more tasks, and although it will also include text and/or images, its main purpose is to provide interactive tools that let you get something done.

Websites may also incorporate a mix of static content and interactive tools. But in this book, we're going to concentrate on teaching you how to code a standalone responsive web application.

How do you build a responsive web app?

The key to responsive websites and applications is the *media query*[1], a CSS element that allows you to set different behavior for different screen sizes (among other parameters). Let's say that you want your <h1> header to be 24px on laptops and desktops but only 16px on mobile devices. To achieve this, you'd write your initial CSS like this:

```
h1 {
    font-size: 24px;
}
```

Then you'd add a media query to specify the behavior at a small size:

```
@media screen and (max-width: 39.9375em) {
    h1 {
            font-size: 16px;
    }
}
```

You can see from the code example that anything wider than 39.9375 em will use the default <h1> size. By convention, these *breakpoints*—literally, the point at which a layout "breaks," or changes—are usually set up with a "mobile-first" philosophy that specifies how wide a screen can get before the CSS shifts, but if you get deep into development, you may find you need to write many more breakpoints using different approaches. It all depends on the screen sizes and device types you're targeting.

But why write these fussy breakpoints if you don't have to? Shouldn't there be an easier way?

---

[1] One exception to this rule is sites or apps built with the CSS Flexbox standard, which don't absolutely have to use media queries to reflow across screen sizes. However, Flexbox can be used in conjunction with media queries as well. We cover Flexbox a little more in Chapter 5.

There is: you can use what's called a *responsive framework,* a toolkit of HTML, CSS, and JavaScript® code that gives you a standard set of breakpoints as well as set of common responsive design elements, such as menus that collapse on smaller screens or grids of thumbnail images that automatically reflow as pages expand or contract. The responsive web framework we use in this book is Bootstrap (getbootstrap.com), a popular framework powering millions of sites and apps worldwide. There are many other responsive web frameworks out there as well, each with their own strengths and weaknesses—but once you've mastered the concepts in one responsive framework, you can usually apply that same knowledge to pick up the others.

HOW IS A RESPONSIVE WEB APP DIFFERENT FROM A MOBILE APP?

Responsive web applications aren't the same as a mobile app that runs on your phone . . . usually.

Android and iOS each have different capabilities and different methods and rules for accessing phone elements such as the camera, the accelerometer, or GPS coordinates. To take full advantage of these capabilities and elements, you need a *native mobile app*—an app designed and optimized specifically for a mobile device's operating system.

But building a good native app takes time. Not only do you need to determine the app's purpose, features, and flow, you also need to figure out how it should look (partially determined by the operating system's interface guidelines), which operating systems and versions it should run on, and which phone and tablet devices it should support—and then you have to debug on the OS versions and devices you plan to support. You might need to learn a new language to build a native app, and that includes learning how to hook into all those special phone elements. Native apps can provide the smoothest mobile-app experience, but they can be challenging to develop.

Within the past few years, however, web applications and their ability to access parts of the phone have become more powerful. If there were a way to harness that power and still make a web app feel like a native app, you could code, test, and release more quickly.

Hybrid mobile apps are the solution. With these apps, you build a web app in the framework of your choice and then use special software to "wrap" your app in code a phone can understand. Hybrid mobile apps have a reputation for slower performance than native mobile apps, but that hasn't stopped Instagram®, Twitter®, Uber, and other major brands from developing hybrid apps that you probably use every day.

Because this book focuses on getting you started in web app development, we don't cover all the gritty details of hybrid mobile apps (though we discuss them briefly in Chapter 9, page 268). But if you're feeling adventurous, you can use software like Apache Cordova™ to turn your finished code into a hybrid app.[2]

---

[2] For a more in-depth discussion of hybrid mobile apps and their capabilities, we recommend developer John Bristowe's article "What is a Hybrid Mobile App?" (developer.telerik.com/featured/what-is-a-hybrid-mobile-app/).

WHAT YOU'LL FIND IN THIS BOOK

In this book, we walk you through the design and development of a restaurant spending tracker. We go step-by-step, starting from learning about who's going to use your app, moving on to visual design and the "front-end" code that displays it, and finishing with the "back-end" code that makes the app run. Along the way, you'll have homework to complete that will help you follow along and build your first web app; we provide downloadable code and templates when you need them.

Here's what you'll learn in the upcoming chapters:

Chapter 1: User Experience Basics

How to use what you learn about people's characteristics, desires, needs, and behaviors to create application features that work the way your audience expects. How do you learn about your audience? What's a user scenario, and how does it help you understand which features you need? Simple and free and/or cheap user-research approaches. Introduction to the case study.

Chapter 2: Application Features and Flow

What wireframing is and how it lays the foundation for page structure and code. Brief review of free and inexpensive tools available for wireframing.

Chapter 3: Visual Design Basics

Why consistency, hierarchy, and personality are important to helping people understand how an application works. Simple tips for applying color, font choice, and imagery to support these meta-principles.

Chapter 4: Preparing to Code: Installing and Configuring

Installing Bootstrap 4, Angular 2, and necessary tools with a package manager. Review the role of each package being installed.

Chapter 5: Bootstrap

Bootstrap basic concepts. Tips and techniques for identifying and fixing errors in your HTML and CSS. Building the physical structure of the case-study web app.

Chapter 6: Getting Started with Angular

JavaScript, TypeScript, and Angular, and how they interact with one another. How Angular's organizational units—or *components*—work. Planning the code in terms of these components.

Chapter 7: Coding the App

Writing a functional but designless test version of the app. Incorporating outside libraries for certain features. Basic testing of the functional app.

Chapter 8: Putting It All Together

The functional app from Chapter 7 now gets combined with the design and user interface built in Chapter 5. Running final user research to confirm your app works the way people expect.

Chapter 9: Deployment

How to bundle the application for release. How to release your application into the world using cloud-based services or repositories. Where to go with what you've learned, including connecting the code to a data service. Brief discussion of building hybrid mobile apps with Cordova.

USER EXPERIENCE BASICS

If you're reading this book, you probably grew up using software every day.

Some of that software will have felt truly tailored to your needs and the way you like to work; some of it will have felt like you were in a canoe paddling upstream, fighting the interface (or simply failing to understand it) every time you had to use it.

User experience design, also known as *UX design,* is one of the disciplines that makes the difference between the software you love and the software you hate. UX designers work to understand the people who need to use an application: the characteristics that make them similar or unique, the situations in which they use the software, and the tasks they need to accomplish while they use it. Then, based on their understanding of users' motivations and typical patterns of behavior, they design the application in a way that feels natural, efficient, and satisfying to the target audiences.

In this chapter, we introduce you to the techniques and tools UX designers apply to understand audiences, and we get you started using them for the app you'll be creating in this book.

USER RESEARCH

User experience design encompasses a lot more than user research, but that's where it all begins. UX designers employ a wide range of research techniques to explore audience perceptions, preferences, needs, and patterns of use. These techniques may be *qualitative*, in which the ultimate *conclusions* focus on observations rather than statistics, or *quantitative*, which focuses on capturing statistical data.

No matter which technique designers use, their goal is to hear user voices in order to build *empathy*—that is, the ability to put themselves in a user's shoes when they use an application. UX designers rarely design applications for themselves; they almost always design apps for other audiences. Understanding what drives an audience is critical to designing a successful application.

Each technique has strengths and weaknesses, and although one technique alone is sometimes enough to learn about an audience, UX designers may employ multiple techniques simultaneously or over the course of a project. Not every technique works for every situation, but here are a few common ones, some of which we use in this and other chapters.

TECHNIQUE	PURPOSE	STRENGTHS	WEAKNESSES
Individual interviews	One-on-one discussions about audience perceptions and behavior	Reveals in-depth information untainted by what fellow interview participants might say	Time-consuming to perform, record, and analyze
Focus groups	High-level feedback about perceptions and preferences	Uncovers group perceptions quickly . . .	. . . but participants can "feed" off each others' answers, sometimes leading to inaccurate results
Surveys	Reaching a broad audience with a standard set of questions	Excellent for gathering statistical data; also good for gathering a lot of information at once	Long surveys are time-consuming to fill out and may be abandoned; good surveys can be difficult to write
Diary studies	Tracking user behavior and perceptions over a specific time period	Provides a deep look into how people think and what they feel	Time-consuming to perform and analyze
Usability testing	Assessing how easy or difficult an interface is to use	Supplies immediate feedback on how audience perceptions differ from designer/developer/client perceptions, indicating what application elements need to change	Can be (but isn't always) time-consuming to perform and analyze

USER RESEARCH WITHOUT BREAKING THE BANK

User research doesn't have to involve a special usability lab, or nationwide recruitment, or an expensive subscription to an online testing service, although of course all of those things can be helpful for the right project. What you really need for user research is one thing only: a willingness to listen. Research, especially for small projects, can be done inexpensively or sometimes even for free. Here are a few tips and tools for getting three of the simplest techniques—interviews, surveys, and usability testing—done without having to open your wallet too far.

Interviews

Although it's best to do interviews in person so you can observe body language, you can also interview people very effectively over the phone or via Google Hangouts™, Skype, and so on. Free conference-call utilities like UberConference® even offer screen-sharing so that you can show an interview participant prototypes, designs in progress, or other online materials to gauge perceptions. Free or inexpensive screen-sharing tools are also available outside of conference-calling sites; join.me has a free option, and two of the biggest players in the field, Cisco WebEx® and GoToMeeting®, offer inexpensive monthly plans you can cancel at any time.

Surveys

One of the most popular survey tools is SurveyMonkey®, which offers free surveys for up to ten questions and one hundred responses. The free plan doesn't offer a way to export the survey data, but an inexpensive upgrade to this plan offers that option and can be billed (or canceled) on a monthly basis. Google Forms is another free way to build a survey, and its data can be automatically imported into Google Sheets™.

Usability testing

Usability testing involves having people use your interface to try to accomplish specific tasks so that you can tell what's intuitive and what's not. It can be performed in person, online with a moderator to ask questions and record results, or remotely without a moderator, where the participant either uploads a video of the test, or the system records where they clicked and the responses they gave to short-answer questions. It doesn't have to take long or cost a lot of money to get immediate feedback on how well an interface is working. Even sitting with someone for five minutes and asking them to perform one task—say, "Show me how you would add the cost of today's lunch to the spending tracker"—is enough to give you useful data, and an advantage of doing quick tests like this is that you can do them multiple times during the design and development process to make sure you're on the right track and to rework things if you're not.

If you can't sit down with your participants to get testing done in person, the next best thing is to use a screen-sharing tool, like the ones discussed previously, to conduct the test remotely.

It's generally best to have a participant test your app on their own computer, where they're most comfortable—but you can still do this remotely provided your screen-sharing tool supports giving the participant control of the screen so that they can click and move the mouse themselves.

There are also numerous remote options available, although they vary widely in cost. Optimal Workshop's Chalkmark tool is available via a free plan that allows three tasks per study with up to ten responses. Plunk App is a free testing service that allows you to upload one mobile device screenshot, ask the users to perform one task, and find out where they tap on the screen to accomplish that task. And remote testing services such as UserTesting®, Loop[11]®, and WhatUsersDo offer pay-as-you-go online tests, although their costs generally start around a few hundred dollars, which moves them outside what we'd consider to be an inexpensive service for someone just dipping their toes into UX waters.

Compensation

For five- or ten-minute sessions or surveys, you don't necessarily need to offer participants compensation for their time. But if you're taking up twenty to thirty minutes of someone's day (or longer), then it's polite—and accepted practice in the user research world—to offer the participant compensation. Compensation varies depending on time, difficulty of recruitment, participant employment role, and institutional norms; Debby has worked on studies where CXO-level participants were compensated $200 for half an hour of their time, as well as studies where students got a $10 gift card for on-campus use. For the type of informal research you'll be doing for this book—you'll likely be relying on friends and family as participants—it may be enough to buy participants lunch or a cup of coffee or even offer homemade cookies while they sit and look at your interface. People are usually happy and excited to help with user research, but they're giving you valuable time and insight and should be compensated in some way for their work.

DEFINING AUDIENCES AND SCENARIOS

Every person who's worked in application design has asked a client who their audience is and has heard "Our audience is everyone!" in reply. And although it's true that many applications must appeal to a very wide group of people, even those audiences can be broken down into *personas* or *user types*: a set of audience members with similar work-style preferences and task requirements that can be summarized in an archetype.

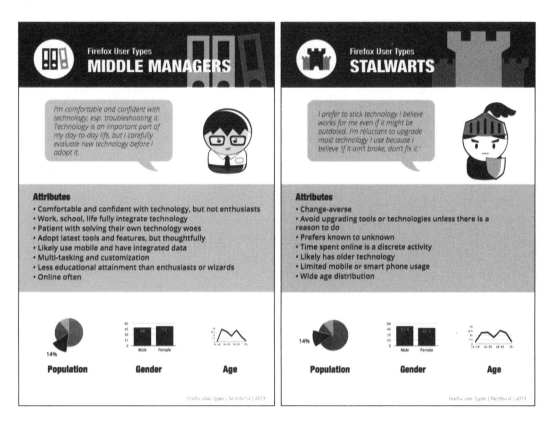

Two of the six user types Mozilla developed for its Firefox browser. Each user type includes a first-person statement summarizing what makes that user type unique, a set of bullet points outlining additional attributes, and demographic data determined from extensive qualitative and quantitative research. For more information, see blog.mozilla.org/ux /2013/08/firefox-user-types-in-north-america/.[3]

How do you uncover those patterns? Look closely at what people tell you about themselves:

■ What questions do they need the application to answer for them? Are they the same types of questions, or are they very different?

■ When do they need to use the application? Every day, every week, a few times a year?

■ When they need to use it, are they sitting at a desk? Or are they browsing a smartphone on the walk to the subway station? Listening to it talk to them in the car? Giving it limited attention on their tablet while they watch TV at the same time?

[3] User type images created by Zhenshou Fang available at blog.mozilla.org/ux/2013/08/firefox-user-types-in-north -america/ under a Creative Commons Attribution-ShareAlike 3.0 Unported license. Full terms available at creativecommons.org/licenses/by-sa/3.0/legalcode.

- How similar are their problem-solving approaches? Do they always call someone for help? Do they muddle around the interface until they find the answer? Do they use one tried-and-true method for performing a task, even if it's not the most efficient one, and if so, why?

- Are they confident with technology, afraid of it, or somewhere in between?

- What similarities or differences in education level or other demographics make it easier or harder for them to use this or other applications?

Documenting these archetypes should include a description of each audience group's characteristics, its needs, and the types of questions its members have or problems they face. This can be done in paragraphs or simple bullet points, much as Mozilla did for its Firefox archetypes (see page 19), although another method[4] involves writing the persona from the perspective of the user themselves. This first-person approach helps build empathy by emphasizing the user's goals, obstacles, and personality characteristics—not their demographics. For example, here's a brief persona Debby created for a development firm looking to evaluate a dashboard application they'd built for marketing teams at small businesses:

> I'm Maria, and I'm responsible for managing and tracking email marketing campaigns. I'm the middle-level person in a small team—it's just me, my manager, and a junior marketing person who writes most of our copy and assists me. Because we're such a small team, we're really busy; in fact, we'd like to bring another junior-level marketer on, but we simply haven't had time to write a job description and get it to HR.
>
> One thing that attracted me to marketing is that I like using words and pictures to tell a compelling story and persuade people. I'm a visual learner myself, and I understand complicated concepts more quickly when there's a picture or a chart to help me grasp the essence of a situation. But part of my job involves tracking campaign clickthroughs on Google Analytics, and that software is a nightmare—it's so complicated, and it gets worse every time they upgrade. They have some charts to give me the quick picture, but drilling down for more information is complicated; I hardly know where to begin! I need simplicity and guidance.

Maria is a composite of marketing staff members Debby has worked with over the years. Her profile includes details—"Google Analytics . . . is a nightmare," "we're really busy," "we don't have time to hire help"—that suggest she needs software that holds her hand and gives her the big picture without forcing her to stop and think about how to set numerous filters to find information. Because the marketing application was designed without Maria specifically in mind, the first-person approach can help the development team focus on the human beings who use their

---

[4] Indi Young, "Describing Personas," *Medium*, Mar. 15, 2016, medium.com/@indiyoung/describing-personas-af992e3fc527.

application every day—and their corresponding desire for simplicity that will need to inform every new and revamped feature in the app.

Scenarios

In order for an application to help its audiences, it has to offer features that work the way those audiences expect and that support the specific tasks they need to perform. When UX designers understand an application's audience, they can begin to imagine how those people might interact with the app.

This imagination exercise takes the form of *scenarios*: short stories that describe how someone interacts with one or more features. Scenarios paint a picture of what using the application could be like and begin to give the UX designer and the rest of the design and development team something firm to grab onto while they continue to plan the app.

Scenarios should be grounded in reality—what you learned during user research, especially specific examples gleaned from storytelling questions—but they should also explore how to push a site or application's feature set into something new or enhanced to help the user base.

The quickest way to explain a scenario is to share an example. Here's one Debby drafted for the Massachusetts Institute of Technology (MIT). The project's "Researcher" archetype wanted historical data and downloadable charts.

A typical Researcher role.

As her department's administrative officer, Andrea helps plan an annual gathering of research sponsors. Before the meeting happens, she helps her department head prepare his introductory presentation by tracking down MIT's research expenditures for the past five years. Knowing she's previously found similar info in MIT Facts, the university's factbook, she reaches for the printed guide to get the most recent numbers but turns to the website to view PDFs of old guides to get earlier ones.

A Researcher task pulled directly from focus group comments.

Researcher's solution, also pulled from focus group comments.

When her department head asks for a chart representing this year's numbers, Andrea's worried she'll have to scan in what she found in the book. She wonders if there's a chart on the web she could download, and goes to the website to look. Sure enough, there's an interactive chart of research expenditures, and beside it is a link suggesting she download the chart. She clicks it, chooses the file format she wants, and a PNG appears on her desktop, ready for her to import into PowerPoint.

Andrea's on deadline, and scanning takes time and might not work reliably. How do we make her life easier?

The proposed solution: downloadable chart graphics.

Here's how the solution might work.

It's important to note that some popular software development methodologies, such as Agile, define *scenario* in a slightly different way. Agile's *user stories* are closer to our definition of *scenario* but are less detailed; a typical user story might be "As a user, I want to download a chart PNG so that I can put it in a presentation," whereas an Agile scenario would outline every step in the chart graphic download process. The Agile perspective makes a lot of sense for developers, who need those clearly defined steps to program the feature, but it can chafe at designers, who want room to imagine and explore possibilities without being confined by details (at first). Both approaches are valid and useful and, most critically, can coexist. But for the purposes of this book, we're sticking to our definition of *scenario*.

DESIGNING YOUR FIRST RESPONSIVE WEB APP

Throughout the course of this book, we're going to design, develop, test, and deploy TastyTracker, a responsive web app that allows a user to track what they spend on meals outside the home. (While images in this book use only two colors, TastyTracker was designed in full color. To see full-color versions of these and other images, visit goo.gl/dODTV3.)

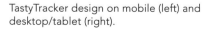
TastyTracker design on mobile (left) and desktop/tablet (right).

Because the goal of this book is to teach the basics of web application development, TastyTracker does less than a full-fledged spending tracker might. It's two pages long, it works only for one person (no login required), its data is stored in a text file instead of a database, and it doesn't automatically integrate with bank or credit card accounts. But it still does quite a lot for such a small application:

- Allows you to enter a restaurant name, date, price, and meal type (breakfast, lunch, dinner, or snack)

- Instantly updates a chart showing how much you've spent that day on meals

- Allows you to view meal spending history by time period (current day or current week)

Simple or not, all application design should begin the same way: by understanding the user.

TastyTracker's user base

We began with an assumption: People who keep an eye on their spending probably also keep an eye on how much they spend on meals or would be open to the idea of tracking that information. So we contacted four friends, all women in their early thirties to early forties, who we knew were closely tracking what they spent on various household expenses. To understand how they currently tracked their meal spending, we drafted an interview protocol.

TastyTracker interview protocol

Goal: Understand how people track their restaurant spending and how their existing tools meet or fall short of their needs.

1. How often each week do you buy something to eat outside your home (including morning coffee or tea, midday snacks, etc.)?

2. How do you currently track what you spend on these meals?

3. Where is your current tracking system most helpful to you?

4. Where is it least helpful?

5. What goals, if any, have you set for yourself in terms of tracking your meal costs, and has your current system helped you do that?

6. If you use a different method or tool to track spending in other parts of your life, what tool or method are you using, and why don't you use it to track meal costs?

Let's break down how this protocol is organized and why we chose the questions we did.

Research protocols should always begin with at least one goal statement. Writing out what you want to learn helps you focus the questions and tasks you draft, and each part of the protocol should work toward those initial goals.

Question 1 is based on implicit knowledge: The interview participant is spending money eating outside the home. Most people do, including our participants, so it's not much of an assumption. But understanding how often someone does this helps us gauge whether people like this would be TastyTracker users; the more someone concerned about their finances spends money on meals they didn't cook, the more likely they are to want to track what they're spending.

Questions 2, 3, and 4 are deceptively straightforward: They seem like simple questions, but what they really get at is someone's thought process. The answers tell us why someone chose their current tracking system, how it supports the way they prefer to work, and where it gets in their way instead. If we know this, we can design TastyTracker to appeal to its user while avoiding pitfalls.

Question 5 is exploratory: We were wondering whether a goal-setting tool might be useful in

TastyTracker. We'd already planned for simple charts or graphs to track spending status, but a goal-setting tool could make those charts or graphs even more useful.

Finally, question 6 reinforces questions 2–4 by approaching them in a different way: If someone prefers to track meal spending by using a different tool than the one she uses for other living expenses, what value is she getting from her current meal-spending tracking system that she's not getting from her alternate one, and vice-versa? Is it a matter of habit, or preference?

What we learned

All four participants used bank and credit card statements to capture spending information, but each had a different and variably successful method for tracking overall spending: Rose relied on her memory, Martha used her bank's software, Clara kept an Excel spreadsheet, and Amy used "an old-school budget on paper." (For privacy reasons, all participant names in this book are pseudonyms. Fans of the TV series *Doctor Who* will have already figured that out.) Rose and Martha's attention to their bank accounts (and in Martha's case, spending categories in the bank's software) kept them on top of meal expenses, whereas Clara said she did it "intermittently, when I want to guilt myself into cutting back."

Only Amy was fully satisfied with her tracking method. Rose said that when she was tired or not paying attention, she could lose track of where things stood. Martha wanted longer-term tracking analysis she couldn't get in her bank's software. Clara's Excel spreadsheet was "cumbersome and annoying" (though not enough to keep her from using it), and, like Martha, she yearned for "something [that] could do a little more analysis."

No one kept any specific spending goals for meals beyond overall spending goals, though Rose and Martha occasionally set informal goals limiting the number of meals they purchased. All said they were disciplined about this spending, however, and volunteered different motivations: not just money, but a desire to eat healthier as well.

The answers began to present a picture we could compile into a persona and scenario:

- Our participants wanted to keep an eye on their spending. They weren't always consistent about it, but they were motivated by finances and other reasons that reminded them to stay on task.

- Bank and credit card statement exports, or software the bank offered itself, made viewing and tracking expenses easier.

- Each participant had a different system, but even if they acknowledged that it was a flawed one, it met their needs.

- Although some participants found goal-setting useful, these were generally limited-time goals ("I'll eat out only twice a week for a little while") rather than longer-term goals focused on spending ("I'm not allowed to spend more than $50 a week on takeout for the next six months").

- Two participants specifically mentioned a need for trend analysis.

- Three of the four were essentially seat-of-the-pants budgeters: Tracking their spending was important to them, but it wasn't always at the top of their minds, even if they felt it should have been or if they felt their own abilities were holding them back. "I'm a terrible budgeter," said Martha, adding, "I really do rely on the online banking system for most trends." Rose said, "Since I don't have an organized system, it may seem . . . chaotic? And it probably would be for some. But it works for me." And Clara felt that more detailed tracking would feel "oppressive"—"it's useful for a reality check now and then, but I don't like to do it all the time."

Our persona: Donna

Based on the interviews, our previous knowledge of the participants, and creative assumptions that felt in keeping with both, we drafted the following persona:

My name is Donna. I'm an administrative assistant, and since 2009, I've lived with two housemates near Davis Square in Somerville, Massachusetts. Housemates have come and gone over the years, and, you know, I'm thirty-five, and it's past time I got a place of my own. These Davis rents are the worst, though, and I don't want to leave the neighborhood, so I'm saving up for a studio—not a one-bedroom. Finally, my own space! No one to fight with for the bathroom first thing in the morning! Maybe I'll even get a cat.

Utilities and rent never get any cheaper in this town, so I check my bank and credit card accounts weekly or sometimes daily. I don't want to go over the "magic number." Okay, I don't know exactly what that number is all the time, but I know when it feels like too much, and that's the important thing. I've got the household expenses down pretty far, so where else can I cut back for that apartment deposit? . . . Oh, there it is in my statements: I've already spent $30 for takeout Chinese this week; my large coffee and blueberry muffin at Dunkin' Donuts every day; and, okay, $50 on cocktails and pulled pork at the fancy new barbecue place, even if it was Gramps's birthday, was probably too much. I need to rein it in.

Someone like Donna could find TastyTracker helpful, but how would she use it? That's where a *scenario* comes in:

Donna has resolved to keep a better eye on her meal expenses, and that begins with tracking the first meal of the day: breakfast. She'd meant to buy coffee pods and a six-pack of muffins at the grocery store over the weekend, but Season 7 of *Game of Thrones* wasn't going to watch itself, was it? So on Monday morning, she's back at her usual Dunkin' Donuts to order a large coffee and a muffin, and, while sitting on the subway with her coffee wedged between her knees, she pulls out her phone to log what she bought in TastyTracker. She selects the meal (breakfast), enters "Dunks" in the restaurant name field, picks today's date (selected by default, thank goodness), enters the cost of her breakfast in another field, and taps a **Save** button. She instantly sees a tally of what she spent and where, as well as **Edit** and **Delete** icons—good things for those times she fat-fingers the phone keyboard. She also sees a chart showing how much she's spent today, organized by meal, and tapping the word "Today" shows her an option to display "This Week" instead—helpful for keeping on top of the magic number.

When she buys breakfast again the next day, she's delighted to see that, instead of having to enter "Dunks" again, it appears in a drop-down menu she can select from. She still knows she needs to hit the grocery store for muffins and coffee, but at least the software is making expense-tracking easier for her.

Although this scenario may not describe every aspect of TastyTracker in detail, it covers the major features and situations of use:

- Must be able to track meal type, restaurant name (which gets added to a drop-down for future use), cost, and date (default to current date)
- Must be mobile-friendly
- Must allow entry editing and deletion
- Must instantly display results to the user
- Must offer charting by day and week

It's more than enough to get started, and we take it to the next level in Chapter 2.

YOUR ASSIGNMENT

You'll hear a lot from us in this book about how knowledge gained in one area can be applied to an entirely different one, and the same goes for TastyTracker itself: You can build a meal-spending tracker along with us, or you can use the same techniques to design your own app to track spending elsewhere—downloaded music, in-game purchases, or whatever else appeals to you. Either way, your first assignment is to:

- Draft a protocol to interview three to five potential users for your app. You can use or edit ours if you want; just make it short and simple (no more than ten questions). Keep your questions open-ended, avoid leading questions, and to see someone's thought processes in action (and get detail for your scenarios), consider focusing at least one question on storytelling: "Tell me about a time when you . . ."

- Interview your participants. We offered our friends the choice between doing the interview via email or over the phone; work with whatever communication method is most comfortable for you and your participants.

- Synthesize what you've learned into one or two personas with at least one user scenario each.

APPLICATION FEATURES AND FLOW

We've reviewed how user research gives you a picture of an audience's mindset and needs, as well as how personas and scenarios begin to explore the features that help people accomplish their goals.

But words are just an early sketch; to paint the full picture, you literally need to draw how the features will work and how people will move from screen to screen. You don't need to be a skilled artist to do this. Pencil and paper are an excellent way to start, but plenty of digital tools exist to help you map out how an application will work, and that's how we do most of our wireframing.

WIREFRAMING

A *wireframe* is a bare-bones mockup of a layout that shows where text, images, and features appear on the screen and which shows how screens change in response to the user or system. Wireframes include little to no visual design; they're generally black and white and kept deliberately sparse to help people focus on how the pages work rather than distracting them at this early stage with colors, photos, and other design choices.

For example, Debby designed the following wireframe page for an updated version of MIT's Infinite History video archive, an oral history of the Institute.

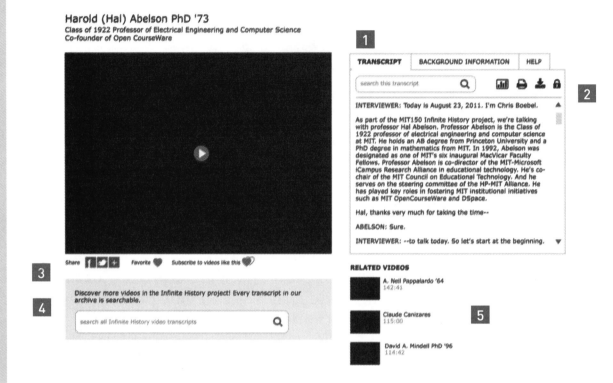

This wireframe shows one option for a "video detail" screen to display an individual video, as well as additional information and tools related to that video. The wireframe demonstrates the following features:

1. A tabbed area for the searchable transcript tool, background information about the video's subject, and help using the transcript tool

2. Transcript search and existing icons for transcript tool features in use on what was then the current Infinite History site: a "list view," print, download, and the ability to disable the transcript's automatic scrolling while the interview subject spoke

3. Sharing and favoriting tools, as well as a new feature allowing visitors to subscribe to videos like this one

4. Search field for the complete video library, helpful to the researchers who used the current site

5. A list of related videos

Each of these features was not just visually represented on the screen; it was also discussed in sidebar notes so the team could build a common understanding of how the app should work and how these design choices supported the user. The sidebar notes read:

- Move interview subject/video title directly above the video to reinforce the connection between the two. (It's also more visually prominent at top left.)

- Link to three–five related videos to encourage exploration.

- Don't present the full scrolling library of Infinite History content at right; only display search results when the user requests them. Displaying less content focuses the user's vision on the few elements that are there—like the search box. Treat the full-transcript search as a promotion to draw attention to it. Results would appear below the search box.

- This layout moves the transcript and related information higher on the screen to give it more prominence.

- Alternate placement/sizing for social media tools shown. With this placement and sizing, it's easier to incorporate future features, like favoriting and subscriptions.

As the app evolved, so did the documentation, though, in this case, not by updating the text but by demonstrating it in responsive HTML and CSS. Printable documentation is valuable, but sometimes people need to test out an app for themselves before they fully grasp how it could work, or how it should work, instead.

Wireframes don't have to be neat and detailed, especially if you're acting as both designer and developer. Even quick paper sketches that demonstrate how you want a feature to work can be enough to work from or enough to get you started on a more complex sketch. Here's Debby's initial paper wireframe and notes for the Infinite History video detail page:

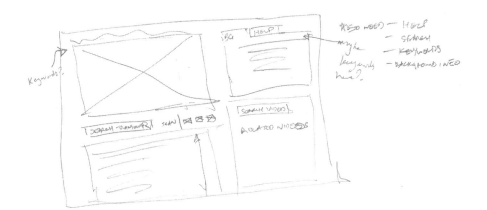

Despite Debby's appalling handwriting outlining the need for help, search, keywords, and background information in the wireframe, there's an obvious relationship between this sketch and the more refined one on page 32. The video area is in the same position, background information and help are tabbed, and related videos appear at the lower right. Other items, like the search bar and the transcript area and its tools, moved from the initial sketch, but these original pencil scribbles laid critical groundwork.

Mapping out features and flow

The Infinite History screen is simply one page in a set of wireframes that demonstrate how the app works. How do you figure out where to start? Your personas and scenarios point the way.

For Infinite History, Debby knew that two of the user types—a researcher and an undergraduate student—would either search the main MIT website or the Infinite History site itself to find video about specific people and topics. The existing Infinite History video archive provided limited search "collections" based on affiliation with the Institute (alumni, faculty, Nobel laureates, etc.), but there was no way to search by topic, different awards, or other criteria. There was also no way to perform a common task researchers would expect: a search to show all videos that matched multiple types of criteria.

There's a standard design solution for this type of problem called *faceted search*. Faceted search allows you to choose multiple criteria simultaneously to narrow down choices. Most people have encountered it on e-commerce sites, but it's a good search option for any large data set with distinct groups of characteristics: everything from shoes to library books.

zappos.com uses faceted search (left column) to help shoppers find shoes by size, width, style, and other categories. Numbers in the styles category display how many shoes of the selected size exist in each facet.

From the scenarios, Debby knew that faceted search would be a must-have feature for researchers and undergraduates to use the app successfully, so it was the logical starting point. Coincidentally, the current home page displayed the complete set of videos, so it made sense to graft on faceted search there as well so that users could immediately find the videos they were looking for. Other than this coincidence, however, there was no particular reason to begin designing the UX with the home page. The entry point to the most vital feature, no matter where it fell in the overall flow of the application, was the right place to start.

After we know the entry point, we can map users' flow through the application. Although experienced UX designers may visualize user movement entirely via wireframes, if you're new to the process, a standard flowchart can help. For example, the basic Infinite History flow would look like this:

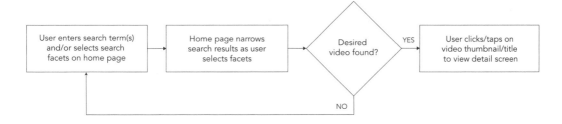

This set of steps represents the following wireframe pages, mapping one-to-one to the flowchart rectangles:

- The search interface
- A depiction of what the search interface looks like as the user selects facets
- The video detail screen

You can use variations on each of these basic screens to show different states; for example, what the video detail screen looks like by default and what it looks like after the user searches for more videos. Alternatively, if the answers to these questions are easily described in text, provide annotations that address them. Either way, when wireframing, you'll have to look beyond your default option to answer at least the following questions:

- How do different parts of the default screen change when the user manipulates interface elements (checkboxes, buttons, sliders, etc.)?
- If there's error messaging, where does it appear on the screen?

▓   Does any success messaging need to display when the user completes a task?

▓   If the app allows login, how does the screen look or behave differently for logged-in users? How does it look or behave differently to administrators logged in to maintain the app?

Your goal with these wireframes is to create a picture of the system—how it's organized and how it works—that everyone on the team understands and can follow. The tools you use for this don't matter as long as everyone ends up with the same picture in their heads.

Wireframing tools

Pencil and paper are perfectly fine tools for wireframing, but you'll probably find it faster and neater to use software. There are a plethora of wireframing programs available, but frankly, any tool that allows you to draw simple shapes and add some text will work just fine. We've provided a short list of inexpensive options, but use whatever you're most comfortable with, regardless of whether we've discussed it. (For what it's worth, Debby prefers the Mac program OmniGraffle®.)

▓   `Balsamiq®:` Balsamiq Mockups is one of the oldest wireframe-specific tools, and it's still very popular. Its wireframes have a deliberately rough, hand-drawn look that helps reinforce that wireframes are sketches of possibilities and are not actual visual design. And like many wireframing toolkits, Balsamiq includes a library of interface stencils you can drag and drop into place to make wireframing as easy as possible.

▓   `Protoshare® Mockups for Drive:` Protoshare is a powerful wireframing tool that also allows you to simulate JavaScript interactions like rollovers, accordions opening/closing, etc. Google Chrome™ users can try a limited Protoshare version via an add-on.

▓   `Google Slides and Google Drawings:` As we mentioned, all you need to create a wireframe is the ability to draw simple shapes and add some type. Google offers two free web-based programs that can help: Google Slides, their presentation program; and Google Drawings, a Chrome-based drawing program for flowcharts and other diagrams. Neither is specifically designed to create wireframes, but Google Drawings' minimal interface is easy to understand, and Microsoft® PowerPoint® or Apple® Keynote® users may find that laying out a page is easier and faster in a familiar interface like Slides. (Slides also allows you to add simple clickable buttons to mimic screen transitions and other actions.) Neither Google program offers interface stencils, but they're good options for people who find Balsamiq or Protoshare intimidating.

MockFlow® : MockFlow is a web-based wireframing tool. Like Balsamiq and Protoshare, it supplies a drag-and-drop library of interface components, and it also allows you to set up a project with key default elements for Twitter Bootstrap and various other mobile and web platforms.

DESIGN PATTERNS

If you've never worked in user experience design before, the idea of tackling the design of an entire application, even a small one, can feel daunting. How do you know how the search interface should work? How do you display several categories of related information in a small space that works across different device types? How should the navigation flex from mobile phones to giant desktop monitors? These are common interface requirements, and no one wants to design new ways to solve these problems over and over again.

The good news is that you don't have to. *Design patterns*—libraries of standard solutions for everyday interface problems—exist online and in print, and designers rely on these patterns to provide audiences with familiar experiences and expectations no matter what type of app they're using. Although many sites and applications include unique interface solutions, it's a good idea to start with a pattern and only modify it if you absolutely have to; this speeds design and development and, more critically, means it's more likely that people won't need additional instructions to start using what you've built. Responsive web frameworks (like Twitter Bootstrap) and JavaScript libraries (like jQuery) include code that supports common paradigms for forms, navigation, and many other interactive elements to make implementing a design pattern that much easier.

SKETCHING OUT TASTYTRACKER

TastyTracker began as a paper sketch well before a single word of this book was written. It didn't have a name yet; it simply had a concept: a small, self-contained tracking application with different elements that responded to user input. Elements in area 1 (identifiable in the scribbled wireframe below) would drive the display of elements in area 2, and charts in area 2 would include drop-downs that allow people to change the time period or meal information depicted in the charts. The interviews discussed in Chapter 1 confirmed that the initial feature set could work for our draft persona.

Obviously, a few notes and some squiggly rectangles aren't enough to use as a coding and visual design reference, not even for experienced designers and programmers. So we focused on the most important part of the flow—meal entry—and we also started with the mobile view of the interface, knowing that Donna, like an increasing number of people, could be using her phone as her primary method of Internet access. How would she enter a restaurant name, especially a new one? How would she select a meal, enter the amount she'd spent, and identify what day she spent the money? And what order would make the most sense for that set of tasks?

Because what Donna cares most about is her spending, we put a field to track that as the very first item on the screen after a logo and subhead. We also considered language that would make the app feel friendly. Donna doesn't enjoy tracking her spending (who does?); although form-field labels reading "amount spent" and "date spent" are perfectly clear, they also sound formal and a little unwelcoming. Phrasing the labels so that they made a complete sentence beginning with the word "I" could help Donna feel more connected to the app and take a tiny bit of the sting out of tracking her daily coffee and muffin habit.

Each of the tracking areas uses an appropriate form element to enter the data:

- Spending is easiest to enter as a number in a text field, and the $ outside the field helps cue that Donna doesn't need to enter it in the box.

- Restaurant names could be entered individually in a text field, but it would be annoying for Donna to enter the restaurant name every time she visits it, especially if she's visiting the same place multiple times a week. So a drop-down that stores the restaurant names she's already entered and makes adding new ones easy both simplifies her restaurant selection process and ensures that the integrity of the data we store is preserved.

- The meals drop-down only has four options—breakfast, lunch, dinner, and snack—and Donna won't be entering spending info for multiple meals at the same time. Although radio buttons are a good way to handle single-choice situations, they're less compact than a drop-down.

- A text field with a calendar widget takes care of date entry, and a default date set to today could make for one less tap on Donna's part to track her spending. Displaying the date also provides a cue about what sort of text entry the field would accept, though realistically, Donna is likely to rely on the calendar widget exclusively. For those few cases when she doesn't, intelligent code on the back end can accept dates in multiple formats, or error messaging can help remind her how the date should be entered.

- Finally, Donna needs a way to save her entry, so we added a Save button.

Adding some CRUD to the interface

Applications that allow users to store data usually have to allow them to modify or delete that data as well. In the programming world, these are called *CRUD operations,* where "CRUD" is an acronym standing for "create, read, update, and delete." We've covered the primary "create" task already, so let's look at one of its subtasks: adding a restaurant for the very first time.

How would Donna do this? We considered two possibilities:

1. There could be an Add New Restaurant button or link that appears near the restaurant dropdown. (Always keep related items near each other!)

2. There could be an Enter New Restaurant option in the drop-down. When selected, it would display a text field allowing Donna to add the name.

When dealing with mobile screen layouts, a good rule of thumb to keep in mind is to only show the interface elements that are absolutely necessary. This way you don't clutter up your screen. Thus, an Add New Restaurant button or link was a less ideal solution than one that showed an additional field only on demand. Tapping the Save button at the end of the tracking process would also save the new restaurant name and add it to the drop-down for future use.

There are two other CRUD elements on this part of the screen that we haven't yet described: an Edit Meals button or link, and a pencil icon to allow for restaurant name editing. We cover the latter next. (The former will be part of your assignment at the end of this chapter.)

We all make mistakes when entering information, so it's important to allow users a way to fix them. If Donna writes "Donks" instead of "Dunks," the steps she follows to correct her typo should roughly look like this:

1. Find the restaurant

2. Edit its name, or delete it entirely

3. Return to main screen

Broken out into a flowchart, the steps get a little more detailed:

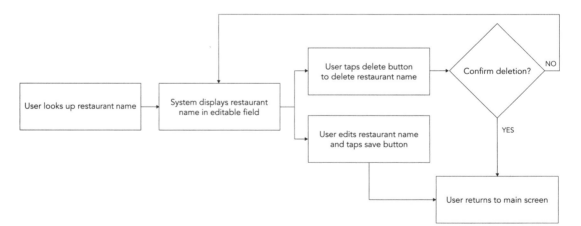

Here we can see some additional steps in the flow. Donna must tap a Save button to save her edited changes, or tap a Delete button to delete the restaurant name entirely. Before she can complete deleting the item, she must confirm that it's what she really meant to do. Confirming a deletion isn't always a necessary step, and in fact, the initial TastyTracker wireframes didn't include one. Why? Adding a restaurant name is fast and straightforward enough that, from Donna's perspective, there were few consequences to accidentally deleting the name. Unfortunately, when a restaurant is deleted, all of its meal entries must also be deleted. (They would become unfindable and unusable). Because of this, we added the confirmation, which gives Donna only one more button to tap in order to finish her task anyway—not a terribly difficult or time-consuming step.

The final issue to address was where to display all these editing controls in the first place. Displaying them on the same screen could cause interface elements to shift around—not necessarily a problem but potentially confusing. At the same time, the editing interface didn't need *that* many elements, so it didn't seem worth moving to a screen of its own.

We settled on a lightbox that would display in a floating window above the main interface. The lightbox approach provides a similar experience to having the editing interface appear on the main screen but without the possible visual confusion of new elements suddenly shifting.

Left: the initial Edit Restaurants lightbox. A darker background appears behind it to focus Donna's attention on the lightbox window itself. Middle: the restaurant name displays. At this point, Donna can choose to edit/save or delete it. Right: If Donna decides to delete the restaurant, she's presented with a confirmation in the lightbox. Confirmation messaging and button text clearly explain the consequences and process of deletion.

Displaying progress

Tracking what Donna spends on meals is useless to her unless she can also see how much she's spent so far. Her scenario suggests that instantly displaying results and allowing her to chart her progress by day and week would be valuable; the former gives her a heads-up if she's exceeding that "magic number" in her head for daily and weekly spending, and the latter lets her see how much money she's saving over time.

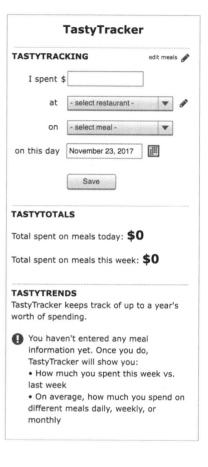

Because current progress is time-sensitive, it's more important than chart display. And because we read from top to bottom, information should be ordered to reflect that priority: the current totals should appear above the trend charts.

The first time Donna uses the app, it's not going to have any information to display about totals or trends, so we need to show this default state. Although a wireframe isn't a visual design, it incorporates some elements that support usability and should make it into the final design:

- No matter the total, numbers should appear in a larger and possibly bolder/darker font to help them, the most important part of the totals area, stand out from the text.

- Alert messaging should explain why the TastyTrends area is useful and what Donna has to do to get trend information to show up. Messaging should also be called out separately from introductory text ("TastyTracker keeps track of up to a year's worth of spending") through use of an alert icon to draw attention to the area.

With the default organization and information in place, we can turn to what the screen looks like *after* Donna has started to use it.

The wireframe now includes a horizontal bar chart comparing Donna's spending this week to the previous one, as well as a chart showing, by default, how much she spends per meal type daily, but which she can fine-tune. Charts like these that show a relatively limited amount of data are good candidates for pie charts instead of bars. However, pie chart labeling uses screen real estate less efficiently than a bar chart with labeling inline, and the bars are every bit as understandable as traditional pies. The situation of use—a mobile phone—has to drive how content is displayed.

THINKING RESPONSIVELY

Although Donna is likely to use a mobile phone most of the time she uses TastyTracker, she may not use it all the time. People like Donna might use a tablet to access the app, or open it up on their desktop machine at work to track the lunch they just bought. We could use the exact same thin, vertical layout across all devices, but imagine how ridiculous that narrow column would look on a 26-inch-wide screen. The layout needs to flex intelligently across devices instead.

As we mentioned in the introduction to this book, the point of responsive design is not to replicate the exact same experience across different screen sizes; it's to deliver the right experience no matter the screen size. Sometimes that means re-ordering, resizing, or even removing or hiding parts of the design, such as collapsing a horizontal menu into a "hamburger" menu instead.[5]

---

[5] Responsive web design guru Ethan Marcotte provides a more detailed look at how layouts and functionality shift across screen sizes in his article "Frameworks" on A List Apart (alistapart.com/article/frameworks). The article is an excerpt from his book *Responsive Design: Patterns & Principles.*

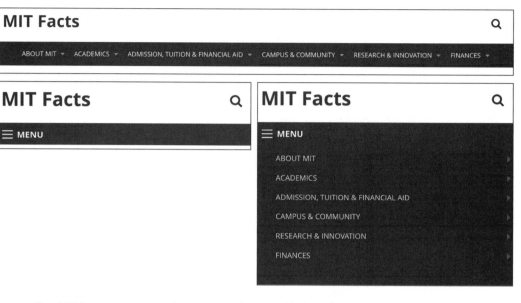

Top: MIT Facts prototype navigation on widescreen (desktop/laptop) devices. Lower left: Navigation, or *nav*, on small screens collapses into a three-line "hamburger" with the word "menu" to guide people there. Lower right: When the user taps the menu, it opens below the hamburger; tapping nav items slides them left to expose submenus.

When reworking a layout across devices, it helps to consider these questions:

- Which features are so important that they absolutely must be displayed, even if that display may shift around somewhat depending on screen size?

- Which features can be removed or collapsed, as with hamburger menus or accordions that show or hide information at a tap?

- How can features and other page elements be broken up into "boxes" or "modules" of functionality to simplify moving them around the page?

TastyTracker has relatively limited functionality, and all of it is available on a mobile device. Because of this, we don't have to think about the first two questions other than keeping in mind that the order of elements on TastyTracker's screen mirrors their hierarchy: tracking meal expenses is most important, seeing current status is the next most important, and seeing longer-term status is the least important. With these questions addressed, we need only consider the third one: how elements can be thought of as single units of functionality.

Consider a fairly typical site layout: a large promotional image at left, a smaller text or feature block at right, and three smaller text or feature blocks below it. Depending on the audience's situation of use, not every block of functionality will be important on every device—nor will it need to take up the same amount of space or even be visible at all.

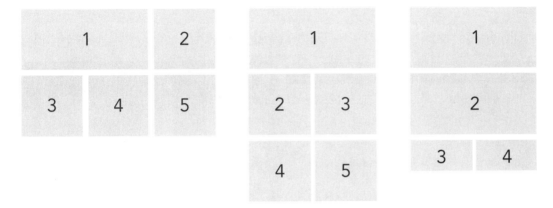

Left: desktop layout; center: tablet layout in portrait (vertical) mode; right: mobile layout.

You'll note that in our example, the boxes all fall neatly into columns, with larger boxes taking up the exact width of multiple columns. The literal foundation of visual design is the *grid*, a set of invisible columns that help elements line up in order to guide the eye and create a harmonious layout.

Responsive web frameworks rely on grids as well—they determine how elements flex in size as screens change. These are frequently twelve-column grids no matter what the screen size, so columns on a phone will be significantly narrower than columns on a desktop monitor. However, frameworks allow you to code your pages so that, for example, an item that takes up all twelve columns on a mobile device takes up only six on a medium-size screen, or four on a large one. We go into this in more detail in Chapter 5, but for now, you may want to use your wireframing tool's guide or grid lines, or even a Twitter Bootstrap grid overlay (a literal picture of the grid), to help determine how elements should be laid out and lined up across screens.

Some wireframing tools come with these overlays, and many are available for download. Just search the web for "twitter bootstrap grid overlay."

YOUR ASSIGNMENT

We've supplied you with wireframes for most of the TastyTracker mobile experience. To practice mapping out features and flows across devices, we'd like you to:

- Design the Edit Restaurant screen. Tip: We put this on a screen of its own because we felt some of the interactions it required got too complex and confined when in a lightbox.

- Design how TastyTracker's screen elements reflow onto tablet and desktop devices. Don't forget that the tablet can be held in portrait (vertical) or landscape (horizontal) mode, though also keep in mind that it's okay to repurpose a desktop screen layout.

- Alternatively, if you're designing your own tracking app, wireframe it for mobile, tablet, and desktop devices. If you need help, use our layouts as a starting point.

While working on your wireframe, you may find the following specifications helpful:

- If your wireframing tool doesn't include device templates, use these dimensions as a guideline: 320 pixels wide for your smallest screen, 576 pixels wide for a tablet screen in portrait mode, 720 pixels wide for a tablet screen in landscape mode, and 1,140 pixels wide for a large screen. (These specs are based on minimum widths; it's easier to scale a layout up and make it look good and work well than it is to squeeze it into a space that's too tight.)

VISUAL DESIGN BASICS

I f you've never studied visual design or worked with a visual designer, you might not have considered how good visual design makes the digital tools you use more usable and enjoyable.

Visual design is much more than colors, fonts, and "decoration"; there are rules and guidelines at work even if the viewer doesn't always perceive them. Although no single chapter of a book can turn someone into a professional web designer, in this chapter, we discuss some basic design principles that affect application usability, as well as review tips for how to apply design elements to make what you build easier and more pleasant to use.

THE META-PRINCIPLES: CONSISTENCY, HIERARCHY, AND PERSONALITY

Before we dive into how to choose colors, fonts, and images, we need to briefly review some foundational principles that profoundly affect application usability and enjoyability. These *meta-principles*—consistency, hierarchy, and personality—are covered in depth in *Visual Usability: Principles and Practices for Designing Digital Applications*, written by Debby and her colleague Tania Schlatter.

Consistency

Consistency, as its name suggests, addresses whether the flows and interface elements that perform specific application tasks always work the same way throughout. Not only should visually similar parts of an application behave similarly no matter where you are in the application, but an application may also need to be *externally consistent* with the way other applications work. As we discussed in Chapter 2, design patterns are common solutions to interface tasks, and every application we use that relies on those patterns teaches us how new applications we've never used before are likely to work. Diverging from those patterns, or from new patterns or systems a designer has consciously set up in an application, must be done thoughtfully, because every divergence can create a "stop and think moment"—and as usability expert Steve Krug famously proclaimed in his First Law of Usability, "Don't make me think!"[6]

Consistency is more than just trying to use the same selection pattern throughout, however. A consistent application:

- Uses similar layouts for similar types of content, just as all individual product pages on amazon.com are arranged the same way

- Has primary headers that are all the same size or color within header levels and application sections, and doesn't change font sizes, types, weights (e.g., bold, italic), or color without reason, as in the difference between body content and a footnote

- Applies colors purposefully rather than arbitrarily, so that, for example, users know that Save buttons will always have green backgrounds, whereas Cancel buttons will always be white

- Has images that feel like they're part of a cohesive set and that support a particular mood or tone, which is why an app using icons chosen from a single icon font feels neater and cleaner than one that chooses icons with many different illustration styles

- Uses drop-downs, buttons, and other interface elements appropriately and uses the same type of interface element to perform similar tasks throughout the application

Although there are occasionally times when an application can't be consistent—for example, when a specific feature is so unique that it can't follow the flow patterns you've already set up— relying on other visually consistent elements, like shared screen layouts, button colors, and so on, minimizes the level of effort required to understand the new flow. Each part of your application feeds into the unspoken language people must learn to use your application, and the more consistent you are about the rules of that language, the easier your application will be to use.

Hierarchy

Hierarchy refers to the relative importance of visual elements on a screen: not just which items are more important than others, but which ones are related to each other. At its most basic, hierarchy can be expressed through comparative size (larger elements are more important than smaller ones) and position onscreen (headers and text near the top of the page are more important than text near the bottom). But hierarchy also comes into play when there are multiple points of interaction on a screen, because people need to know which controls apply to which parts of the page. Like

---

[6] Steve Krug, *Don't Make Me Think!: A Common Sense Approach to Web Usability* (Berkeley, CA: New Riders Pub, 2006), p. 10.

consistency, good visual hierarchy supplies vital clues that tell people what requires their attention and when.

An application with a strong hierarchy:

- Gives its most vital features the highest and/or largest position on the screen, as in our placement of the TastyTracker meal entry form

- Sizes and formats type appropriately to guide the eye to headers and clarify what text or features they introduce, as in labels placed directly beside or above form fields rather than halfway across the screen

- Sets up rules for color use that support the hierarchy, such as only using red for alert icons and error messages

- Displays images, including icons, at an appropriate size relative to the text and purpose of the application; for example, a photo displayed on image-sharing application Flickr is far bigger than the information about the photo

- Groups and orders interface elements in a way that allows users to enter and configure information naturally, without presenting them with apparently editable elements before they can be used; for example, only displaying the TastyTracker "enter restaurant name" field after a user selects "add new restaurant"

Personality

If consistency and hierarchy lay the ground rules for how an application functions and is organized, then *personality* sets the tone of the application, literally and figuratively. People have personalities, and so, in their own way, do applications: Are they fun-loving? Thoroughly serious? Your best friend? Your teacher? Are they quiet and restrained, only there to help you get something done? Or are they warm and supportive, encouraging you to complete your next task? Personality uses visuals and language to create a tone and infuse it throughout the application.

To know what kind of personality to set in your application, consider the app's user base and what will appeal to them, as well as the purpose of the app itself and whether it needs a unique personality to set itself apart from its competition. Although a trained visual designer is best equipped to translate these requirements into an appropriate look and feel, it's important for developers (as well as the rest of an application team) to understand personality and its foundational elements so that every part of the app, right down to the text in Submit buttons, helps set a tone that appeals to the user and supports the organization's goals.

Because the right personality is so dependent on each application's business needs and user base, not every application needs a strong, in-your-face approach; for the right application, subtlety is every bit as effective an approach. But an application that defines its personality well does the following:

- Uses a layout that reflects underlying elements of its personality, such as a weather app that provides plenty of white space surrounding its map and forecast to help it feel clean and well-focused

- Chooses appropriate type for its purpose and audience, like a charting tool that picks a sans-serif instead of a serifed font to feel casual and modern instead of staid

- Has colors that reflect brand requirements as well as subtler requirements, like using highly contrasting colors (e.g., blue and orange) to provide visual energy

- Displays icons and images that contribute to, rather than conflict with, the personality; for example, using rough illustrations instead of stock photos to give an app a handcrafted feel

- Applies the personality's color and type specifications to interface widgets so that the personality filters down to the smallest elements

USING THE VISUAL DESIGN TOOLS: LAYOUT, TYPE, COLOR, IMAGERY, AND STYLED CONTROLS

In *Visual Usability*, Debby and Tania broke down the elements of visual application design into five tools: layout, typography, color, imagery, and styled controls. Careful choices in each of these areas based on a rationale—a set of rules about how, when, and where to apply a tool to support consistency, hierarchy, and personality—result in a more usable application.

The tips offered in this chapter are by no means comprehensive. Our goal in this book is to teach you how to build your first web app, not to turn you into a full-fledged user interface designer, so the tips we've chosen are the ones we believe will help you most as you work on TastyTracker (and, hopefully, other applications in the future).

Layout

As we discussed in Chapter 2, the grid is the literal foundation of any well-designed page. A grid's columns give you invisible guides for where to place items onscreen and how wide those items should be. The columns are separated by small amounts of white space called *gutters* so that page elements aren't squished together and it's easier for someone's eye to follow each column.

Although responsive web grids are frequently twelve columns by default, they can include more or fewer columns or may group grid columns together to create wider ones that still feel visually harmonious simply because they're based on a multiple of the original column size. The code typically used for responsive grids also makes it easier to align elements vertically across grid columns, which neatens the page and helps expose relationships between similar items. However, it's important to remember that you don't need to use a responsive web framework to use a grid. Because grids are simply underlying, virtual columns, any page that's been designed with a grid in mind, and which translates that invisible set of columns into page elements of specific widths matched to those columns, is using a grid.

> Responsive web grids typically rely on the concept of a *row* (much like a table row) to group column elements, and the row will naturally give elements across grid columns the same top line. Bootstrap 4, as well as some other responsive frameworks, also supports the CSS Flexbox layout mode, which enables similar alignments. We cover this more in Chapter 5.

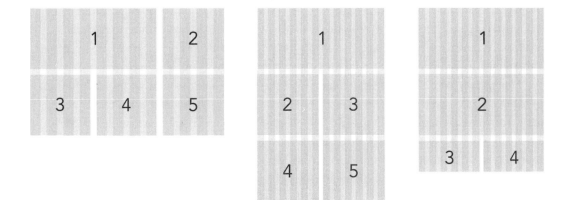

The responsive reflow example from Chapter 2, now with grid lines overlaid. Each screen has twelve columns; the width of a grid column changes with the width of the device.

Grids may sound like they'd make a page incredibly boxy, and in some cases, they do. But by varying column widths, applying color and images or textures, and, most important, leaving white space for the eye to "rest," a page with a strong underlying grid can still feel pleasant to use.

White space

White space is literally blank space on the page—but that makes it one of the most essential layout tools. We've all seen PowerPoint presentations and websites crammed full of text and images, and the reason we dislike them is because there's too much to look at; our eyes need that white space to guide us to individual items.[7] White space directs the eye to what's important, provides valuable

---

[7] For a slightly more detailed look at white space in UX design, see Jerry Cao et al., "Why White Space Is Crucial To UX Design," *CO.DESIGN*, May 28, 2015, fastcodesign.com/3046656/why-white-space-is-crucial-to-ux-design.

breathing room between items, and helps us determine which items are related to each other; we perceive items further away from each other as less related.

White space and grids work hand-in-hand to create usable layouts. White space used without a grid may appear haphazard and won't direct the eye effectively; grids without white space are cluttered and unpleasant to look at and use.

Templates

In a small application like TastyTracker, *templates*—screen layouts that can be applied to different pages—are less important. But in larger web applications, templates are vital. Not only do they simplify the design and development process by allowing you to repurpose the same layout for multiple screens, they also allow you to create pages rapidly by populating them with information from databases. Amazon and other online retailers don't have warehouses full of people writing new HTML pages for every product; they have databases in which they enter product information, and the website's page-generation code automatically pulls that product information into a template to display it.

Whenever you've got an app that has multiple pages that serve the same purpose, it's time for a template. And templates don't always have to be created on a page-by-page basis; they're also necessary for smaller onscreen "fragments," where content changes without reloading a page. For example, all tweets in someone's Twitter timeline include the Twitter user's name, avatar, tweet content, and various buttons and links to perform tasks with that tweet. The HTML used to code the layout of that tweet is stored as a fragment that gets displayed over and over on the page as the user reads through their timeline. Dynamic sites that rely on databases for content must also rely on fragments if they want to work efficiently, because no human could possibly code this level of content and keep up with demand.

We come back to fragments later in this book, when we work on adding Angular to TastyTracker.

Type

The right *typeface*—a set of fonts that may have different levels of boldness (*weight*) and *styles,* like italics or obliques—has a big impact on an application's personality, primarily because type has so much personality of its own. Typefaces designed for body text have different characteristics from those designed for distinctive headlines, which in turn have different characteristics from those designed for use displaying computer languages, and so on. That doesn't mean you can only use a typeface for its intended purpose, but it does mean that you need to be *aware* of that purpose and use the typeface carefully to support your desired personality.

Lobster is designed for distinctive headlines, not paragraphs.

Avenir is designed for paragraphs and also works for headlines.

Although separating groups of type into three categories (body, display, and monospace), as we've done in the chart below, is an oversimplification of the way typographers and designers catalog type, these categories are a simple way to explain the difference between typefaces and their roles.

	BODY TYPE		DISPLAY TYPE	MONOSPACE TYPE
	Sans-serif (no edges extending from letter ends)	Serif (small, pointed edges extending from letter ends)		
Purpose	Readable text and headlines. Space between letters varies to improve readability.		Visually distinctive, attention-grabbing headlines. Space between letters varies.	Computer code, which needs differentiation from body text and may also need the precise alignment that comes with not varying space between letters
Examples	Calibri Helvetica Trebuchet MS	Georgia Palatino Times New Roman	Brush Script Chalkboard Lobster	Courier Consolas Monaco
Personality	Modern (but can be perceived as plain)	Conservative (but can also feel elegant)	Varies widely by typeface	Technical (but may also be perceived as modern or stylishly retro)

We'll show examples of type's influence on TastyTracker's personality later in this chapter.

Web fonts

You should already be familiar with the small set of web fonts common across platforms, but it's now easier than ever to incorporate more interesting typography via free and paid services. Google Fonts and Font Squirrel are free and have a huge variety of attractive fonts available for web projects, but the most refined and well-designed choices are usually on sites aimed at professional designers: Typekit®, Hoefler & Co.®, MyFonts®, and others.

Color

Experienced designers will work out color palettes on their own, but people who don't have that level of expertise can start with online color palette generation tools, like Adobe®'s free Color CC. The great thing about using online color generators is that they take the guesswork out of it, using algorithms to base palettes on color complements, shades of a single color, and so on, so that you know the colors will always work together. But they don't take into account *how* you plan to use those colors (nor can they), and that's where more subjectivity comes in.

When developing your color palette, you'll need:

- One body text color with sufficient contrast against the page background color to be readable (e.g., black or dark gray on white)

- One or two additional colors that complement the text color and could be used for headers, backgrounds, logos, navigation, form elements, and anything else that isn't body text

- One or two tints (lighter versions of the color) for each of the additional colors—these are good for use as background highlights

- One "accent color" used only for error messaging and alerts

Start with an online color palette generator, and think about how you can apply the color rules listed above to what you see. Remember, just because a generator gives you five separate colors doesn't mean you have to use them. One body text color, one additional color, and the accent color may be enough.

Color and accessibility

Another drawback to online color generators is that they don't take into account a vital factor for people with visual impairments: there must be sufficient onscreen contrast for people to be able to read your text and interact with your app. Color contrast is critical for people with visual impairments, and it helps the rest of us as well by improving legibility.

This text is too dark and fails contrast tests.

This lighter text will pass a contrast test.

Websites, browser extensions, and desktop software can help you determine whether your color choices have enough contrast. (Our preferred tool is the Paciello Group's Colour Contrast Analyser tool, paciellogroup.com/resources/contrastanalyser/.) The tools will take into account text size as well, because a color choice applied to type at a small size might be too dark to pass but could be legible at much larger sizes.

Another important accessibility consideration for color use in app design is color blindness. Eight percent of men and 0.5 percent of women with a Northern European background have red-green color blindness.[8] Because of this, the World Wide Web Consortium's web accessibility guidelines state that color should never be "the only visual means of conveying information, indicating an action, prompting a response, or distinguishing a visual element."[9] Color should instead be used in conjunction with other elements, such as text and icons, to help app users understand what they're looking at regardless of whether they can perceive the colors accurately.

Images

If you're focusing on functional application design, the type of imagery you're most likely to use to help people identify tools and services they can interact with is icons. In modern apps, using icons often means employing icon fonts or SVG-format images that allow you to control their size and color via CSS.

Technically, *icons* are different from *symbols*; icons are a direct representation of an object or task, whereas symbols use a metaphor to represent a concept, such as a dove representing peace. Because icon sets used in application design may also incorporate symbols, we're going to use the term *icon* throughout this book to keep things as simple as possible.

Sample of some of Font Awesome's icons.

[8] "Facts About Color Blindness," *National Eye Institute*, Feb. 2015, nei.nih.gov/health/color_blindness/facts_about.
[9] "Guideline 1.4.1: Use of Color—Level A" in "How to Meet WCAG 2.0," *Web Accessibility Initiative*, July 20, 2016, w3.org/WAI/WCAG20/quickref/#qr-visual-audio-contrast-without-color.

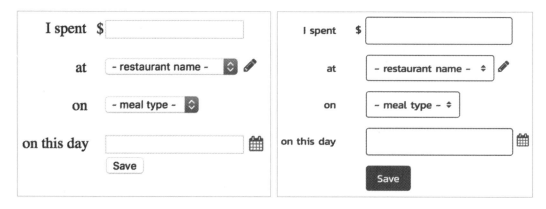

An unstyled TastyTracker form (left) feels perfunctory. A styled one (right) that applies rounded edges, colored borders, and type matching the body-font specs feels like a well-integrated part of the application.

The icon font supplier we use most frequently—and the one we'll use on TastyTracker—is Font Awesome, originally developed as part of the Twitter Bootstrap system and now a project in its own right. Font Awesome includes hundreds of icons of different styles for common tasks (editing, closing windows, etc.), social networks, and much more, and its friendly, rounded edges feel at home in modern web apps.

No matter what icons or other images you use in your app, the most important consideration is that they need to share the same visual aesthetic. Using icons (and photography) with different styles together yields results that look chaotic, undermine an application's personality, and, worst, feel less trustworthy.

Styling controls

Without CSS (and sometimes JavaScript), form elements default to browser base styles, which all look different. To promote consistency and apply your app's personality throughout, style interface controls to help them feel like a cohesive part of a whole.

Some responsive web frameworks, like Bootstrap and Foundation, include basic form-element styling and animated focus effects to bring an extra touch of refinement to the framework look and feel. JavaScript libraries and tools such as jQuery also provide the ability to customize form elements to harmonize with an app's visual design.

At a minimum, your buttons should be styled, and this can be done with pure CSS. When styling buttons, consider that you may need multiple levels of button; for example, your "level one" button design might apply only to primary actions, a "level two" button design would apply to secondary or cancel actions, and so on. The more complex an application, the more detailed the button hierarchy might need to be to promote user understanding. But practically speaking, anything more than four or five levels of button may be hard for users to grasp, difficult for designers and developers to maintain consistently, and also suggest an overly complex application.

SOFTWARE FOR YOUR VISUAL DESIGN

When you're ready to start designing your application, you'll need software to do it. If you're comfortable enough with CSS that you don't mind designing directly in your code, this is a perfectly fine (and efficient!) way to do it, especially if you already have a strong vision of what you want your app to look like. But using an image editor outside the code allows you to experiment with multiple options first, which, for many of us, is the best way to narrow in on the right solution for the audience.

- Adobe Photoshop® is the most well-known software program visual designers use and the one people who aren't designers are also most likely to be familiar with.

- GIMP, the GNU Image Manipulation Program, is a free, open-source image editor whose control scheme will be familiar to Photoshop users. In our experience, it's more challenging to use than Photoshop, but it's hard to beat "free, Photoshop–level capabilities" as a selling point.

- Pixlr® Editor is a free, Flash®–based image editor that runs in web browsers. Like GIMP, it will feel familiar to Photoshop users.

- Sketch, Mac–only software, is the priciest of our inexpensive design options, and it doesn't offer the pixel-based image editing capabilities of Photoshop, GIMP, or Pixlr. Instead, it's based on vectors, so it's possible to create designs that scale smoothly at any size, and it allows users to export design specs in CSS. It's also the tool we used to design TastyTracker.

DESIGNING TASTYTRACKER

We began TastyTracker's design by teasing apart what we knew about Donna and beginning exploration of TastyTracker's language. Both of these would create a foundation for TastyTracker's personality, which would then inform the rest of its design. We knew:

- Donna would want something that felt supportive and didn't shame her for her choices, which implied a warm personality.

- At the same time, Donna wasn't using TastyTracker for fun; she needed its help to meet a specific goal, so it should have a serious side.

- Some language we'd already used—including the name of the app itself—had a friendly tone, though not one that was overly familiar.

- There was an element of playfulness to using "tasty" in alliterative header phrases ("TastyTotals," "TastyTrends").

These observations suggested that we needed something approachable and inviting but that had a no-nonsense side as well. So we developed the following initial criteria for conveying this personality visually:

- Use a sans-serif typeface that includes at least four fonts and has a touch of flair but not so much flair that it becomes distracting.

- Develop a palette based on "warm" colors (colors tending toward red, orange, or yellow), provided they aren't too bright—something that supplies visual energy while retaining a soothing quality.

- Explore icon fonts to see if we can find one with more playfulness than Font Awesome, although if Font Awesome ultimately feels right, we'll use that.

For an application as minimal as TastyTracker, this felt like plenty to start with.

The TastyTracker typeface and logotype

Because type has such a strong influence on visual personality, we started by searching Google Fonts for the right typeface. Standard sans-serif faces like Arial, Helvetica, and Verdana are fine (in fact, we used Verdana in our wireframes) but are so well-worn that they lack the oomph we were looking for. We also considered whether this typeface could handle being used for TastyTracker's *logotype*—a "logo" consisting only of typeset text—or whether we would need something more adventurous.

We started with five options, one of which (Lobster 2) was explicitly a script display face and suitable only for logotype and header use—not for body text.

Arima Madurai

Exo 2

Lobster 2

Kanit

Quattrocento Sans

Arima Madurai and Exo 2 felt likely to have too much personality of their own for our purposes, but they were attractive enough to continue to explore further. So we typeset TastyTracker's name in each one's regular weight and compared them:

TastyTracker

TastyTracker

Tasty Tracker

TastyTracker

TastyTracker

This exercise immediately narrowed down our choices from five to two. The Arima Madurai felt too flowery and the Exo 2 too technical, whereas the Lobster 2 option looked like a logo for a hamburger chain. It was time to see how the logotype could work in different weights of Kanit and Quattrocento Sans instead.

TastyTracker QUATTROCENTO SANS REGULAR

TastyTracker QUATTROCENTO SANS BOLD

TastyTracker KANIT THIN

TastyTracker KANIT LIGHT

TastyTracker KANIT REGULAR

TastyTracker KANIT SEMIBOLD

Comparing the logotypes side-by-side told us that Quattrocento Sans wasn't the right choice; its rounder letterforms, especially of the lowercase *a* and *e*, felt inherently less interesting to us than the corresponding, more squared-off characters in Kanit. The logotype didn't have to be exciting, but it did need a little more zip than Quattrocento Sans was providing.

From there, our choice narrowed to the elegance of the Kanit Thin option, which we feared might be too thin onscreen, and the slightly stronger Kanit Light. We decided we'd choose one after seeing it in place in the design, where we'd also work on body and header type size.

The TastyTracker color palette

With type selection relatively complete, we moved on to color choice. We started in Adobe Color CC, working with warm options as a base for the palette and settling on orange as a compromise between red (too strong) and yellow (difficult to work with because of its brightness).

When we'd found options that looked good together, met our personality criteria of "soothing with a hint of energy," and followed accessibility guidelines, we added a few tints of the colors—necessary not just for possible backgrounds but also for the chart graphics—and finalized the palette. (You can see our original and final palettes at goo.gl/dODTV3.)

Laying out the screens

Working with the wireframe layouts as a guide, we applied our color and type choices to the mobile screen and developed two design directions to consider (see following page).

During visual design, it's normal to explore and consider alternative layouts to what's been covered in a wireframe; the wireframe represents feature and information requirements and hierarchy, whereas visual design must flesh those out by using type, color, and other tools to make that hierarchy as apparent as possible. The circular backgrounds and reversal of information as shown in the wireframe—totals first rather than explanation—emphasized the numbers but still made the explanation easy to find.

Compared to the design direction with the teal header, the gold-background option felt *blah*. The circles and centered headers of the second option felt fresher, so we chose that direction and looked at how it could expand to wider screens on tablets and desktop devices.

The portrait-mode tablet and desktop layouts took the same approach, shifting the first two modules of the app to equal-dimension sections at the top left and right and using the extra space at the bottom to display the charts side-by-side. This still kept the most important task in the quadrant of the screen people look at first[10], but gave more breathing room and prominence to secondary information. The desktop layout used larger type than the tablet but was otherwise the same.

---

[10] Eye-tracking studies performed with people who read languages written left-to-right show that people generally first look at the upper-left quadrant of the page (Jakob Nielsen, "F-Shaped Pattern for Reading Web Content," *Nielsen Norman Group*, Apr. 17, 2006, nngroup.com/articles/f-shaped-pattern-reading-web-content/).

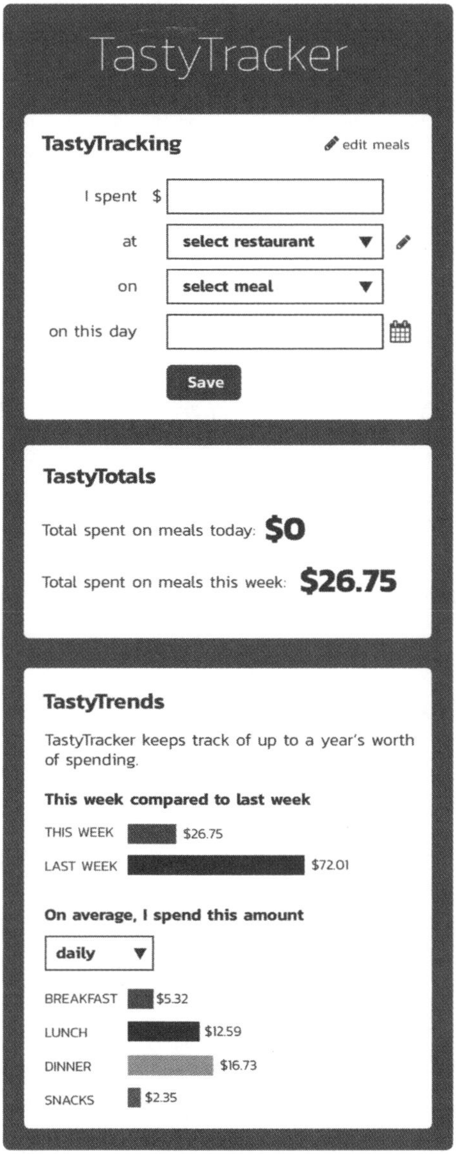
TastyTracker
TastyTracking
edit meals
I spent $
at
select restaurant
on
select meal
on this day
Save
TastyTotals
Total spent on meals today: $0
Total spent on meals this week: $26.75
TastyTrends
TastyTracker keeps track of up to a year's worth of spending.
This week compared to last week
THIS WEEK $26.75
LAST WEEK $72.01
On average, I spend this amount
daily
BREAKFAST $5.32
LUNCH $12.59
DINNER $16.73
SNACKS $2.35

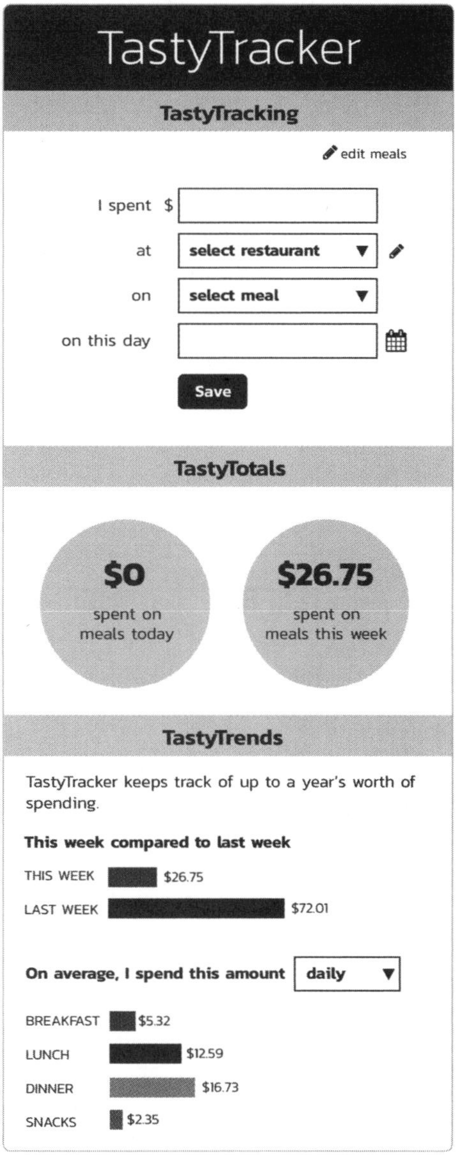
TastyTracker
TastyTracking
edit meals
I spent $
at
select restaurant
on
select meal
on this day
Save
TastyTotals
$0
spent on meals today
$26.75
spent on meals this week
TastyTrends
TastyTracker keeps track of up to a year's worth of spending.
This week compared to last week
THIS WEEK $26.75
LAST WEEK $72.01
On average, I spend this amount
daily
BREAKFAST $5.32
LUNCH $12.59
DINNER $16.73
SNACKS $2.35

You can view both of these images in full color at goo.gl/dODTV3.

Defining rules for applying the design

As we laid out the screens, we also considered how to apply color and type consistently throughout the app. We knew red would be reserved for alerts and brown would be the text color, but we had to set rules for how to display form elements, buttons, headers, icons, and so on; these rules would help Donna use the application, even if she only unconsciously made a connection that all interactive links, icons, and buttons were teal.

- Body text would be set in Kanit Light with headers in Kanit SemiBold. Kanit Bold would help TastyTotals' large numbers stand out.

- The header hierarchy moved from most important/largest (TastyTracker logotype), to 16pt Kanit SemiBold section headers, to 12pt Kanit SemiBold body text headers, to all-caps 10pt Kanit Light chart labels. (When using all-caps labels, you can often use a smaller body text size than normal and maintain readability.)

- Other than form elements, interactive parts of the screen would use teal. This included buttons, links, and icons. Form elements, which incorporated text, would remain brown. (This also called attention to the buttons and links, because their color would visually differentiate them from the elements on which they exert action.) The only other exception would be the delete X icon, which would be red to emphasize its destructive action.

- Secondary buttons, such as the Cancel button used for restaurant deletion, would be white with a teal border and teal text. This created a relationship between the two while maintaining the visual prominence of the teal primary button.

- Icons would use Font Awesome. Its icons looked at home in the app, and Font Awesome's massive catalog and ease of use made it the simplest choice.

Adding alerts

The last part of the design we considered was how alerts would display onscreen. As we discussed in Chapter 2, there were two instances where we knew there would need to be alert messaging: the message shown in the TastyTrends area before Donna has entered any data, and the warning message when she tries to delete a restaurant name. There might also need to be error messages associated with the form fields, but if we could set a visual style for the two cases we were certain of, then that same style could be applied to other messages later.

We'd already decided on the red background tint for alerts, as well as red for icons associated with them. So designing the alerts themselves (full color versions at goo.gl/dODTV3) was simply a matter of applying those specs and confirming that they were readable and stood out without being overly aggressive.

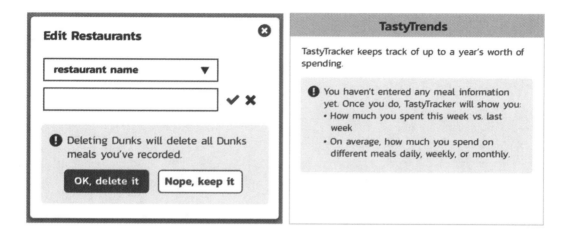

YOUR ASSIGNMENT

Although you're welcome to use our designs and specifications for TastyTracker—our original file is available in PDF and Sketch form—you probably have your own design rationale and preferences to apply to the app. For this chapter's assignment, you should:

- Pick a typeface to use in your app. It should have at least three font weights (regular, bold, italic). Set rules for use of your type styles, and create your logotype.

- Pick a color palette. Choose one text color, a secondary and/or tertiary color, and one accent color. Create tints of the secondary and tertiary colors. Set rules for use of your color palette.

- Apply your font and color selections to your screens in the image editing tool of your choice, adjusting your layout if needed to work effectively on mobile, tablet, and desktop devices.

PREPARING TO CODE: INSTALLING AND CONFIGURING

We've reached the point where we're about to leave the design-and-planning phase of this project.

Next we'll enter the phase where we actively write things—both the visual UI implementation in Bootstrap and the behind-the-scenes operational code in Angular, which we'll write using a language called TypeScript. Before we can begin any of that, however, we have to do some preparation.

It's certainly possible to just sit down with a text-editing program and start writing raw HTML, CSS, and JavaScript and create a web app that way. But few people do—not even the most masochistic programmers. There exist any number of tools to make the process easier, and we'll be installing them in addition to the major ones named in the previous paragraph—compilers, package managers, support libraries, and other things that are probably mystifying to you right now. Don't worry! We explain what they all do. Many of these tools are "install and leave alone." We won't go deeply into their workings, but we will give you a reasonable idea of what it all is and why we're asking you to install it.

STEP 1: INSTALLING THE PACKAGE MANAGER

We're installing so many tools and systems that it's worth our time and pain to install a tool just to wrangle other tools. A bundle of files that make up a single tool or application and all its other required resources—its *dependencies*—is sometimes called a *package,* and the wrangling tool we're about to install is called a *package manager.* The one we're using is *npm,* and we use it to install our other tools as well as to run some of those tools when we need them.

The npm package manager requires a tool called *node.js* (sometimes *nodejs* or even just *node*). This is a JavaScript *library* that primarily handles communication between processes ("How can this thing get data from or send data to this other thing?"). In fact, "npm" stands for "Node Package Manager."

Downloading node.js

Node.js is available from nodejs.org. The node.js website will try to detect your operating system and offer you some easy buttons to install a version that is appropriate to you. If it guesses wrong, you may need to go to the "other downloads" page and pick the right version. Note that node.js usually offers both an LTS (long-term support) version and a Current version. The LTS version is preferred for our purposes.

The download will be a self-contained installer: an .msi file for Windows, a .pkg file for Mac. Save the file to your desktop so you can get to it easily. After you've downloaded it, run it. You will need administrator/sudo rights in order to do this.

In general, installing software requires "administrator" rights. Normally on single-user Windows machines, the main user also has administrator rights, but if this isn't the case, before installing node.js, you'll either need to:

- Change to a user who does have administrator rights.
- Give/acquire administrator rights for your current user.
- Right-click the installer and select "Run as Administrator," if that option is available.

If you *do* have an issue with administrator rights, be aware that this will affect several later steps in our installation instructions.

For Mac users, the equivalent warning is that some tasks in our instructions, including installing node.js, will require you to use the sudo command to run the process as super-user; you'll be asked for your administrator password when doing so. You can confirm whether you have administrator rights by going to System Preferences > Users and Groups and checking to see whether the word "Admin" appears below your username. If you don't have the ability to use sudo, you'll need to obtain it.

Installation choices

Windows users

You will be asked to specify an installation directory (folder). Both node.js and npm will be installed into that location. Pick a location you can get to easily, because immediately after we install, we'll need to make a few changes. In this example, we assume you've decided to install it into `C:\nodejs`. But choose your own *path* (directory location) as you like, and substitute accordingly.

This installation directory has *nothing to do with* the working directories we're going to set up later in this chapter, and in fact should *not* be the same location.

The installer will also eventually ask you which parts of node.js you want to install. Set it to install everything. In particular, you need node.js itself, npm, and the feature which adds npm to your path so we can run it from anywhere.

Mac users

The installer doesn't give you a choice about installation paths. It puts the base node.js under `/usr/local/nodejs` and the npm program in `/usr/local/bin/npm`.

By default, it will install both node.js and npm, which is what you want. It does *not* alter your path, which may interfere with your ability to run npm; if `/usr/local/bin` isn't already in your path, you'll have to alter your path so that you can run npm from anywhere.

To find out whether **/usr/local/bin** is in your path, open **Applications > Utilities > Terminal** and type the following command:

```
echo $PATH
```

This displays the list of directories in your path. If it doesn't include **/usr/local/bin**, you'll have to add it, which fortunately is easy to do with a text editor. (See Chapter 5, page 90, for our list of suggested text editors.) In that program, go to **File > Open File By Name** and enter the following filename:

```
/etc/paths
```

When you try to edit the file, you'll be asked if you're sure you want to unlock it; confirm that you do. Add **/usr/local/bin** to the file and save it. (You'll have to type your administrator password to do this.) Open a new Terminal window—any changes to **/etc/paths** are not automatically reflected in previously opened windows—and type **echo $PATH** again to confirm that your changes were successful.

When the installer has installed everything and finished running, it's safe to delete the .msi or .pkg file. We no longer need it.

STEP 2: SETTING UP THE PROJECT DIRECTORY

It's time to pick the location where we do all our actual work. This should be a directory with an easy-to-get-to path, for reasons that will soon be obvious. It should be on a drive with enough space to hold the tools and dependencies we're about to install (around 200MB, as of this writing). For this example, we use `C:\tastytracker` (Windows) or `~/tastytracker` (Mac) as our project directory. (You can choose your own directory name if you prefer.)

Windows users

Select Computer from the Start menu, choose drive C:, and create the `tastytracker` folder on drive C: in the file manager. Go into the folder you just created.

It will be *greatly helpful* to you later if you make a shortcut to a command window which starts in this directory. Here's how you do it:

1. Go into the `tastytracker` folder you just created.

2. Right-click (anywhere in the file-listing pane) and scroll to New in the menu that pops up, then select Shortcut.

3. When asked for the program to run, type `cmd` (no need to browse for it); when asked for a name to give the shortcut, name it anything you like.

4. Right-click the shortcut that was just created. Select Properties from the menu.

5. Select Shortcut from the tabs at the top if it isn't already selected. In the "Start in:" field, enter the path you've chosen as the project directory, including the drive letter (e.g. `C:\tastytracker`). Press OK.

6. Now when you run that shortcut and the command window opens, the prompt should show the path of your project directory.

If you don't do this, every time you open a command window to do something in npm, you'll need to remember to change to the project directory first. The npm manager works *relative to the path where you currently are*. That is, if you install or run things with npm, unless you go to some trouble to tell it otherwise, it will install or run them *in your current directory*. That's what we want it to do, but it's very important that you be in the right place when using it!

If you have to run the command window using "Run as Administrator" (see remarks in the node.js instructions, page 68), you will *not* start in the correct location, despite the settings we've just made. Windows always starts cmd in C:\Windows\system32 when run as Administrator, for obscure reasons. Pay attention to the path in the prompt, and use cd to change directory as needed. You definitely do not want to install packages in the system32 directory!

Mac users

Go to your Home directory in the Finder. It's the directory listed with a house symbol, or you can choose "Home" from the Finder's Go menu. Create the tastytracker folder under the Home directory.

The Terminal command window should always start in your home directory. To check on this, open a new Terminal window and enter the command ls. Among the files and folders listed, you should see the tastytracker directory you just created. You can move into that directory with cd tastytracker, which you will have to do every time you're about to do command-line work on this project (including the rest of these instructions).

In case you didn't read the Windows part, we'll repeat: npm works *relative to the path where you currently are;* that is, it installs or runs things *under your current directory.* That's what we want it to do, but this makes it very important to be in the right directory when using it, so keep track of where you are. Remember, pwd always shows you your current directory.

STEP 3: SETTING UP AND RUNNING THE PROJECT CONFIGURATION FILES

We've posted three premade project configuration files, as well as Bootstrap HTML and CSS files and our final application code, on the npm website, so you can download and install them as you would any other package. Follow these steps:

1. Go into your tastytracker folder.

2. While in that directory, type this command: npm install tastytracker-demo-pkg

Assuming there weren't any errors with the installation process (and there shouldn't be, though there may be warnings, which you can ignore), you should now have a tastytracker -demo-pkg directory within your tastytracker folder's node_modules subfolder. Our demo files are divided up by chapter.

We provide you these premade configuration files because they're complex enough that you won't want to write them from scratch. Even when you go on to design and build future apps (which we hope you will), you will likely want to copy old versions of these project files and edit them to fit your new needs. We got them from Angular's quickstart (angular.io/docs /ts/latest/quickstart.html) and adapted them to suit this project. Others will borrow and adapt ours. It's the circle of life.

But you do need to have an idea of what they do and why we need them.

The package description file (package.json)[11] describes your project to npm. If you were bundling up your project as a package so that other people could install it using npm, the file would be required; here, it's only needed as a convenience . . . but it's a big convenience. It keeps us from having to run some twenty separate npm installs by hand and also allows us to create shorthand commands to run other tools via npm easily.

The package.json file should look like this:

```json
{
  "name": "tastytracker",
  "version": "1.0.0",
  "description": "Dependencies for the TastyTracker project",
  "scripts": {
    "start": "tsc && concurrently \"npm run tsc:w\" \"npm run lite\" ",
    "lite": "lite-server",
    "tsc": "tsc",
    "tsc:w": "tsc -w",
    "typings": "typings"
  },
  "license": "UNLICENSED",
  "private": true,
  "dependencies": {
    "@angular/common": "2.x",
    "@angular/compiler": "2.x",
    "@angular/core": "2.x",
    "@angular/forms": "2.x",
    "@angular/platform-browser": "2.x",
    "@angular/platform-browser-dynamic": "2.x",
    "@angular/router": "3.x",
    "bootstrap": "4.0.0-alpha.5",
    "core-js": ">=2.4.1",
    "moment": ">=2.13.0",
    "reflect-metadata": ">=0.1.3",
    "rxjs": "5.0.0-beta.12",
```

[11] We'll review how our package.json file works, but for more information on package configuration in general, see docs.npmjs.com/files/package.json.

```
    "systemjs": ">=0.19.27",
    "zone.js": ">=0.6.17"
  },
  "devDependencies": {
    "concurrently": ">=2.2.0",
    "lite-server": ">=2.2.2",
    "typescript": ">=2.0.2",
    "typings": ">=1.3.2"
  }
}
```

The name, version, and description items are all set as we please to describe this project, but "name" is important—there are other parts of the project that will need to match it, so if you change it, you'll need to make changes in a couple of other places later. We've started the version at 1.0.0, although some people would start "prerelease" versions of software at 0.1.0. If we were sending this app out into the world in a package, "license" would be important; for now it is "UNLICENSED," which means "no one else has permission to use this."

The "scripts" list has some shortcuts we will run later via npm. *tsc* means "TypeScript Compiler" and does just that; *typings* is a necessary setup tool for TypeScript; *lite-server* is used to test our application locally (more on that in the Angular chapters); and the "start" shortcut is used when we do those tests. It runs lite-server and tsc at the same time, and to do so, it needs another tool called *concurrently*.

The packages that these tools come in (tsc is part of the *typescript* package) are all listed in the "devDependencies" list at the bottom of the file. The difference between "dependencies" and "devDependencies" is that development (dev) dependencies are things you need to create and test the application, whereas dependencies are the things the application itself needs to run properly.

This may be the first time you've encountered a file in JSON format; it's a safe bet that it won't be your last. The curly braces { } in the file mark the beginning and end of a list of named values. (Some people call this type of data an *associative array* and others a *hash*.) You'll see an outermost set of those braces, meaning the whole file is one big list; some items on that list, such as "name," are single values, and others, like "scripts," are lists of values themselves, with their own braces. Items in a list are separated by commas; the last item in the list must *not* have a comma. For our purposes, both the name and value in any item are enclosed in quotes, but the colon is not part of the name and is outside them. There are other wrinkles to JSON, but this is all we need.

If you were bundling the app as a package, you'd need to bundle the dependencies, but not the dev dependencies.

Our dependencies are:

- Various parts of Angular (we only install the parts we need)
- Bootstrap, which has dependencies of its own that we'll install separately
- *systemjs*, which tells our app where to look to load the various things it needs
- *moment,* a date/time handling library
- *rxjs* (Reactive Extensions for JavaScript), which is used by Angular
- *core-js,* which enables older browsers to handle our code properly
- *reflect-metadata,* which is needed by TypeScript
- *zone.js,* which enables Angular's bindings

In each case, the file specifies what version of a particular package we need, although only two of the items have exact specifiers. It's better to allow npm to get the most recent suitable version where possible. We believe the version requirements in our project file will be handled correctly by npm without needing any intervention from you. However, more information about how npm reads version specifications, and how to obtain specific versions from npm as needed, are contained in the `about_versioning.txt` file in the `tastytracker-demo-pkg` directory you have just installed.

The second premade configuration file, tsconfig.json,[12] contains a set of rules which determine how TypeScript, and tsc in particular, will behave. The tsconfig.json file should look like this:

```
{
    "compilerOptions": {
      "target": "es5",
      "module": "commonjs",
      "moduleResolution": "node",
      "sourceMap": true,
      "emitDecoratorMetadata": true,
      "experimentalDecorators": true,
      "removeComments": false,
      "noImplicitAny": true
    }
}
```

---

[12] For more information on tsconfig.json, see typescriptlang.org/docs/handbook/tsconfig-json.html.

Boolean values (true or false) take a value of true or false *without enclosing quotes*. If you put quotes around the value, you would instead be setting the property to the text *string* "true" or "false"—which is not the same thing.

These are the settings preferred by Angular, and we won't discuss them in detail. The "target" option says that when tsc compiles TypeScript to JavaScript, it creates JavaScript in the ES5 standard instead of the newer ES6. This is done for compatibility reasons and won't affect us operationally at all.

The third premade file is systemjs.config.js.[13] JSON files do not permit internal comments, but .js files do, so rather than explain what it does here, the explanation is right in the file! (The comment lines are the ones which begin with //.)

The systemjs.config.js file should look like this:

```
// The SystemJS config file tells our Angular modules and components
// where to find the things they will use/include!
(function (global) {
  System.config({
    // Paths are useful aliases which will be used in the map below.
    // They are relative to the root of the system, e.g. the 'npm:'
    // path will refer to a 'node_modules' directory in the SAME
    // directory as this config file!
    paths: {
      'npm:': 'node_modules/'
    },
    // The map tells the System loader where to find stuff.
    map: {
      app: 'app', // OUR stuff lives here.
      '@angular/common': 'npm:@angular/common/bundles/common.umd.js',
      '@angular/compiler': 'npm:@angular/compiler/bundles/compiler.umd.js',
      '@angular/core': 'npm:@angular/core/bundles/core.umd.js',
      '@angular/forms': 'npm:@angular/forms/bundles/forms.umd.js',
      '@angular/platform-browser':
'npm:@angular/platform-browser/bundles/platform-browser.umd.js',
      '@angular/platform-browser-dynamic':
'npm:@angular/platform-browser-dynamic/bundles/platform-browser-dynamic.umd.js',
      '@angular/router': 'npm:@angular/router/bundles/router.umd.js',
      'moment': 'npm:moment',
      'rxjs': 'npm:rxjs'
    },
```

---

[13] For more information on systemjs, see github.com/systemjs/systemjs.

```
// The packages section tells System loader how to load when there is no
// filename and/or no extension. The main.js in the app section is very
// important because we don't explicitly specify it anywhere else in the
// section; this is the only place System can learn how to load it.
packages: {
  app: {
    main: './main.js',
    defaultExtension: 'js'
  },
  moment: {
    main: 'moment.js',
    defaultExtension: 'js'
  },
  rxjs: {
    defaultExtension: 'js'
  }
 }
});
})(this);
```

Notice the line that says app: 'app'. This line is important because it says that for all our own Angular code—the bulk of the work we will be doing later in Angular—this loader will expect to find the files in a subdirectory of the project directory called app. Go ahead and create that directory (folder) under the project directory now.

STEP 4: INSTALLING DEPENDENCIES

Now that those three files are in place in the project directory, we're finally ready to install all the dependencies we listed in package.json.

You're still in your project directory, right? Open a command window (Windows users: use the shortcut you've made; Mac users: open a Terminal window), and make sure you're in the project directory there, too. Enter the command:

```
npm install
```

After you enter the command, npm reads the dependencies you listed in the package file, finds them all, and installs them. It could take a while.

As already noted, any WARN messages npm generates are okay to ignore for our purposes. But ERR messages will stop the process, and then we have to fix whatever is wrong and try to install again. We have run this install many times with no ERR messages, and we hope you will, too, but things do change.

The most common source of an ERR message is the user not having sufficient rights to run the install; see remarks in the node.js section about administrator rights (page 68). The second most common problem is a version mismatch issue.

Imagine, for example, that the maintainers of the Angular "core" module suddenly decide they're going to require version 3.x of Angular's "common" module. (This type of decision would be very bad practice, by the way.) Since we require version 2.x of "common," the installer can't install the version that "core" requires. Fortunately, if this happens, the npm error is lucid, and you should be able to adjust the versions in package.json to do what it needs.

Don't close the command window when the npm install is finished. We're not done.

Installing Bootstrap

In the command window, enter:

```
cd node_modules/bootstrap
```

node_modules didn't exist a few minutes ago; it's the directory npm made when it installed all your dependencies and dev dependencies. But Bootstrap has dependencies of its own, and for various reasons, we need to install those separately. So now that you're in the Bootstrap directory, enter the command:

```
npm install
```

a second time.

This reads a separate package.json file that's in the Bootstrap directory (you didn't create it; npm installed it) and follows its instructions to install what Bootstrap needs.

When npm is finished, we have to install one more package so that Grunt, the tool that compiles parts of Bootstrap, can be run from anywhere without having to deal with path issues. Enter the following command:

Windows: `npm install grunt-cli --global`

Mac: `sudo npm install grunt-cli --global`

The `--global` option tells the npm install to put a package (the Grunt command-line interface) in a globally available location rather than under the current directory. This is an option we don't want to use in any other situation, but it's important here. (It's also why this command requires administrator rights and the previous ones didn't.)

At this point, Mac users may run into a bug with some 3.x versions of npm. If you get an error that contains the message "uid must be unsigned int," then you have encountered this issue. This means `sudo` is having trouble putting files in that global npm installation directory, and the easiest solution is to use the following command to make you the owner of the directory instead of the root (administrator) user:

```
sudo chown -R $(whoami) $(npm config get prefix)/lib/node_modules
```

After you've done that, try the install command again, but *don't* prefix it with `sudo`—now that you own the directory it's writing to, you don't need it!

Don't close the command window yet. We have one more task.

Configuring typings

The typings[14] utility enables TypeScript to play nicely with other JavaScript libraries that aren't part of TypeScript or Angular. It's not always necessary, but we have two libraries in this project—*core-js* and *moment*—for which it is.

We didn't provide you with a default typings.json configuration file because we're going to make one from scratch. This will also show you how to run some outside commands via npm.

In your command window, assuming you're still in `node_modules/bootstrap`, go back up to your project directory like this:

```
cd ../..
```

which just means "go up two directories."

Now, after confirming that you're back in the project directory, enter the following commands in order. (Note that the spacing is important, and the character following `dt` in the latter two commands is a tilde, not a hyphen.)

---

[14] For more information about typings, see github.com/typings/typings.

```
npm run typings init
npm run typings -- install dt~core-js --save --global
npm run typings -- install dt~moment --save --global
```

The first command creates a skeleton typings.json file in our project directory. Each of the latter two commands adds a line to that file and also installs necessary files in a typings folder.

You can finally exit that command window.

WHERE ARE WE NOW?

At this point, you should have the following subdirectories (folders) in your project directory:

- An app directory, which you created and is empty at the moment

- A node_modules directory, which contains everything installed by npm

- A typings directory, which was created in the previous step

You should also have the following four files in your project directory:

- package.json

- systemjs.config.js

- tsconfig.json

- typings.json

plus, if you're a Windows user, you should have your shortcut to a command window.

Most of what you have just done and installed is now "set and forget"—we need it, but we can leave it alone and let it do its thing. Your work from here on out will almost all be either creating more files in the project directory, or creating files in app.

It may seem like we've installed an awful lot of stuff, especially as you learn more about what some of these tools do and realize there's significant overlap between their functions. (Bootstrap requires jQuery, which covers some of the same ground as TypeScript and Angular; node.js, which we don't even use directly at all, handles some of the same things Angular does; and so on.) This is unfortunately the way the world of web development works. Certainly there are "purer" methods—we could, with some fuss, restructure our use of Bootstrap to not require jQuery at all and we could write Angular (painfully) without using TypeScript. We have chosen tools that we believe will continue to be relevant, but we have also made some choices in favor of ease of use. We did not opt for conservation of install space, nor for programming purity.

Obviously, when your app is finished, if you want to distribute it, you shouldn't bring along all of the ~200MB of files you've just installed. What you have here is a *development environment,* and those are always much, much larger than a *production* application package. At the end of this book, we discuss what's involved in trimming out all the bits you no longer need and distributing only the set of files the app needs to actually run.

But there's more work to do before we get to that point.

5

BOOTSTRAP

If you're already comfortable with HTML and CSS, writing pages in Bootstrap will feel familiar to you.

Most of your time coding TastyTracker will be spent creating a layout structure and then applying CSS classes to it to get your desired behavior across screen sizes, which isn't any different from creating a web page in plain-vanilla HTML and CSS. Bootstrap's magic—and the magic of similar responsive frameworks—lies in its pre-created classes, which simplify developing responsive layouts and page elements like forms, alerts, and accordions.

Bootstrap's documentation (v4-alpha.getbootstrap.com/getting-started/introduction) is excellent, and it would be pointless for us to fully replicate it. Instead, we concentrate on the key classes you need to know to build TastyTracker and other web applications. You also get a taste of SCSS ("Sassy CSS"), an extension of CSS that allows you to set variables that propagate CSS values throughout your files; for example, you can set master colors that will then apply to headers, buttons, and so on automatically.

We installed Bootstrap 4 alpha 5 in the previous chapter. You'll find it in your `node_modules` directory, which includes the following subfolders in a `bootstrap` folder:

- `dist`: Bootstrap's default CSS and JavaScript

- `grunt`: Files necessary to support Grunt, the tool you'll use to compile Bootstrap's SCSS and JavaScript

- `js`: JavaScript files to support individual Bootstrap components

- `scss`: Individual SCSS files for different components and aspects of Bootstrap

When you're ready to start coding, store your files in the main `tastytracker` directory rather than any of the Bootstrap subfolders; otherwise, the compiler will delete your files as it does its work. The only file you'll need to edit and store in a Bootstrap folder is `_custom.scss`, which lives in Bootstrap's `scss` directory. (Later in the book, we'll move the code you create in this chapter into other locations within the project structure.)

BOOTSTRAP BASICS

Document structure

In order to use Bootstrap, your HTML will have to reference Bootstrap's CSS and JavaScript, as well as a couple of other JavaScript libraries (jQuery and Tether). But the file's structure is otherwise straightforward; apart from these few inclusions, it's a pretty typical HTML document.

We've provided a basic index.html file for you to start your TastyTracker work. (Our final code is available, too.) The initial contents of the basic index.html look like this:

```
<!DOCTYPE html>
<html lang="en">
  <head>
    <!-- Required meta tags always come first. -->
    <meta charset="utf-8">
    <meta name="viewport" content="width=device-width, initial-scale=1,
shrink-to-fit=no">
    <meta http-equiv="x-ua-compatible" content="ie=edge">
    <!-- Bootstrap CSS -->
    <link rel="stylesheet"
href="node_modules/bootstrap/dist/css/bootstrap.min.css">
    <title>TastyTracker</title>
  </head>
  <body>
<p>Your code goes here.</p>
    <!-- The following code should be at the end of your body section. -->
    <!--Load jQuery first, then Tether, then Bootstrap JS. -->
    <script src="node_modules/jquery/dist/jquery.min.js"></script>
    <script src="node_modules/tether/dist/js/tether.min.js"></script>
    <script src="node_modules/bootstrap/dist/js/bootstrap.min.js"></script>
  </body>
</html>
```

Apart from the Bootstrap–specific CSS and JavaScript links, the only other unusual elements in this file are the three <meta> tags at the top. These tags identify the language character set for the document, set *viewport* (browser width) size and scale, and enable a special compatibility mode to force Internet Explorer® to use the latest rendering engine for Microsoft Edge®. You shouldn't have to change anything about these or the CSS or JavaScript links to use this file; just delete our initial paragraph tag and start coding.

Containers and grids

Bootstrap expects your page elements to be nested within a container. Using a container `div` to set margins and padding for an entire page is a well-established approach to front-end web development, and Bootstrap offers two container classes for this purpose: a general `container` class with a fixed maximum width at each responsive breakpoint, and a fully fluid `container -fluid` class that takes up 100 percent of the page width no matter what the screen size. For most cases (including TastyTracker), you need only one container class.

As we've mentioned in previous chapters, Bootstrap's primary structural elements are its grid classes, just as they are in other responsive web frameworks. Grids have twelve columns by default no matter what size the screen and must be enclosed within a `<div class="row">` tag. A "row" `div`, just like a table row, groups a horizontal set of `div` or other structural elements and ensures that they all line up correctly; the column declarations within the row are analogous to table columns. You can (and often should) use multiple column classes on a single `div` to determine how it reflows on screens of different sizes.

The default set of responsive breakpoints [15] in Bootstrap 4 alpha 5, the version used in this book, is as follows:

BREAKPOINT	WIDTH	COLUMN CLASS
Extra-small	< 544px	`.col-xs-#`
Small	544px–767px	`.col-sm-#`
Medium	768px–991px	`.col-md-#`
Large	992px–1199px	`.col-lg-#`
Extra-large	>1200px	`.col-xl-#`

The number sign # included in each class is a placeholder for the number of columns, so if you wanted to create a layout with three boxes that reflowed over small, medium, and large screens, it might look like this:

```
<div class="row">
  <div class="col-sm-12 col-md-6 col-lg-3">
    I take up full width on small screens, 1/2 width on medium
ones, and 1/3 width on large ones.
```

[15] "Layout," *Bootstrap*, published 2016, accessed Sept. 12, 2016, v4-alpha.getbootstrap.com/layout/grid/. As of January 2017's release of Bootstrap 4 alpha 6, the breakpoints have changed slightly, with extra-small set to anything less than 576px and small running between 576px–767px.

```
  </div>
  <div class="col-sm-12 col-md-6 col-lg-9">
    I take up full width on small, 1/2 on medium, 2/3 on large.
  </div>
  <div class="col-sm-12">
    This div always takes up the full width of the screen.
  </div>
</div>
```

The output from this code would look like this:

SMALL

I take up full width on small screens, 1/2 width on medium ones, and 1/3 width on large ones.

I take up full width on small, 1/2 on medium, 2/3 on large.

This div always takes up the full width of the screen.

MEDIUM

I take up full width on small screens, 1/2 width on medium ones, and 1/3 width on large ones.

I take up full width on small, 1/2 on medium, 2/3 on large.

This div always takes up the full width of the screen.

LARGE

I take up full width on small screens, 1/2 width on medium ones, and 1/3 width on large ones.

I take up full width on small, 1/2 on medium, 2/3 on large.

This div always takes up the full width of the screen.

As you can see by comparing the code with its output, chaining together the CSS grid classes is the key to setting your layout preferences. Generally, you'll want the number of columns to sum up to twelve across sizes—for example, the first two divs are specified as col-med-6, which adds up to the full twelve grid columns—but you can reduce or exceed that number. If you do, the row will either not take up the full width of the grid or push a div to the next line accordingly, which is what's happening with our bottom div.

This bottom div is also special because it only specifies one size, col-sm-12, yet it consistently takes up full width on medium and large screens. This is because of Bootstrap's mobile-first approach: in the absence of other grid width specifications, the smallest available specification will apply to all breakpoints above it.

Bootstrap's grid is immensely flexible. For example, there may be times when you want to skip a few grid columns to place something more precisely onscreen. In that case, you can use offset classes with the syntax offset-[size]-#. For example, let's say you want to make a layout with a lot of extra space on the left:

```
<div class="row">
  <div class="col-xs-4 offset-xs-3">
    This is a div offset three columns from the left.
  </div>
</div>
```

This is a div offset three columns from the left.

As with regular grid classes, offset classes are mobile-first as well, so if the offset applies consistently across breakpoints, you only need to set it at the smallest size.

You can also nest rows inside of rows, a handy feature that ensures all parts of your layout are neatly aligned. Nested rows still use the same twelve-column grid, but their grid's full width is based on the width of the parent element, not the width of the page.

```
<div class="row">
  <div class="col-xs-6">
    This is a six-column div.
  </div>
  <div class="col-xs-6">
    This is also a six-column div.
    <div class="row">
      <div class="col-xs-3">
        Name:
      </div>
      <div class="col-xs-9">
        Duggan
      </div>
    </div>
  </div>
</div>
```

This is a
six-column div.

This is also a
six-column div.

Name: Duggan

Beyond the Bootstrap grid: Flexbox

As of Bootstrap 4, the framework supports an emerging CSS layout standard called Flexbox (w3.org/TR/css-flexbox-1/)—and as of January 2017, the date of Bootstrap 4's sixth alpha release, Flexbox is Bootstrap's default. Flexbox attempts to solve some of CSS's core layout problems by creating a markup language that enables boxes to change sizes smoothly across screens, as well as change sizes relative to each other. However, because the Flexbox standard is relatively young compared to CSS itself, it isn't perfectly supported across browsers and platforms. Older browsers, especially versions of Internet Explorer prior to version 11 (which itself still has compatibility bugs), don't always support Flexbox. (See caniuse.com/#search=flex to get the most up-to-date list of browsers supporting Flexbox.) Thus, before relying on Flexbox to lay out your app, you should be sure that your audience is using browsers and platforms that can view Flexbox content properly.

To get a sense of Flexbox's power, take a look at Flexbox in 5 Minutes (cvan.io/flexboxin5/), an interactive tutorial that shows off Flexbox's capabilities and allows you to play with its configurations. You don't need to know all these configurations to use Flexbox in Bootstrap, but it helps to see them so that you can understand Flexbox's model, which takes the direction of the "flex" (row or column) into account along with how the boxes align on the screen and with each other.

Conveniently, the way Flexbox works in Bootstrap is almost completely analogous to the way the traditional Bootstrap grid works. The biggest difference is that you don't have to set column numbers unless you want to; instead, grid elements will distribute themselves equally based on the number of column divs you create. Use column number settings when you want a grid element to be proportionally larger or smaller than other items, or when you want a column to be full width (col-[size]-12).

Here's how our nested grid code would be rewritten using Bootstrap's Flexbox classes—almost exactly the same, barring use of col-xs for the two primary divs instead of col-xs-6:

```
<div class="row">
  <div class="col-xs">
    This is a six-column div.
  </div>
  <div class="col-xs">
    This is also a six-column div.
    <div class="row">
      <div class="col-xs-3">
        Name:
      </div>
      <div class="col-xs-9">
        Duggan
      </div>
    </div>
  </div>
</div>
```

Bootstrap also includes three Flexbox-specific vertical alignment classes—flex-items-[size]-top, flex-items-[size]-middle, and flex-items-[size]-bottom—to manage vertical alignment within divs, a particular bugbear for developers. The Bootstrap grid documentation (v4-alpha.getbootstrap.com/layout/grid/) covers these and other Flexbox classes in more detail.

Flexbox isn't enabled by default in Bootstrap 4 alpha 5, so if you want to use it, you'll have to change the value of the SCSS variable $enable-flex from false to true and then recompile. If that sounds new and intimidating, don't worry; we cover SCSS and compilation later in this chapter.

TEXT EDITORS

To code Bootstrap and Angular effectively, you need a text editor. A text editor designed for coding is different from one designed for word processing; it displays text in a monospaced font; its default save format is plain text; and it includes *syntax coloring,* a visual convenience that color-codes different types of programming terms to make them easier to spot. (It also makes it easier to spot errors, because nothing says "I've made a huge mistake" quite like half of your program turning pink because you forgot to close a quotation mark.)

Good-quality text editors are available relatively inexpensively, or even for free. Here are a few options:

- Notepad++ (notepad-plus-plus.org)—free, Windows only
- Sublime Text—free to evaluate before purchase; available for Windows and Mac
- BBEdit (barebones.com/products/bbedit)—free to evaluate for 30 days and use with a limited feature set afterward until purchase; Mac only (and Debby's preferred text editor)

Text utility classes

Bootstrap includes numerous "components" for common website and app needs, but because TastyTracker has a relatively simple layout and custom functions that rely on Angular instead of Bootstrap's JavaScript, we're not going to cover most of these components in this book. Instead, we recommend perusing Bootstrap's library of components (v4-alpha.getbootstrap.com/components /alerts/) to get the full picture of what Bootstrap offers.

However, no matter whether a website or app includes these packaged components, it includes text that needs formatting, and that includes ensuring that page elements of all sorts are positioned correctly onscreen. Bootstrap classifies these tools as *utility* classes, and TastyTracker makes extensive use of some of them.

The ones we use most often in TastyTracker are spacer classes. Anyone who's spent time coding web pages will recognize that sometimes you need to manually push items right, left, up, or down to get the precise layout you want. Bootstrap's spacers simplify the process by using a standard syntax to create a mix-and-match set of classes: `[CSS property]-[sides]-[size]`[16].

---

[16] As of Bootstrap 4 alpha 6, the spacer syntax has changed to remove the hyphen between `CSS property` and `sides`; for example, a left-margin spacer with value 2 would be `m-l-2` in alpha 5, but `ml-2` in alpha 6.

Property is margin or padding, abbreviated m or p; sides are top, bottom, left, or right (abbreviated t, b, l, r), among other options. Size is a little less straightforward; whereas the default values you can use range from 0–3; these values are as follows:

0	delete margin or padding entirely
1	use the default spacing setting (1rem)
2	multiply the default spacing setting by 1.5
3	multiply the default spacing setting by 3

Thus, if you wanted an item to have right margin of 1.5 times the default horizontal spacing number, you'd add the following class to your code: m-r-2. A class name that abbreviated can look confusing at first, but once you get the hang of the spacer syntax, it's fast and easy to apply. You can also use SCSS to customize the default horizontal or vertical spacing, or even add more spacing numbers to the library if you need them.

There's one more spacing utility we used in TastyTracker that also covers a common need in many websites and apps: a horizontal centering tool for a div. Often, developers center such divs with code like this:

```
.className {
    margin: 0 auto;
}
```

In Bootstrap, you can accomplish the same goal by adding the m-x-auto class to the div and specifying its width inline or with a separate class.

Forms

Form elements are among the most common components you'll need for a web app, and TastyTracker is no exception. Bootstrap provides basic and custom form styling that looks consistent across browsers and platforms, includes focus highlight states to improve usability, and also includes special classes to help form input and label tags align properly.

Coding form elements in Bootstrap is essentially no different than coding them in straight HTML; you're coding pairs of label and input (or select, etc.) tags. However, Bootstrap expects you to wrap each set of label and associated inputs with a div or fieldset to which a form-group class has been applied. Using this class ensures that there's a consistent bottom margin applied to the label/input pair.

Controls should have a form-control class applied to them in most cases, or special form-check or form-control-file classes for checkboxes/radio buttons and file-upload controls. Sizing controls is as simple as applying standard grid column classes to the input. And alignment is a snap with the col-form-label class applied to labels to vertically center them next to their related inputs, or the form-inline class applied to forms or their elements to ensure plain text runs alongside inputs instead of below it.

Let's take a look at code to create the following form:

This form uses two classes we haven't yet discussed: a placeholder class for "type your name here" text that disappears when the user clicks into the form field, and a text-muted class for small instructional text appearing near a field. Otherwise, however, its classes should look familiar.

```
<form>
    <div class="form-group row">
        <label for="name-input"
class="col-xs-2 col-form-label text-xs-right">Your name</label>
            <div class="col-xs-5">
                <input type="text" class="form-control"
id="name-input" placeholder="type your name here" />
                <small id="name-input-help"
class="form-text text-muted">We won't share your name, we promise.</small>
            </div>
    </div>
    <div class="row">
        <fieldset class="form-group col-xs-5 offset-xs-2">
            <legend>Choose a Kang! Which is best?</legend>
                <div class="form-check">
                <label class="form-check-label">
                        <input type="radio"
class="form-check-input" name="kang-radios"
id="red-kangs" value="red-kangs" />
                            Red Kangs! Red Kangs are best!
                </label>
```

```
                            </div>
                            <div class="form-check">
                                <label class="form-check-label">
                                    <input type="radio"
            class="form-check-input" name="kang-radios"
            id="blue-kangs" value="blue-kangs" />
                                        Blue Kangs! Blue Kangs are best!
                                </label>
                            </div>
                            <div class="form-check">
                                <label class="form-check-label">
                                    <input type="radio"
            class="form-check-input" name="kang-radios"
            id="cant-decide" value="cant-decide" checked />
                                        I can't decide!
                                </label>
                            </div>
                        </fieldset>
                    </div>
                </form>
```

EDITING AND COMPILING SCSS

Your app will undoubtedly include your own classes for some design elements, but Bootstrap provides a way for you to control huge swaths of the app's look and feel through editing SCSS. Within Bootstrap's scss directory, you'll find two very important files: _custom.scss, which is empty, and _variables.scss, which is where you copy the Bootstrap variables you want to customize.[17]

The _variables.scss file includes Bootstrap's default settings for the following items:

▪ Colors

▪ Options (global styles for Flexbox, gradients, transitions, etc.)

▪ Spacing

▪ Body

▪ Links

▪ Grid breakpoints

---

[17] For people downloading Bootstrap 3 instead of installing via package manager, the Bootstrap team provides a more newbie-friendly way of customizing its look and feel with a massive form at getbootstrap.com/customize. Because Bootstrap 4 is in alpha as we write this book, that customization tool is not yet available for this version.

- Grid containers

- Grid columns

- Fonts

- Components (numerous individual settings to customize each component)

Customizing your app through SCSS involves these three steps:

1. In `_variables.scss`, locate the variables you want to edit.

2. Add a copy of those variables to `_custom.scss` and edit appropriately, being sure to remove the `!default` attribute from your edited variable.

3. Save your file and compile with Grunt to propagate your changes throughout the other SCSS files.

Here's an example. Let's say you want to enable Flexbox. You know from this chapter (and the Bootstrap documentation) that you'll need to edit the `$enable-flex` variable, so search for it in `_variables.scss` and add a copy of it to `_custom.scss`. It should look like this:

```
$enable-flex:       false !default;
```

In `_custom.scss`, delete the `!default` attribute, change `false` to `true`, and save your file. Then go to the command line, navigate to the `bootstrap` directory, and type `grunt`. You should get output that looks similar to what is shown on page 95.

If you don't spend much time on the command line, this output looks a little terrifying. (Even for those of us who do spend time on the command line, it's a little terrifying.) But Grunt is just sharing its status as it compiles the different parts of Bootstrap, telling you how long it took to perform its tasks, where it succeeded, and where it ran into trouble. We can see that it succeeded at most of what it wanted to do, either creating new files or running tasks that required no status output beyond "Running [taskName] task." It also ran into a few problems, but neither were serious: it couldn't find the Bundler software it needed to run an SCSS syntax-checker (a *lint-checker*, here called "scss-lint"), and it couldn't find any tests to run for the QUnit QA tool. Because we deliberately chose not to install Bundler for this project (it's primarily needed for Bootstrap's Ruby–based documentation), and we aren't running QUnit's automated QA-testing software, either, we can safely ignore both of these errors.

```
Running "clean:dist" (clean) task
>> 1 path cleaned.

Running "sass:core" (sass) task

Running "sass:docs" (sass) task

Running "exec:postcss" (exec) task

> bootstrap@4.0.0-alpha.4 postcss /Users/debby/node_modules/bootstrap
> postcss --config grunt/postcss.js --replace dist/css/*.css


Running "cssmin:core" (cssmin) task
>> 1 sourcemap created.
>> 1 file created. 137.4 kB → 111.11 kB

Running "cssmin:docs" (cssmin) task
>> No files created.

Running "babel:dev" (babel) task

Running "concat:bootstrap" (concat) task

Running "babel:dist" (babel) task

Running "stamp:bootstrap" (stamp) task

Running "uglify:core" (uglify) task
File dist/js/bootstrap.min.js created: 100.5 kB → 44.9 kB
>> 1 file created.

Running "scsslint:core" (scsslint) task
Running scss-lint on core
>> scss-lint failed with error code: 10
>> and the following message:Error: Command failed: /bin/sh -c bundle exec
>> scss-lint -c scss/.scss-lint.yml scss/_alert.scss scss/_animation.scss
>> scss/_breadcrumb.scss scss/_button-group.scss scss/_buttons.scss
>> scss/_card.scss scss/_carousel.scss scss/_close.scss scss/_code.scss
>> scss/_custom-forms.scss scss/_custom.scss scss/_dropdown.scss
>> scss/_forms.scss scss/_grid.scss scss/_images.scss scss/_input-group.scss
>> scss/_jumbotron.scss scss/_list-group.scss scss/_media.scss scss/_mixins.scss
>> scss/_modal.scss scss/_nav.scss scss/_navbar.scss scss/_pagination.scss
>> scss/_popover.scss scss/_print.scss scss/_progress.scss scss/_reboot.scss
>> scss/_responsive-embed.scss scss/_tables.scss scss/_tags.scss
>> scss/_tooltip.scss scss/_type.scss scss/_utilities.scss scss/_variables.scss
>> scss/bootstrap-flex.scss scss/bootstrap-grid.scss scss/bootstrap-reboot.scss
>> scss/bootstrap.scss

Running "qunit:files" (qunit) task
Warning: 0/0 assertions ran (0ms) Use --force to continue.

Aborted due to warnings.


Execution Time (2016-09-14 15:19:09 UTC-4)
sass:core       123ms    ███ 3%
exec:postcss     1.3s     ████████████████████████ 30%
cssmin:core     257ms    █████ 6%
babel:dev        1.2s     ██████████████████████ 27%
babel:dist      742ms    ██████████████ 17%
uglify:core     376ms    ███████ 9%
scsslint:core   359ms    ██████ 8%
Total 4.4s
```

However, if an error affects an SCSS or JavaScript file you're working on, you'll need to pay attention. For example, if there was a problem with your _custom.scss file, you might see something like this:

```
Running "sass:core" (sass) task
>> Error: Invalid CSS after "$btn-primary-bg": expected 1 selector or at-rule, was
":                #"
>>          on line 21 of scss/_custom.scss
>> >> $btn-primary-bg:                #00746B;
>>     ^
Warning: Use --force to continue.

Aborted due to warnings.
```

Grunt tells you exactly where it sees an error—line 21 of _custom.scss—and what it found there. In this case, the source of the error was actually above line 21 (we'd deliberately left out a semicolon to generate an error message), but knowing the line number where Grunt had a problem gives you a starting point.

_variables.scss is a big file—830 lines of customizations!—so we can't go over each and every variable it offers you. But the Bootstrap team has done a good job commenting (or adding explanatory comments to) the file and naming variables intuitively (many variables match class names exactly), so if you plan to customize your app extensively, spend some time reviewing what _variables.scss includes.

TRACKING DOWN ERRORS

Unless you're already a star coder (and, frankly, even if you are), it's very likely you'll make a few mistakes with your HTML and CSS as you start to build your pages. In our experience, the most common types of errors are:

- Misspelled code and/or class names
- Case-sensitivity errors
- Missing or incorrectly positioned closing tags or elements (e.g., missing quotation marks or angle brackets)
- Redundant code overwriting changes you made elsewhere
- Pathname errors

Although there's no single tool that can look at your code and identify both what's wrong and how to fix it to give you the desired layout and visual effects, a few sites and techniques can help you track down the problems.

HTML and CSS validators

The World Wide Web Consortium has provided HTML and CSS validation tools for years. Although neither tool can locate Bootstrap-specific errors (say, if you've used the wrong Bootstrap class name), they'll both catch several of the common problems on our list. The HTML validator is available at validator.w3.org and accepts input as a URL, file upload, or code pasted into a window.

Not everything the HTML validator identifies needs to be addressed. It will warn you about minor issues, and some errors, such as the use of obsolete tags, can be ignored if there's a genuine reason to preserve the code as written. But it will also tell you about more serious problems, such as mismatched opening and closing tags, which must be fixed for your code to work reliably.

The CSS validator at jigsaw.w3.org/css-validator/ works similarly to the HTML one. Although it, too, sometimes flags non-fatal errors like using occasionally necessary vendor extensions (such as `-webkit-box-sizing`), it also catches all those times you forgot to close a curly brace or add a semicolon.

Isolating the problem

Even with the validators to identify issues, you can still end up with perfectly valid code that still doesn't work the way you expect. One way to track down these issues is through careful use of HTML and CSS comments to isolate the problem. Start by commenting out half the layout or CSS of your file (whichever one you suspect is the source), save, reload your HTML page in the browser, and see if the problem still exists. If it does, then the problem is in the active code; keep commenting out half the remaining code until the problem goes away, at which point you'll know the most recently commented portion is the source of the issue. Conversely, if the problem goes away when you first comment out part of the code, you'll know the problem lies in the portion you commented out, and you can un-comment as necessary until the problem reappears. Either way, literally cutting down what the browser renders allows you to home in on the issue.

A FEW FINAL NOTES ON CODING

For now, you're just learning to code Bootstrap and Angular, and you're the only one who'll be reading your code and using your app. But if you decide to pursue development full-time, there are a few best practices you should follow in your code to keep it neat, readable by others, and accessible to everyone.

Formatting and commenting

A professional development team usually has several developers, and you may have to review or debug each other's work. When writing your code, we recommend indenting it whenever you open a new tag, which draws attention to the tag and keeps closing tags lined up neatly and easy to find. (You may or may not find indentation helpful in small HTML files, but it's valuable in larger ones and essentially required for readability in programming languages like Angular.)

　　Similarly, adding comments to your code helps you and others understand what parts of the code perform different functions, as well as why you've written things in a particular way. As a colleague of Debby's says, leaving yourself comments is a way to not be a jerk to your future self. You may come back to your code months or even years after writing it and not have the faintest clue why you wrote parts of it; comments fill in your own memory gaps and tell others what you were thinking.

```html
<!-- BEGIN LOGO -->
    <section>
        <div class="row">
            <div class="col-xs-12 text-xs-center tealBG">
                <h1>TastyTracker</h1>
            </div>
        </div>
    </section>
<!-- END LOGO -->
```

Indents in this TastyTracker code make it easy to tell where the row and column begin and end. Comments surrounding the section explain its purpose.

Accessibility

We've already covered how to make accessibility-friendly color choices, but that's just a small part of accessibility best practices. Writing accessible code that labels elements appropriately for screen readers—including hiding those elements when necessary—is every bit as important as making accessible design choices. Here are a few tips for improving the accessibility of your code.

- Always use `alt` attributes to provide a simple description of your images. (Longer descriptions of more complex images should use `longdesc` instead.) If your image is purely decorative rather than informational, use an empty `alt` attribute instead: `alt=""`.

- Follow HTML5 and general HTML semantic standards as much as possible, labelling regions and headers appropriately in your code.

- Use `label` tags with your forms, or use the `aria-label` attribute when a form or other interactive element doesn't have a visible label. `aria-label` provides the equivalent of label text to screen readers if there's no label text to display.

- Use Bootstrap's `sr-only` class to display items only to screen readers, such as hidden navigation menus. (Bootstrap provides a few other accessibility tips at v4-alpha.getbootstrap. com/getting-started/accessibility/.)

- Use an accessibility evaluation tool to confirm that you've provided appropriate tags and identify areas for improvement. Web Accessibility in Mind provides a free site called WAVE (wave.webaim.org) to check URLs for accessibility compliance; there are also numerous browser plugins and add-ons available to help you, too.

There's lots more to learn about accessibility than we can cover, but for a brief, clearly written set of recommendations, we suggest the MIT Accessibility and Usability Team's web accessibility guidelines at goo.gl/VimMLF, as well as Web Accessibility in Mind's excellent article on writing accessible forms (webaim.org/techniques/forms/). For a more in-depth look at the specific requirements and techniques involved in the World Wide Web Consortium's Web Content Accessibility Guidelines, see the WCAG version 2.0 page at w3.org/WAI/WCAG20/quickref/.

GETTING TASTYTRACKER OFF THE GROUND

We like to start our web development projects by coding the skeleton of a page first—a grid that maps out the main content/feature areas and includes only temporary content—to make sure we've got a layout that reflows the way it should before we start to add final content, features, and design. TastyTracker started no differently: we began by using Bootstrap's grid to create a completely bare-bones version of the four main sections of the page (logo, TastyTracking, TastyTotals, TastyTrends).

TastyTracker

TastyTracking   **TastyTotals**

form stuff goes here   circular results go here

TastyTrends

intro text goes here
chart 1 goes here   chart 2 goes here

TastyTracker skeleton page in desktop/tablet view.

This skeleton code told us immediately that even though we had a long way to go visually, our page was reflowing into the correct layouts no matter what screen size we used. (We tested using the simple method of resizing the browser window; no need to post this to a live server yet, although that also would have been a perfectly fine way to test.)

There was one last consideration before we moved on to CSS: Should we have used Flexbox instead of Bootstrap's default grid? Although Donna would mostly be using this app with her phone, where she probably had a Flexbox–compatible browser, if she had a computer at home, it would likely be an older model that might not have a browser capable of displaying Flexbox layouts correctly. And if she'd been hanging on to an older phone as a way of stretching her money rather than investing hundreds of dollars on a new smartphone, she could well have an older, less Flexbox–friendly browser, too. For those reasons, we stuck with the Bootstrap grid.[18]

With basic grid layout decisions settled, we added form elements and began investigating what parts of `_variables.scss` we'd want to override in our `_custom.scss` file; we wanted to rely on Bootstrap's variables as much as possible to minimize the amount of TastyTracker–specific CSS we'd have to write. After all, with Bootstrap providing so much CSS essentially for free, it would be pointless to duplicate effort! But in addition to changing colors, we were also going to need to load our Kanit font, which meant heading to Google Fonts to get the right code to import.

---

[18] All that said, we did try a Flexbox version of the grid. For the most part, it worked flawlessly, but alignment issues with the text in the TastyTotals circles cemented our decision to stick with Bootstrap's grid.

Fleshing out the skeleton with basic CSS

If you haven't used Google Fonts before, adding a font is a four-step process:

1. Search for the typeface you want to use.

2. Click the Select This Font button. When you do, a small window appears that is docked to the bottom of the screen and tells you how many font families you've selected.

3. Open the window, and you'll have the option to embed or customize the font family. If you only want the basic text weight of the font, you're all set with the default Embed choice; if, like us, you wanted to choose specific fonts, click Customize and check off the ones you want.

4. Click Embed again to copy and paste the code you'll need to add the font via a `link` tag, or for direct import into a CSS file, click the `@import` link to view code you can paste into your CSS.

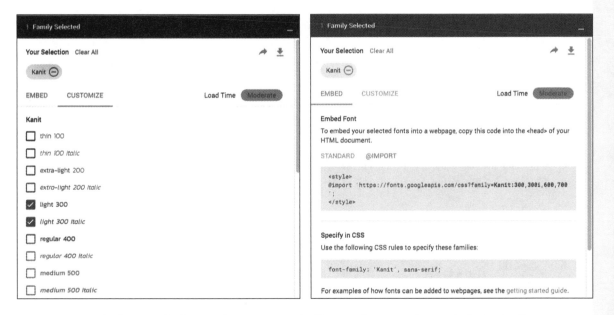

Left: choosing the fonts in the **customize** tab. The more fonts you choose, the longer it will take people to download your webpages, so keep an eye on Google's load-time warning. Right: the "@import" sub-tab provides the code and specs we need for our CSS.

We pasted Google's @import code into _custom.scss and copied some basic variables from _variables.scss into the file as well—body text color, button colors, link colors, etc.—along with the typography variable that allowed us to set the default body font.

```scss
// Bootstrap overrides
//
// Copy variables from `_variables.scss` to this file to override default values
// without modifying source files.

@import 'https://fonts.googleapis.com/css?family=Kanit:300,300i,600,700';

// Body
//
// Settings for the `<body>` element.

$body-color: #4F430F;


// Buttons
//
// For each of Bootstrap's buttons, define text, background, and border color.

$btn-primary-bg:            #00746B;
$btn-secondary-color:       #00746B;
$btn-secondary-border:      #00746B;
$btn-box-shadow:            none;


// Colors
$brand-primary:         #4F430F;
$brand-success:         #4F430F;
$brand-info:            #9F0316;
$brand-warning:         #9F0316;
$brand-danger:          #9F0316;


// Forms
$input-color:               #4F430F;
$input-border-color:        #4F430F;


// Typography
//
// Font, line-height, and color for body text, headings, and more.

$font-family-base:      "Kanit";
```

We saved the file, ran the grunt command to propagate our changes throughout Bootstrap's CSS, and also added FontAwesome's CDN link to our skeleton page. Now it looked a little more attractive in our browser.

TastyTracker

TastyTracking

✏ edit meals

I spent $ [   ]

at [– restaurant name – ▾]

on [– meal type – ▾]

on this day [   ]
📅

[Save]

TastyTotals

$0

spent on meals today

$0

spent on meals this week

TastyTrends

TastyTracker keeps track of up to a year's worth of spending.

This week compared to last week

chart 1 goes here

On average, I spend this amount on

chart 2 goes here

TastyTracker

TastyTracking

✏ edit meals

I spent $ [   ]

at [– restaurant name – ▾]

on [– meal type – ▾]

on this day [   ] 📅

[Save]

TastyTotals

$0

spent on meals today

$0

spent on meals this week

TastyTrends

TastyTracker keeps track of up to a year's worth of spending.

This week compared to last week

chart 1 goes here

On average, I spend this amount on

chart 2 goes here

Partially styled TastyTracker skeleton in mobile (top) and desktop/tablet (bottom) views.
You can see both in full color at goo.gl/dODTV3.

It still had a ways to go—we had none of our colored header bars or the TastyTotals circles, and the form clearly needed some alignment help—but just a few simple changes in _custom.scss had taken us much further without having had to write a single CSS class of our own. We continued to update _custom.scss to refine header sizes and spacer specifications, and in the end, it took a mere fourteen custom classes in a styles.css file we created to give TastyTracker the look and feel we wanted.

ADDING A MODAL WINDOW

TastyTracker comprises only two pages: the main screen, and an Edit Meals screen. With our main screen complete, we could use it as a foundation from which to build Edit Meals, but the main screen was still missing one small sub-screen of its own: the Edit Restaurants lightbox that overlaid it whenever Donna needed to edit or delete a restaurant name (page 41).

To add this, we'd need to use Bootstrap's modal component (v4-alpha.getbootstrap.com /components/modal/). Bootstrap provides the following example of the code used to create a modal, which consists of three main sections—header, body, and footer—defined by the named classes modal-header, modal-body, and modal-footer, respectively.

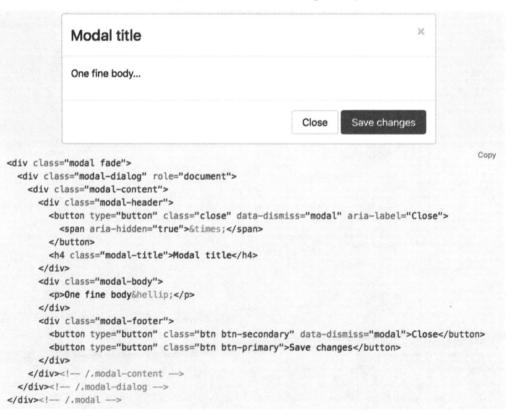

```
<div class="modal fade">
  <div class="modal-dialog" role="document">
    <div class="modal-content">
      <div class="modal-header">
        <button type="button" class="close" data-dismiss="modal" aria-label="Close">
          <span aria-hidden="true">&times;</span>
        </button>
        <h4 class="modal-title">Modal title</h4>
      </div>
      <div class="modal-body">
        <p>One fine body&hellip;</p>
      </div>
      <div class="modal-footer">
        <button type="button" class="btn btn-secondary" data-dismiss="modal">Close</button>
        <button type="button" class="btn btn-primary">Save changes</button>
      </div>
    </div><!-- /.modal-content -->
  </div><!-- /.modal-dialog -->
</div><!-- /.modal -->
```

This needed a little customization on our end, but creating the Edit Restaurants modal was as much a matter of pasting in the right content and form elements as anything else; Bootstrap had done the structural and formatting work for us. We changed the header to an H3 to match similar styles we'd set up, added our form code, and deleted the modal-footer area we wouldn't need. We also added two custom classes to our styles.css file to override aspects of the modal design we couldn't change with parts of _variables.scss: an opacity change to the .close class on the Close button to make it 100 percent teal instead of only 20 percent, and a class that removed the unnecessary border below modal-header. With that done, there was only one piece left to complete: the alert shown to confirm that Donna wants to delete a restaurant.

Alerts

Bootstrap's alerts come in four varieties: alert-success, alert-information, alert-warning, and alert-danger. Each of these uses a different color to distinguish itself, with the expectation that an alert's text will help convey its level of seriousness to people who can't perceive the colors.

To display an alert to a Bootstrap page, add a div with the appropriate class. You can include headers, buttons, or other HTML elements, and variables within _variables.scss allow you to customize alert background, text, and border color.

```
<div class="alert alert-warning row" role="alert">
  <div class="col-xs-1">
    <i class="fa fa-exclamation-circle large" aria-hidden="true"></i>
  </div>
  <div class="col-xs-11">
    <p>Deleting $RESTAURANTNAME will delete all $RESTAURANTNAME meals you've
recorded.</p>
    <button type="button" class="btn btn-primary">OK, delete
it</button><button type="button" class="btn btn-secondary m-l-1">Nope,
keep it</button>
  </div>
</div>
```

With the alert in place in our modal, it was now complete, and so was our draft code for TastyTracker, which was now ready to be included in an Angular project.

Coded TastyTracker modal and alert.

Coded TastyTracker page shown in desktop/tablet view.

YOUR ASSIGNMENT

It's finally time to start coding!

- Code TastyTracker or your own tracking app in Bootstrap. We provided a basic `index.html` file you can use as a starting point, and complete source code is also available if you need a peek at our solution. Your final code should include your CSS styles and be able to reflow across mobile, tablet, and desktop devices. (Not sure how to make the CSS circles? There are many techniques for this available online, but we used the one described at davidwalsh.name /css-circles, which sets `border-radius` to 50 percent of the circle's width and height.)

GETTING STARTED WITH ANGULAR

It's time for a change of routine.

This book has two authors, and the second one is now going to take over for a while. This may feel strange at first, since Todd does things a little differently from Debby. As a user experience designer, Debby thinks in terms of user flow: What will the user expect to see here? What tasks will they want to perform? Todd, as a programmer, thinks in terms of operational tasks: How do I make this control do what the UX designer wants it to do? How are we going to store and retrieve the data we need? Both are valid approaches for their respective jobs . . . and if you're the sole developer of a web application, you'll have to do both jobs, so you should learn both approaches.

We'll temporarily set aside the work that you did in Chapter 5 to concentrate on making an ugly-but-functional "smoke test" version of the app. Then, in Chapter 8, we'll merge the Bootstrap work into the bare-bones code to arrive at the ultimate form of the app.

Although this chapter is mostly about basic principles of the code you'll be writing, we also do some work that will become part of the app, work that we progressively build upon. In other words, there *is* actual coding in this chapter. That requires us to take one preparatory step.

After the previous chapter, assuming you adhered fairly closely to the design we set out, you've likely created three files in the project directory: two HTML files (the main page and the edit meals page) and a styles.css file. Your main page, however, is probably called index.html, and you need to temporarily rename it, because for the moment we're going to create and use a different index.html.

Go ahead and rename index.html to something else. Perhaps chapter5index.html?

We'll make another, temporary index.html shortly.

THE WAY ANGULAR THINKS

Back in the Stone Age (perhaps a slight exaggeration), programming was *linear* and *procedural*. You started at the beginning of the script or program and worked your way down, instruction by instruction, to the end. You might have encountered instructions that sent you back to a previous instruction, or ones that told you to jump ahead, or ones that looped through the same set of instructions multiple times. Or you might have diverted temporarily to execute a *function*, a self-contained set of instructions that performed a task and returned some result back to the main program.

In a web application, though, it doesn't make sense to write code that way. There is no start or end point. Code is executed in response to *events*: the user clicked here, the user changed a value there, the page has been reloaded. The closest we have to "begin here" is the "page is being freshly loaded" event, and we have no "end"—we respond to an event and then we wait for the user to do something else. The user could close the page entirely, and we wouldn't even know it.

If you were coding in straight JavaScript, the result of this would be a set of functions that are all linked, directly or indirectly, to events. Everything in the code happens in response to user action (or even just the page being loaded).

For example, you could have this code in your HTML:

```
<button onClick="doTheThing()">Click this</button>
```

which means there had better be a function somewhere in your JavaScript—in a location where that HTML page can find it—called doTheThing:

```
<script>
function doTheThing() {
    alert("Hi there!");
}
</script>
```

which does something useful in response to that button being clicked. (In this case, it pops up a message window which says "Hi there!"—not exactly useful, but you get the point.)

The problems with this approach come when you have many controls across many pages responding to many events. If you have a page with five different buttons and you want to have them all do exactly the same thing when clicked, that would only require a single function, but if they all needed to do slightly different things, you'd have to take one of two approaches.

You could write five different functions, each with a different name: doTheThingButton1, doTheThingButton2, and so on. This would get messy and, if the functions did *almost* the same thing in each case, wasteful.

A better approach would be to write one function which took a *parameter* and then did something customized for that parameter. Notice how our function doTheThing() had those empty parentheses after its name, both in the function declaration and when it was called by the onClick event? The empty parentheses indicate that it doesn't accept any parameters. Let's change that.

```
<script>
function doTheThing(buttonNum) {
  alert("Button #" + buttonNum + " was clicked");
}
</script>
```

You would send the parameter to the function when it was called by each control:

```
<button onClick="doTheThing(1)">Button 1</button>
<button onClick="doTheThing(2)">Button 2</button>
```

The first button would produce a message "Button #1 was clicked," and so on. The button number is passed to the function as the buttonNum parameter.

Let's pause for a bit of syntax. We'll be working in TypeScript, not JavaScript, but these basics are the same in both.

A function, and any other things that may have multiple instructions, always encloses those instructions in curly braces: {}. The curly braces are the start and end markers of the *block* of instructions. They are needed even if the block only has a single instruction inside it, as in the button example.

Single instructions end with a semicolon, as shown at the end of the alert() line.

Parameters provided to a function are enclosed in parentheses, both in the function definition and when it is called. If there are multiple parameters, they are separated by commas. alert(), which is a function, too, sort of looks like it's taking three parameters, doesn't it? But it's actually only taking one—a single *string* (text) which is made by gluing three parts together using the + operator. We discuss strings versus numbers and how + behaves differently with each in the next chapter.

This is fine for an example this simple, but as an application gets bigger, it becomes harder and harder to keep all the functions and events untangled. The odds of a *name collision* get higher. A name collision is when you have a function or *variable*—an item of data which has a name—with the same name as a function or variable somewhere else in your code. It's confusing at best, and possibly leads to fatal errors at worst.

Angular's approach to this problem is to divide the entire app into chunks called *components*. Each component has its own HTML, possibly its own CSS, its own functions, its own variables, and so on. A component isn't *entirely* self-contained, or there'd be far too much duplication—you can use functions and data that have been defined elsewhere. But as a general rule, each component is its own little universe.

This helps avoid name collisions. If each of your components has a `getUserName()` function, then it isn't a name collision the way it would be in a straight block of JavaScript, because the components can't "see" each others' functions. Similarly, if your component declares that it uses a variable called `restaurants`, it won't matter if every other component also has a variable with that name . . . because each of them is considered *local* to its own component, and they don't conflict with one another.

The flip side of this is that it's hard to create variables which are *global*—visible to the entire body of code—in Angular. Angular's developers don't want you to do that, and they're right. Instead, we either use Angular's mechanisms to explicitly make selected items of data in one component visible to some other component, or we use a data *provider* that makes its data available to any component that calls it.

THE APPLICATION MODULE AND WHAT IMPORTS WHERE

All of the parts of Angular that we'll be using are organized into *modules*. You can think of a module as a collection of code that performs a set of related tasks. "Related tasks" is the important bit: a module is organized around a purpose. The Angular router module handles all tasks that belong to its router. The Angular forms module handles all tasks related to web forms. The Angular core module handles all the basic Angular tasks not specific to any other module.

We also work with a few *libraries* that are not part of Angular. These are called and used in a slightly different way from modules, but a library is also a collection of code organized around a particular purpose.

Finally, we use a couple of *providers*. Unlike the modules and libraries, we write these ourselves. The providers we'll make are also data *services*—they allow their callers to both set and access data through a set of functions. More on data services and why we need them later in this chapter.

All of the components, modules, and providers we use must be *imported* (that is, we say "we'll be needing this") into the *application module*—the only module we write ourselves. We also sometimes call this the *root module*. This is a "master" module required by Angular and by the rest of the application. Libraries, and individual parts of the various modules, need to be imported in the components when used; each component imports only the specific things that it needs. A few things, like our data services, get imported in both the application module and in the components that use them. This can be a little confusing ("Do I import this here, there, or in both places?") but will become clearer as we go.

You'll find the final application module in our repository. It imports three modules, a router, two services, six components, and a pipe. (No, we haven't explained what two of those things are yet; you didn't miss anything.) In the course of your work, as you add new components and so forth, you'll have to periodically go back to the application module and add lines that import them. One of the most baffling ways an Angular app can go wrong is a missing declaration in the application module—it tends to just show a blank page with no explanation when this happens— so if you worry that you've missed something, you can always go check our final file to see if it provides a hint to what you left out.

For now, let's create a bare-bones one, with much to be added later.

Back in the installation chapter, we had you create a subdirectory of the project directory called app. Go into that directory and fire up your text editor of choice. The file you'll be creating will be called app.module.ts—the .ts extension because it will be written in TypeScript, as will all our components.

Create and save app.module.ts in the app directory as shown:

```
import { NgModule }      from '@angular/core';
import { BrowserModule } from '@angular/platform-browser';

import { AppComponent }  from './app.component';

@NgModule({
  imports:      [ BrowserModule ],
  declarations: [ AppComponent ],
  bootstrap:    [ AppComponent ]
})
export class AppModule {}
```

The extra spaces in some of the lines are optional. We put them in so that parts of the various instructions will line up vertically, making the file easier to read. The empty lines are also optional and for readability.

This is an absolutely minimal application module. Let's take it apart instruction by instruction (or *statement by statement*; we use the terms interchangeably).

The first two import statements say we will be using NgModule and BrowserModule.

NgModule is a special module that is *always required*. We need it in order to define the application module itself, further down. It's the Angular "core" module and should probably be called "CoreModule" but isn't. Since it contains the basic guts of Angular itself, it's named NgModule—"ng" in various combinations of upper and lower cases being used in several places as an abbreviation for "Angular."

BrowserModule is required for any web-based Angular app. It tells Angular how to deal with the specifics of various web browsers.

The third line is the import of our *root component*. Just as we must have a root module, we must have a root component. Or, put another way, every Angular app must have at least one component, and at least one component must be imported in the application module. By convention, this root component is called AppComponent and lives in the file app.component .ts, just as the application module is called AppModule and lives in the file app.module.ts. We haven't written this component yet, of course; that'll be next.

The paths that end each import statement are not actual paths in your filesystem. If they were, they'd be a lot longer and more specific. One of the reasons we use the SystemJS loader is so we can abbreviate paths like this in our import statements and let SystemJS figure out which specific files our modules and libraries are contained in. If you went back to look at systemjs.config.js, one directory up, you'd see that @angular/core actually works out to the file node_modules/@ angular/core/bundles/core.umd.js (relative to the project directory).

The path to find AppComponent is different. It begins with ./, which in a path means "the current directory." In other words, we're saying AppComponent is located in a file called app. component.ts (the .ts is implied) *in the same directory as this module*.

Next we have some lines that begin with @NgModule. This is a *decorator*. A decorator is a special marker that says, "I'm modifying the behavior of whatever immediately follows this." The particular style of writing a decorator with an @ sign as @Something() is peculiar to TypeScript; in JavaScript, it's done differently (and much less comprehensibly). We will encounter several more of these decorators as we go. The @NgModule() decorator is modifying the export class line at the bottom—the intended meaning is "the class being defined/exported is a special kind of class with a particular significance to Angular," and it has some extra parameters, which will be enclosed inside the @NgModule() parentheses.

Inside the @NgModule() decorator, we have all sorts of grouping symbols. The parentheses are, as noted, part of the decorator; they enclose its parameters, just like they would for a function. The decorator actually has only *one* parameter: a list of various pieces of data that have names. This list is enclosed in curly braces. You've already seen curly braces used to enclose lists of named data in JSON files in the installation chapter, and they work the same way here. As in JSON, the items in the list are separated by commas, and the last item in the list does not get a comma.

The names of the data items are imports, declarations, one we don't use yet but will be called `providers`, and `bootstrap`[19]. Each of those is an *array*—a list of data *without* names. Where lists of named data are enclosed in { }, arrays are enclosed in [ ].

What is a *class*? Why is it marked with **export**?

A class is a set of code and data united by a common purpose. That isn't the definition you'll find for it in object-oriented programming books, but it suits us. If we had a class called `restaurants` in it you would expect to find all the functions that deal with restaurants and all the data and variables needed for restaurant-wrangling tasks, grouped together in a single bundle called a "class."

In the object-oriented programming world, a class is just a definition—a template—and is not used operationally. Instead, what you do is declare the existence of an object of that class, and work with the object. The class is the ruleset; the object is the actual implementation. In the JavaScript (and, by extension, TypeScript) world, the distinction isn't that rigid. A class here is convenient shorthand for "a bunch of functions and data that belong together." A component, as you'll see in the next file, is just a special kind of class, and when we make objects from component classes, it will happen invisibly when the component is used in HTML. We discuss this more in the next chapter.

The classes we define are all marked with the word **export** so that the Angular system can "see" them. If we didn't export one of our components, we wouldn't be able to use it in our HTML!

The `imports` item is an array of all modules and routers used by the application (except `NgModule`, which is special and need not be listed). The `declarations` item is an array of all components and pipes used by the application. The `providers` item will eventually list all data providers and services used by the application, and the `bootstrap` item lists any components to look for and load when the app starts (which will normally only be the single root component).

After all that, you may be surprised to realize that the class itself has nothing in it!

```
export class AppModule {}
```

---

[19] `bootstrap` is not to be confused with Bootstrap, the responsive web toolkit. (Sorry, we didn't name any of this.) Throughout this book, we're careful to capitalize "Bootstrap" when we mean the toolkit.

The curly braces enclose no statements. This is because all we actually need for the application module is the declaration that it exists, the various lists of what other things will be used by the app, and the import statements. It has no other job.

THE ROOT COMPONENT

Like the root module, the root component is required. In our app, it won't ever do much (and we talk more about why later in this chapter); it's there as a starting point for the application, and all the real work will be done in other places.

Create and save the app.component.ts file in the app directory as shown:

```
import { Component } from '@angular/core';

@Component({
  selector: 'app-main',
  template: `
            <h2>{{title}}</h2>
            <!-- That's all for now. -->
            `
})
export class AppComponent {
  title = 'TastyTracker';
}
```

This is a test version of the root component that doesn't do much. We make it a little more complex in the next chapter, but even once the app is complete, this component will be our smallest and simplest.

Let's take it from the top:

First, we need to import the Component part of the Angular core so that the @Component() decorator below it will have a meaning.

> "Part" isn't an accepted term. Why use it? Because we don't need to care. We just need to know that there's *something* in the core module needed here and that it's called Component. All of these imports are things you have to learn arbitrarily anyway—you don't need to know their internal details, just when you need them and what they provide to you.

The @Component() decorator modifies the class declaration; it says that the class AppComponent is an Angular component. Because it is a component, there are several extra parameters, two of which appear here (and which will appear in every component we create): the selector and the template.

The selector is a string (that is, text; notice it's enclosed in single quotes) that is the name used to refer to this component in HTML. We show you how this works in a moment.

The template is a string that contains the actual HTML *of the component*. When you "insert" the component into some other HTML by using its selector, the contents of the template are what gets inserted and displayed. For this template, we have used a special trick: enclosing the string in *backticks* instead of single quotes. (The backtick is up in the corner of a standard US QWERTY keyboard, just to the left of the 1 key.) This enables us to write the template contents over multiple lines for readability, because a normal string cannot have carriage returns in it without taking special pains.

For other components, we're going to put the template contents in files of their own and thus won't have to worry about those peculiar backticks. The only reason we've put these template contents *inline* (i.e., right here in the component) is because they're so short.

Notice that the template contents are in HTML, and the comment, which is part of the template, is thus an HTML–style comment. Comments are not written that way in TypeScript, as we see in the next chapter.

Notice also that there's something strange in the HTML: {{title}} does not refer to an HTML <title> tag. Instead, it refers to a variable somewhere in the component's data named title—and if we go to the bottom of the file, we see that defining title is, in fact, the only thing the class does.

When a variable is defined, it's always a good idea to specify what kind of variable it is—a string, a number, a Boolean (true or false), an array of something, or other more complex data types. We can specify the type of a variable without setting it to any value, like this:

```
title: string;
```

Or we could *initialize* the variable (set it to a value) with an equals sign, like this:

```
title = 'TastyTracker';
```

Because the value we are initializing it to is a string (notice the single quotes), TypeScript understands that **title** is a variable of the string type—this is *implicit* type declaration. But if you want to be absolutely clear, you can always combine an *explicit* type declaration and the initialization:

```
title: string = 'TastyTracker';
```

If you declare a variable without either an explicit type or an initialization, TypeScript won't know what type it's supposed to be. TypeScript may allow you to get away with this depending on how it's configured, but it's a bad idea. Don't do this.

So we have a variable called title, which, when the template is loaded, gets displayed in place of the {{title}} marker—this is *interpolation* of that variable. The interpolation markup can also contain other things besides variable names, and we show you some in the next chapter.

Your interpolated variable names must be data known to that component (declared or obtained somewhere within the component), and they must be spelled exactly the same as they are within the component, including uppercase versus lowercase letters.

Now we need an HTML file in which we make use of the component.

Unlike the Angular files, the HTML file doesn't go in the app directory. Go up one level to the project directory and create and save index.html as follows (you *did* remember to rename the index.html from Chapter 5 to something else so you wouldn't lose it, right?):

```
<!DOCTYPE html>
<html>
  <head>
    <base href="/" />
    <title>TastyTracker</title>
    <meta charset="UTF-8" />
    <meta name="viewport" content="width=device-width, initial-scale=1" />
    <link rel="stylesheet" href="styles.css" />
    <!-- 1. Load libraries -->
    <!-- The next line makes ES6 stuff work for older ES5-only browsers. -->
    <script src="node_modules/core-js/client/shim.min.js"></script>
    <!-- Angular needs the next line for bindings to work. -->
    <script src="node_modules/zone.js/dist/zone.js"></script>
    <!-- TypeScript's @() decorators need this: -->
    <script src="node_modules/reflect-metadata/Reflect.js"></script>
    <!-- And, of course, our module/path finder is addressed next. -->
```

```
    <script src="node_modules/systemjs/dist/system.src.js"></script>
    <!-- 2. Configure SystemJS -->
    <script src="systemjs.config.js"></script>
    <script>
      System.import('app').catch(function(err){ console.error(err); });
    </script>
  </head>
  <!-- 3. Display the application -->
  <body>
    <app-main>Loading...</app-main>
  </body>
</html>
```

You don't need to copy the HTML comments if you don't want to; we put them in there to show you what all that required overhead does. The actual working bit is the one line inside the <body>. When the page loads, the contents of the <app-main></app-main> tag pair will be replaced by the contents (the template) of the root component, whose selector is app-main. Until it loads, the temporary contents "Loading..." will be displayed instead. Again, the name in the tag pair must match the name in the selector exactly, including case.

With these three files, you now have an extremely minimal, but working, Angular app. Let's try it out. To do that, though, we first have to compile the TypeScript we just wrote.

THE FIRST TEST (AND SOME TROUBLESHOOTING)

Your web browser doesn't know how to read and interpret TypeScript.

We're using TypeScript because Angular can be very messy without it. There are enough advantages of using it to make it worthwhile, but it does add an extra step. Before we can actually look at our work in a web browser, we have to compile the TypeScript *into JavaScript*.

In practical terms, this means that *every time* we change any of our .ts files and test them, we have to compile (using tsc, the TypeScript compiler) and generate a set of JavaScript files.

To help simplify this process, we've installed a small local web server. When we launch the web server, it also runs tsc in "watch" mode, so it not only makes sure that all the TypeScript is compiled, but it also keeps an eye out for any file changes you make while the server is running. If you change any of the files, it will recompile them, restart the server, and completely reload the application.

This is nice for minor adjustments—you can instantly see what your changes did. If you have major work to do, though, and you know your code is going to be broken while you work on it (because of missing components, etc.), it's probably a better idea to *not* keep the server running until you get the code operational again.

Open a command window and make sure you're in the project directory. All our npm commands should be run from the project directory.

You can run tsc on its own—compilation only, without "watch" mode—by entering the command

```
npm run tsc
```

You run tsc, put it in watch mode, and run the local server all at the same time by entering the command

```
npm start
```

Do the latter now. The server will either launch your default web browser if it isn't running, or open a new tab if it is. (If for some reason it doesn't, open your web browser and go to the location localhost:3000/, which is the special URL for the local server we're running.) The browser should show you a new window or tab whose entire text is "Loading . . ." We'll come back to this page after a short break to discuss error messages.

Errors from tsc

npm runs tsc in watch mode and then starts the server. The messages you'll see at the beginning of the output are from tsc. Assuming you entered these three files exactly as listed, you shouldn't see any errors from tsc—but suppose you do?

Any errors from tsc will happen while it compiles your files. If the server hasn't begun running yet, these errors will prevent the server from starting, and npm will tell you so with a chain of ERR messages. Here's an example where we went back and changed a line in app.component.ts to be deliberately wrong (the actual gripe from tsc is the emphasized line):

```
C:\tastytracker>npm start

> tastytracker@1.0.0 start C:\tastytracker
> tsc && concurrently "npm run tsc:w" "npm run lite"

app/app.component.ts(11,10): error TS2304: Cannot find name 'TastyTracker'.

npm ERR! Windows_NT 6.1.7601
npm ERR! argv "C:\\nodejs\\node.exe" "C:\\nodejs\\node_modules\\npm\\bin\\
npm-cli.js" "start"
npm ERR! node v4.5.0
npm ERR! npm  v3.10.8
npm ERR! code ELIFECYCLE
npm ERR! tastytracker@1.0.0 start: 'tsc && concurrently "npm run tsc:w"
```

```
"npm run lite" '
npm ERR! Exit status 2
```

Whenever you do something with **npm** that causes ERR messages, you'll find a file called **npm-debug.log** in your project directory with the same error details you just got. This file can be safely deleted—although you may want to wait until you've first solved the problem in case you need to refer back to it!

Hopefully, any errors that `tsc` reports when it runs are identifiable enough that you can go fix them. The most common problems are:

- Trying to do something with a variable that the component doesn't know about (e.g. the variable was never declared)
- "this" scope on variables (we discuss the special "this" element in the next chapter)
- Forgetting delimiters ({ }, [ ], ( ), etc.) or using the wrong delimiters
- Forgetting to end statements with a semicolon

But the error can be deceiving. In this case, what we actually did was change this line

```
title = 'TastyTracker';
```

to the incorrect line

```
title = TastyTracker;
```

It's legal for the variable `title` to be initialized to a string with quotes or to a number or a Boolean (without quotes), but initializing it to a value without quotes that isn't a number or a Boolean is illegal . . . *unless* there were a variable named `TastyTracker` defined elsewhere in the component and we were setting `title` to the same value as whatever's in `TastyTracker`. So `tsc` tries for that, can't find a variable `TastyTracker` anywhere, and *that's* what it ends up griping about—not the missing quotes.

Fortunately, there are other clues. We're told by `tsc` which file the problem appears in, which line of the file, and how many characters into that line it got before it realized there was a problem.

The (11,10) after the file name in the error means line 11, character 10. (Blank lines count, and spaces in a line count as characters.)

If tsc gets errors after the server is already running, the errors from tsc will be harder to spot because they'll be buried by server requests (described in the next section). But if you scroll up, you'll see them.

Errors from the server

But back to our code *without* the deliberate error. When the server started, you probably got some messages about not finding a browser-sync file, which you can ignore because its defaults are okay as is. Then you should see a whole lot of lines that start with a date and time, followed by a three-digit number, the word GET, and a file name. This is the server requesting and loading files.

```
[1] 16.10.03 14:54:53 200 GET /index.html
[1] 16.10.03 14:54:53 200 GET /styles.css
[1] 16.10.03 14:54:53 200 GET /node_modules/core-js/client/shim.min.js
[1] 16.10.03 14:54:53 200 GET /node_modules/zone.js/dist/zone.js
[1] 16.10.03 14:54:53 200 GET /node_modules/reflect-metadata/Reflect.js
[1] 16.10.03 14:54:53 200 GET /systemjs.config.js
[1] 16.10.03 14:54:53 200 GET /node_modules/systemjs/dist/system.src.js
[1] 16.10.03 14:54:53 404 GET /app/main.js
[1] 16.10.03 14:54:54 404 GET /favicon.ico
```

Ideally, all of those numbers should be in the 200s or sometimes in the 300s. These are fine. Numbers in the 400s (such as in the last two lines) are the ones you have to watch out for. 200s are "success"; 300s are "redirecting to a different place" (but still success); 400s are "a file is missing or can't be read." (500s are "something went wrong on the server," but we won't get those here.)

Having a missing favicon.ico isn't fatal; that's just the browser looking for a custom icon to display in its location bar for this page. But what about that missing app/main.js?

Let's go back to our "Loading . . ." page in the browser. Do you suppose the missing main.js file has anything to do with the fact that the page just shows "Loading . . ." and not the text from the component that we want it to display?

Your friend, the web console

The browser has a diagnostic tool called the *web console* which can help us. Different browsers have different methods for enabling the console; for example, in Chrome, you can find it under View > Developer > JavaScript Console. A web search on "web console" (or "web inspector," if you're a Safari® user) plus the name of your browser should get you an appropriate page of instructions.

Open the web console while your `localhost:3000` window is active. Sure enough, the web console has some probably-not-very-understandable lines about `zone.js` attempting to start and then a more understandable line about an error loading `localhost:3000/app/main.js`. Well, we know why we can't load it: it isn't there.

We'll fix that problem in a moment, but first we must stress that we didn't pull this trick just to torment you. Angular doesn't have any internal error-checking of its own; diagnostics are up to you, the developer.

For some situations, you can do what is called a *try/catch* setup, where you tell the code "Attempt to do this thing (the *try* block), and if it doesn't work, do these things instead as an error response (the *catch* block)." But those aren't really applicable to the app we're building.

We can check for bad user inputs (leave a field empty that shouldn't have been, etc.), and we will, but that won't help us track problems in our own code.

The only kinds of errors `tsc` knows how to spot are gross errors in syntax—the code equivalent of misspelling words or omitting punctuation marks.

Everything else we have to track in the web console, either by seeing the errors generated there or by sending diagnostic messages there ourselves. (We learn how and why we'd want to do that in the next chapter.) So take the time now to learn how to find that web console and use it. It's practically the only troubleshooting tool we have.

SECOND TIME'S THE CHARM

So what is this `main.js`, and why do we need it?

It wasn't a lie to say that the root module was the "starting point" of an Angular application. The problem is that your web browser needs another link to *get* to that starting point. SystemJS is part of that link; it knows where to find things. But we also need to tell SystemJS where the Angular app begins—*we* know what our root module is, but the browser doesn't. As it happens, we actually *did* tell SystemJS where to start! In its config file `systemjs.config.js`, there's a line where we tell it to look for `main.js`. We just forgot to provide a `main.js`. So let's do that.

But we won't write it as JavaScript. We'll write it as TypeScript—`main.ts`, not `main.js`— and let `tsc` compile it like everything else.

In your app directory, create and save `main.ts` as shown:

```
import { platformBrowserDynamic } from '@angular/platform-browser-dynamic';
import { AppModule } from './app.module';
const platform = platformBrowserDynamic();
platform.bootstrapModule(AppModule);
```

Two of the lines here are to figure out what our web browser is and set it as platform. The other two say where to find our application module and what it's called and designate that as the starting point for the whole Angular app (the bootstrapModule for that platform).

Now, all that said, if:

- The browser knows how to load index.html and its inclusions;

- One of those inclusions is SystemJS, which looks for and loads main.js (because we told it to);

- main.js tells the browser what and where the Angular root module is;

- And the root module describes what gets loaded, as well as what and where the root component is . . .

. . . why not combine two of those steps and just tell SystemJS to load the root module? Well, you could, with a little tinkering. But it's bad practice. The little main.js file is a bootstrap file (again, no relation to the responsive web toolkit of the same name) that has to deal with the specifics of our particular *environment*—what browser's being used, possibly what server's being used, any other peculiarities of the local setup where this app is being run. It's best to keep those environment-specific steps separated from the actual operations of the Angular app, the idea being that you've already done anything specific to your server or browser by the time you get to the root module and that the Angular app from there on down is the same for all environments (and, ideally, runs the same way in all environments).

This is the minimal necessary framework to run an Angular app, and all of these parts need to be present in addition to the Angular modules and other dependencies we use.

Assuming you still have the server running—and you probably do—it detected the addition of main.ts. You should have seen it try to fetch a lot more files than before, and now you should see "TastyTracker" displayed in your browser.

THAT'S IT?

This probably seems like a lot of work just to get a test this simple running. Well, it is, but it's a question of scale. The amount of basic overhead we've just gone through is the same whether your app has a single component or five components or fifty components or five hundred. Also, now that we have these files the way we want them, we'll leave them mostly alone. We won't touch main.ts again until we prepare the app for distribution. We'll modify app.component.ts once more functionally, then any changes to it will be UI design elements. We'll revisit app.module.ts only when we need to add new imports and declarations. The scaffolding is in place; now we have to build the parts that actually do useful work.

In addition, you've learned where to look for basic troubleshooting, you've learned some key elements of TypeScript syntax, and you've learned how Angular organizes its universe.

There's one more thing you'll want to learn before we wind up this chapter, however: how to stop the local web server. Sometimes there's no point in leaving it running.

You can stop the server by closing the command window, but a cleaner way is to make sure the window is selected, then press Ctrl+C. You'll be asked some variation of "Terminate batch job (Y/N)?" Press Y and then Enter, and you'll be returned to the command prompt.

You'll notice in the **app** directory that `tsc` has created a `.js` file and a `.js.map` file for every `.ts` file we've created.

You may be wondering: If the TypeScript has all been compiled to JavaScript, which the browser knows how to interpret, what's stopping you from just loading and running the app *without* needing the local web server? Just go to `index.html` in the browser, and the rest should all be JavaScript at this point, right?

In theory, yes; in practice, it doesn't work. If you try it (just open `index.html` in your browser while the server is *not* running), a Windows-based web console will show you a message about not being able to find/load `System`, which is the SystemJS engine. On the Mac, you'll see a series of errors reading "Failed to load resource: Could not connect to the server."

This is a path issue, and it has to do with the way relative (partial) paths are handled in a web server environment versus local filesystem environment. We discuss this a little more later, but the short answer is: *our app is designed to be run from a web server.* Even once you distribute the app, it's still meant to be installed on a web server of some kind. This is a book about designing web applications, after all.

YOUR ASSIGNMENT: PLANNING YOUR CODE

At this point, you've created four new files: an `index.html` file in the project directory, and `app.module.ts`, `app.component.ts`, and `main.ts` in the app directory. We have many more files left to create in the app directory. Your homework is to plan what they will be.

As noted, the files we created in this chapter are used to load and start the application. They don't do much else, and they will continue to not do much else. Yes, we *could* put a lot of operational code into the root component, but it's a better idea not to. Let it concentrate on getting things started; let other components do the heavy lifting.

A component works best if it handles a single set of related page operations. Got an edit form? That's a clump of related things, and the component would contain code to preload data into the form as well as to save it and check it for user errors—any operations having to do with that form as well as the template needed to actually display it.

A component is also indivisible—it will be kept together as a single unit even if it gets relocated on the page due to the responsive grid. Our Totals and Trends areas of the page could easily be written as a single component; they have a lot of calculations in common. But better to write them as two, because sometimes they won't be displayed in the same grid column on the page. They need to be able to move around independently of one another.

Think in terms of what areas of your design from Chapter 5 are indivisible and always operate as a single clump. Each of those is probably a component. Components can be quite small; or they can, in some circumstances, be an entire page on their own.

Another thing you will need to plan is your data service(s). We need *persistent data*—that is, you'll want a way of storing it so it doesn't all vanish as soon as the user closes the browser! When you have a persistent data source—when the data is "saved" somewhere—that means you not only need a way to save new or changed data but also a way to retrieve/load it. In short, you need a real data service with methods for the four CRUD operations: create new data, retrieve data, update existing data, and delete data.

You may, in fact, need more than one! Give some thought to distinct data structures and what their basic unit of data is. For example, if you were writing an app that needed to know about students and the courses they were taking, "students" would be one type of data structure, where a single data unit would be one student, with all that student's data (their major, class year, etc.). But "courses" would be an entirely separate data structure, where the data unit is a single course (including its term, its prerequisites, its meeting times, etc.). You'd have multiple options for how you choose to connect a student with the course(s) they were taking; you could record course choices directly in the student's data, you could record a list of enrolled students in the course's data, or you could use a third data structure which did nothing but link students and courses.

We chose an unrelated example in that paragraph because we want you to figure out what data structures are needed for this app—we don't want to give you the answer yet. Each data structure you come up with will probably demand its own data service.

There's a hint earlier in this chapter which will tell you something about how we divided our version of the app into components and services. Your ideas don't have to match ours exactly; but in the next chapter, we'll be implementing it the way *we* designed it, so if you want to take a slightly different approach, you'll have to adapt your work accordingly.

CODING THE APP

This chapter is long and covers a lot of ground.

Each section ends at a point where the app will run cleanly; that is, it may not do much, but it will compile and run without errors, so you can stop and see what you've done so far. Pace yourself. Stop at the end of each of those sections, and make sure you've absorbed the material and are ready to proceed before you go on.

At this point, you should have at least a rough idea of how you're going to divide the app into components. Here's the way we divided ours:

- A `meal entry component`, which contains the four form fields—amount, restaurant, meal, date—for entering a new meal, plus a modal for adding, editing, or deleting a restaurant. (There's a case to be made for making the restaurant-handling portion its own component. We've chosen to keep it with this one because it makes it easier to instantly reflect changes in the restaurant back to the rest of the meal-entry form.)

- A `totals component`, displaying the two running totals for meal amounts.

- A `trends component`, displaying statistics over time.

- A `meal list component` (the entire second page of the app), which lists all the meals entered for a particular restaurant and allows you to alter or delete individual meals.

- A `datepicker component`, because entering calendar dates is a specialized UI task that's complex enough to carve off into its own thing.

In addition to these components, we also need:

- A data service for restaurant data

- A data service for meal data

- The definition of our meal data structure

- The definition of our restaurant data structure

(Don't worry if that doesn't make complete sense just yet.)

We also need something we referred to a few times already: the *router*, which we explain shortly. And for convenience in displaying dates in one spot, we'll add a small *pipe* to change the way the data is shown.

Since each of the things listed above is its own file, that's eleven files, plus each of the five components will also have its own .html file for its template—so that's sixteen new files in all we'll be creating.

Let's get started.

A SET OF PLACEHOLDER COMPONENTS

We're going to begin by creating all the components, but they won't actually do very much. We do this so we can define the relationships between the components—which component gets displayed where, who calls whom, how we switch between seeing this component and that one—and then we test that before adding operational code.

Make sure you're in the app directory (all the files we make in this chapter, including the .html files, will be in the app directory), and create and save meal-entry.component.ts as shown:

```
import { Component, OnInit } from '@angular/core';
import { Router } from '@angular/router';

@Component({
  selector: 'meal-entry',
  templateUrl: 'app/meal-entry.component.html'
})
export class MealEntryComponent implements OnInit {
  showRestDiv = false;

  constructor(private router: Router) {}

  ngOnInit(): void {
  }
```

```
  showRestaurants(): void {
    this.showRestDiv = !this.showRestDiv;
  }

  gotoList(): void {
    this.router.navigateByUrl('/meal-list');
  }

}
```

Before we discuss its contents, create and save meal-list.component.ts as shown (it's almost the same but not quite, so be careful to make all the necessary changes if you choose to copy and paste the meal-entry.component.ts file instead of writing from scratch):

```
import { Component, OnInit } from '@angular/core';
import { Router } from '@angular/router';

@Component({
  selector: 'meal-list',
  templateUrl: 'app/meal-list.component.html'
})
export class MealListComponent implements OnInit {

  constructor(private router: Router) {}

  ngOnInit(): void {
  }

  gotoMain(): void {
    this.router.navigateByUrl('/meal-entry');
  }

}
```

In both cases, we import Component (because we need to declare a component). We also import OnInit from core for reasons about to be seen; and we import Router from the Angular router module because we'll be using the router shortly (not yet, but we can go ahead and import it now).

You'll notice that in the @Component() parameters, we don't have a template. Instead we have templateUrl, the path to an HTML file which will contain this component's template.

Paths in **templateURL** are relative to the local server's root directory (that is, the project directory)—*not* the current directory. We're looking for a file in the same directory as this component, but in this case **./meal-list.component.html** wouldn't work. We have to use **app/meal-list.component.html**.

Incidentally, we *could* put the component **.html** files up in the project directory where **index.html** is and set the path here accordingly, but we don't for visibility reasons. If you were installing this app on a real web server, you'd need to make everything that's in the project directory visible to anyone who wanted to request it—any user could ask for **index.html** and get it (and thus launch the app). The component **.html** files, on the other hand, should be visible only to your components; on a real web server, everything in the **app** directory would be set with more restrictive permissions so that outside users couldn't just inspect those files at will.

The class declaration has two new words in it. `implements OnInit` indicates that we will be using a special function called `ngOnInit()`, which is called when the component is *instantiated*. (A horrible programming word that means "when the component comes into existence." How that happens, we discuss shortly.) This is why we had to import `OnInit`.

It's good practice to put any variable declarations at the beginning of the block they apply to; that is, variables used in a function should be declared as the first statements in the function, and variables used by the entire component should be declared as the first statements of the component. Even if your particular programming language doesn't outright require that you do so, it makes the code easier to read. At the moment, only `MealEntryComponent` has a variable: `showRestDiv`, which we know is a Boolean because we initialized it to false (without quotes; if we set it to 'false', we would be making a string, not a Boolean). There will be more variables to come in both of these components.

Now we come to something odd.

```
constructor(private router: Router) {}
```

First, let's consider the idea of a class *constructor*. You may recall from the previous chapter that the class is just the definition; to actually use it, you create an object of that class. Normally, if we had some class we wanted to use in our code, we'd handle the object creation just like a variable declaration. Say we had a class defined somewhere called `Restaurant`. We'd make a new object of it by saying:

```
myRestaurant = new Restaurant;
```

. . . That is, the variable named myRestaurant is a new object of class Restaurant.

When we make a new object, the class's constructor is called. The constructor is a special function composed of "things we need to do when making a new object of this class." A class doesn't *have* to have an explicit constructor—at least, not in TypeScript—but if there are special instructions that must happen when the object is created, then that's the place for them.

However, for our component classes, we usually don't *care* about the constructor. Nowhere in this code will you find a new MealEntryComponent declaration, for example. Each component is implicitly instantiated—there's that word again—that is, an object of that class (the component) is created automatically when we refer to the component somewhere in HTML. We don't *need* an explicit new for our components. Also, we have a better way of specifying "things we need to do when the component is loaded," as you'll see in a moment.

So this constructor isn't required, and you'll also notice it isn't *doing* anything. It has a pair of curly braces with nothing in them. The *only* reason we have it is so we can say private router: Router in its parameters.

Dependency injection

Angular makes a lot of fuss about the idea of *dependency injection*. What follows is an oversimplified explanation. Router is a class. (We realize you still don't know what it does. We're getting there.) Our component needs an object of the Router class, which we put in the variable router. In any other language, we might have declared that object inside the constructor:

```
constructor () {
  private router: Router;
}
```

or perhaps even along with the variable declarations in the main body of the component

```
private router = new Router;
```

(The private keyword means that the data is private: nothing outside this class can see this variable.)

All names—variables, classes, functions, whatever—are case-sensitive in TypeScript. .router and Router are not the same thing. Normally we wouldn't use a name that could be so easily confused with another name, but here it makes sense: router (small) is a local instance of Router (big).

Remember, the parentheses are where you supply parameters *to* the function. The constructor is just another function, albeit a special one. So `constructor(private router: Router)` is actually saying that the constructor is depending on having a class called `Router` *passed to it* so that it can make the private variable `router`. Angular uses this syntax for classes which are marked as *injectable*—available for use in just this way by other classes or components.

Angular does this to set up certain kinds of services so that any code which uses them doesn't need to know their internal details. It makes the service more of a "black box," where you just need to know what to put in it and what you can expect to get out of it without having to know or care how it really works. This is a fine principle, but it's worth noting that it'd be good practice to set up services this way *anyway*, and it can be done without needing the "injection" concept. In other words, Angular is trying to enforce something that everybody should already be doing.

But we'll play along. We'll be using three things in this app that are injectables: the router, which is a special case, and our two data services. We'll discuss how to designate something as an injectable when we get to those. In the meantime, you can assume that only these injectable dependencies are declared in the constructor's parameters in this odd way. Any other class we want to use, we'll instantiate in more conventional ways.

ngOnInit

We imported and declared our intent to use `OnInit` so that we could write a function called `ngOnInit()`. It doesn't do anything at the moment in either component, but it will. The `ngOnInit()` function is a special function that gets called when the component is initialized. You may feel that the constructor and `ngOnInit()` seem to handle more or less the same purpose, and you're not wrong. The difference is that the constructor gets called when someone is asking for a new object of the class, and the `ngOnInit()` function gets called once that object is created. In other words, during the instantiation of the object, the constructor gets called first and `ngOnInit()` basically gets called last. (There's another special function called `ngOnChanges()`, and we discuss where it falls in this order when we write the totals and trends components.)

As a practical rule, use the constructor (if at all) just for defining the class's variables and data. To initialize those variables and data or perform any operational "do this when starting" tasks, use `ngOnInit()`.

You'll notice the `void` keyword in the `ngOnInit()` declaration. This means that the function will return nothing. It does its thing, but doesn't pass back any data to whatever called it. It doesn't need to. The other functions we've put in these components so far are also void returns. Later we encounter some functions that do actually return values, and they indicate which types of data they return. For example:

```
transform(value: string): string
```

accepts a string as its parameter and returns a string as its output.

(The constructor doesn't need to show what kind of thing it returns. The constructor automatically returns an object of that class. That's what makes it the constructor.)

"this"

The showRestaurants() function in MealEntryComponent takes the showRestDiv variable defined in the main body of the component and toggles it. The exclamation mark, in a logical context, means "not" or "the opposite of," and a Boolean is always either true or false, so what

```
this.showRestDiv = !this.showRestDiv;
```

means is, if showRestDiv is true, set it to false; if it is false, set it to true. We'll need this in the template. You'll see why.

But why does it need this. in front?

If we'd just said

```
showRestDiv = !showRestDiv;
```

tsc would have given us an error at compile time. It would gripe that there is no variable called showRestDiv *local to the function*. That is, we did *not* declare a variable in the function like this:

```
showRestaurants(): void {
  let showRestDiv: boolean = true;
  showRestDiv = !showRestDiv;
}
```

because that's not what we wanted. That would have created a Boolean which could only be used by the showRestaurants function, which would have existed only while the function was running (and, if you read carefully, would always have ended up set to false just before it vanished).

We want a showRestDiv which *holds its state* (remembers what it's set to) for the lifetime of the *component*, not the function, which is why we declared it up in the component body. Here are some rules about variable *scope*—that is, which code can "see" which variables:

- Variables declared in the main component (class) body are visible to the entire component.
- Variables declared within a function are visible only to the function (we'll help enforce this by using let when we declare them, which we'll discuss more later).

- When a function uses or alters a variable that was declared up at the component level, add prefix `this.` to the name of the variable, or `tsc` will get confused.

- The above rule applies to functions as well; when a function in a component refers to another function in the same component, the function name must be preceded with `this.` or `tsc` won't know where to find the function.

The last function in each of these two components has to do with the router, which we're finally getting to.

The router

The mysterious router! (It's not really that mysterious.)

The router is an Angular module that allows you to associate components with browser paths. Just as you can go to a specific web page via a particular URL, the router allows you to go to a specific component via its own distinct URL.

To configure the router, we need to

- Set up a routing file.

- Call the router as an injectable in each component that uses it in its functions (we already did this in the only two components which need it).

- Add the routing file to the dependencies and imports in the root module (we do this at the very end of this section).

Create and save the file `app.routing.ts` as shown:

```
import { ModuleWithProviders }  from '@angular/core';
import { Routes, RouterModule } from '@angular/router';

import { MealEntryComponent }   from './meal-entry.component';
import { MealListComponent }    from './meal-list.component';

const appRoutes: Routes = [
  { path: '', redirectTo: '/meal-entry', pathMatch: 'full' },
  { path: 'meal-entry', component: MealEntryComponent },
  { path: 'meal-list', component: MealListComponent }
];

export const routing: ModuleWithProviders = RouterModule.forRoot(appRoutes);
```

Notice that, in addition to the required items we need from the core and router modules, we also import *our* two components that we just made. Every component referenced in the routes table needs to be imported here.

Our routes table is small; it only refers to those two components. The path meal-entry refers to MealEntryComponent, and the path meal-list refers to MealListComponent. Once we get to a point where we can test-run the app, this will translate to direct URLs—so, if we went to

```
localhost:3000/meal-list
```

we would see the meal-list component displayed.

The first path in the list of routes controls what happens for an empty path, e.g., if we just go to

```
localhost:3000/
```

then it is considered "empty" because there's nothing else in the URL but the domain. (localhost:3000 fulfills the same purpose a domain name would in a real URL.) We specify pathMatch: 'full' to match the entire empty path (we want to make sure it's really empty), and we tell it to redirect to /meal-entry, so an empty path will show us the meal-entry component.

The routes table is picky about its paths. You'll notice that the **meal-entry** and **meal -list** paths don't begin with a slash. In our case, they *could* and it would still work fine, but in a more complex application, that might be a mistake. The difference is, **/meal-list** is an absolute path that says "start at the top and match from there"; it will only match **our.domain.name/meal-list**. Without the slash, it's a relative path—it just looks for **meal-list** anywhere inside the path; it doesn't care where.

On the other hand, when we redirect to **/meal-entry** from an empty path, we *do* put on the slash, because at that point, we know we want to go to the absolute path.

Path matching happens in the order that routes are listed. This has hazards of its own. If you listed a path for **meal** and then a path for **meal-entry**, the latter would never get used, because the router would see 'meal' in the first part of 'meal-entry,' immediately go to whatever component was associated with **meal**, and go no further. You'd need to list them in the opposite order for it to work as intended. With our empty-path redirect, the **pathMatch: 'full'** parameter avoids this trap, so it can be listed first without causing problems.

It's worth a closer look at `appRoutes` for syntax reasons. The `const` keyword says that the variable we're declaring is a *constant*—it won't change again after it's initialized. The variable, `appRoutes`, is an object of type `Routes` (which we imported prior to that), and `Routes` expects to be an array of lists. (How did we know this? We followed the example Angular itself provided in its documentation, which we discuss on page 139.)

"An array of lists": that is, the outer array in [ ] encloses any number of lists in {}, or the lists being separated by commas (as always, no comma after the last one). Lists contain named data, so inside each list we have several named data items, again separated by commas. Notice that the three lists don't have exactly the same data items inside them—we assume the `Routes` structural definition knows how to deal with that. The whole thing, even though it's on multiple lines for readability, is a single instruction and thus ends in a semicolon.

> We stress "no comma after the last item in an array/list" repeatedly because you'll get a syntax error if you put one there! There are other languages that don't care, but TypeScript does.

`Routes`, were we to dig deep in the Angular code and have a look at it, would contain a definition of a complex data structure. It's also a class; it just happens to be a class that only has a data definition and no operational code. We'll be defining two data structures of our own later. They too will be classes, and we'll see how to use them and refer to them in functions. Here we only have to worry about initializing the structure. It's not our job to use it; it's for the router to use.

The `appRoutes` initialization may look daunting, but don't be frightened by it. Saying

```
const appRoutes: Routes = [complex array contents];
```

is no different syntactically than

```
const myVariable: number = 5;
```

It's still a variable declaration where we give it both an explicit type and an initialization.

There's no functional code in this file, just imports and two variables. The other variable in the file is `routing`, which is exported so that the rest of the code can see it. Its initialization is, once again, something you have to look at an example to learn how to do. What it works out to mean is: `routing` is an injectable object of the `ModuleWithProviders` class, which is used to provide the routings to `RouterModule`, accessible to the entire Angular app, that are defined in the `appRoutes` constant. Whew!

Just enter it the way we've shown and don't worry about it. The key information on that line, for us, is that the variable is called routing—we'll need to know that when we alter the application module shortly.

We won't actually use the router for much. (It's capable of doing a lot of nifty things, but they're out of scope for this app. You should read the Angular 2 documentation[20] if you'd like to know more.) The two components we've made so far each use it. They each have a function that, when called, uses the router to navigate to a different path—which means a different component. For example, the meal entry component has a function that navigates to the meal list component, and vice versa:

```
this.router.navigateByUrl('/meal-list');
```

navigateByUrl() is a function within router (which, remember, is an object of type Router; the function is defined in the Router class). The this is necessary because router is defined in the component and is not local to the function. So the dot notation could be read as "this component's router object's navigateByUrl() function."

When you're using classes you didn't write—or modules, libraries, or anything else you didn't write—how do you know what they do? When we were making the routes list, it was all right for us to tell you "just accept that it wants an array of lists," but in practice, you won't get freebies like that very often. How would you be expected to know that the **Router** class contains a function called **navigateByUrl()**? How do you know what sort of data that function is expecting?

You could, of course, go find the actual code where **Router** is defined, deep in the bowels of the Angular router module, but that code is pretty difficult to read. A better choice would be to go to the Angular API docs (angular.io/docs/ts/latest/api/). API stands for "Application Programming Interface," and people use it to mean several different things, but here it means "everything you need to know to use our classes and functions in your own code." On that page, we find a link for the **Router** class, and that takes us to a page with a definition of every parameter **Router** accepts and every function it contains. The notation is a little strange, but the trickier functions in **Router** all have usage examples, so that helps.

For outside libraries, ideally the people who wrote the library have provided documentation on how to use it. Some documentation is better than others. Sometimes you do have to go into the code and look at it just to figure out what to do, but it's a bad sign when you do. A developer who isn't interested in documenting their code usually also isn't interested in making sure it runs well.

---

[20] More about routers at angular.io/docs/ts/latest/guide/router.html.

The root component will also use the router, but in a different way. Open `app.component.ts` and change the template so it reads like this:

```
template: `
        <header style="background-color: #00746B">
        <h1>{{title}}</h1>
        </header>

        <router-outlet></router-outlet>
        `
```

Don't change anything in the rest of the file, just the template.

We've added a little temporary formatting to get the header to display on a background of our banner color. That's not obligatory.[21] The important part is the `<router-outlet>` tag pair. In place of these, the component currently selected by the router will be displayed. When the app first starts, the path will be empty (just `localhost:3000/`), so the `MealEntryComponent` template will be shown, as we have told it to do in the routes table. Later, if we navigate to a different component (using the navigation functions we've created), the contents of this tag pair will change accordingly.

In other words, we've just set up the root component as a "frame" that will display all our other components, depending on navigation. The only HTML in the root component that doesn't change with navigation is the title banner.

We don't need to import or declare use of `Router` in our root component because we're not using `Router` data or functions anywhere within the component's code. We get `<router-outlet>` "for free"—assuming we remember to add the appropriate declarations to the root module, which we get to shortly.

Finishing up the rest of the placeholders

We still need template contents for `MealEntryComponent` and `MealListComponent`, and we'll go ahead and set up the files for the totals and trends components while we're at it.

First, create and save `meal-entry.component.html` as shown (remember, these template `.html` files go in the app directory with their components):

---

[21] But if you use the styles the way we set them up in chapter 5, you'll need some kind of non-white background color behind `<h1>` contents, because they're currently styled as white text, and otherwise you won't be able to see them!

```
<h2>TastyTracking</h2>
<div>
  <div><button (click)="gotoList()">Edit Meals</button></div>

  <div>
    <label>I spent $</label>
    <input id="amount" value="" />
  </div>

  <div>
    <label>At</label>
    <select id="restaurantID">
    <option value="0">-- select a restaurant --</option>
    </select><button *ngIf="!showRestDiv"
    (click)="showRestaurants()">Edit</button>
    <div *ngIf="showRestDiv">
      Restaurant editing stuff will go here
      <button (click)="showRestaurants()">Close</button>
    </div>
  </div>

  <div>
    <label>On</label>
    <select id="name">
    <option value="B">Breakfast</option>
    <option value="L">Lunch</option>
    <option value="D">Dinner</option>
    <option value="S">Snack</option>
    </select>
  </div>

  <div>
    <label>On this date</label>
    <input id="date" value="" />
  </div>
  <button>Save</button>
</div>

<totals></totals>

<trends></trends>
```

Right now this contains a form that doesn't do anything and a Save button that also doesn't do anything, but it has a few special tricks already. The Edit Meals button at the top (we style it to improve its placement and display in the next chapter) calls the gotoList() function when clicked; as defined in the component, this will navigate you to the meal-list page. And below the restaurant list (which currently has no restaurants), there's some magic going on with something called *ngIf.

We explain *ngIf more when we do more work on this template, but it's a *conditional*, which says "only display the page element it appears in if its condition is met." The condition is the part enclosed in quotes.

To run through the logic here quickly:

- The *ngIf inside the Edit button says to only display that Edit button if the showRestDiv variable is false (remember, the ! in an evaluation context means "not"—i.e., "not true"). We initialized showRestDiv to false in the component, so when this component is first loaded, the button will be shown.

- That Edit button, when clicked, calls showRestaurants(), which toggles the showRestDiv variable. Poof! Suddenly showRestDiv becomes true, and *this button disappears*.

- But just as the button disappears, the <div> immediately below it, which has its own *ngIf that says to only display the div contents if showRestDiv is *true*, magically appears.

- Within that div is another button, Close, which toggles showRestaurants() again when it's clicked. Press it and the div disappears (including the Close button), but the Edit button comes back.

- In short, either the Edit button or the contents of the div will be displayed; never both at the same time. The value of showRestDiv determines which will be shown.

At the bottom of this template, the <totals> and <trends> tag pairs are where the totals and trends components will be displayed. Yes, a component can display the contents of other components. In this case it makes sense, because no matter how our design adjusts responsively, the totals and trends components will always be displayed after this component and always in the same order. This won't interfere with Bootstrap needing to slide them around.

Next, create and save meal-list.component.html as shown:

```
<h2>Edit Meals</h2>
<div><button (click)="gotoMain()">Back</button></div>
<div>
  <select id="restaurantName">
  <option value="0">-- select a restaurant --</option>
  </select>
```

```
    Not done yet
</div>
```

This one's much more obviously a placeholder for now, but note the use of gotoMain(), which will navigate back to the other page.

Because we've referred to the totals and trends components in the meal-entry template, we'll need to set up some placeholders for them, too. We'll need four files: two components and two templates.

Create and save totals.component.ts as shown:

```
import { Component, OnChanges, Input } from '@angular/core';

@Component({
  selector: 'totals',
  templateUrl: 'app/totals.component.html'
})
export class TotalsComponent implements OnChanges {

  ngOnChanges(): void {
  }
}
```

Create and save trends.component.ts as shown:

```
import { Component, OnChanges, Input } from '@angular/core';

@Component({
  selector: 'trends',
  templateUrl: 'app/trends.component.html'
})
export class TrendsComponent implements OnChanges {

  ngOnChanges(): void {
  }

}
```

These both import something called Input, which they don't use yet, as well as having an ngOnChanges() function, which doesn't yet do anything. We cover all that when we get there.

They'll need templates.

Create and save `totals.component.html` as shown:

```
<h2>TastyTotals</h2>
<div>
  Not done yet
</div>
```

Create and save `trends.component.html` as shown:

```
<h2>TastyTrends</h2>
<div>
  Not done yet
</div>
```

Now, with all that done, surely we're ready to pause for a test run, right? Not quite. One more very important step needs to be done.

Back to the application module

If you tried to run the app right now, you'd get a "Loading . . ." window with none of our content. You'd then need to look at the web console and decipher some of the failure messages there to discover that we haven't yet made the application module aware of some of the new things we're using.

You'll need to add all four of our new components to `app.module.ts`, both as imports and as items in the `declarations` section of the `@NgModule()` parameters. You'll also need to import our routing file . . . but not `Router` or `RouterModule`; we don't import those because the routing file does that for itself. And the routing file needs to be added to the `@NgModule() imports` parameter.

It's a little hard to guess the routing file import syntax, but you should be able to figure out how to properly add the four new components by yourself. See if you can do it before looking at the text of the revised file, which follows.

Here's what your `app.module.ts` should now look like:

```
import { NgModule }      from '@angular/core';
import { BrowserModule } from '@angular/platform-browser';

import { routing } from './app.routing';

import { AppComponent }   from './app.component';
import { MealEntryComponent } from './meal-entry.component';
```

```
import { MealListComponent } from './meal-list.component';
import { TotalsComponent } from './totals.component';
import { TrendsComponent } from './trends.component';

@NgModule({
  imports:       [ BrowserModule, routing ],
  declarations: [ AppComponent,
                  MealEntryComponent,
                  MealListComponent,
                  TotalsComponent,
                  TrendsComponent ],
  bootstrap:     [ AppComponent ]
})
export class AppModule {}
```

It's unclear whether it makes a difference what order the router and components are imported in, but modules should always be imported first. We stick to this order:

1. modules

2. router

3. any other services

4. the components, with AppComponent always first

We follow the same order in the @NgModule() parameters.

And now we're ready for a test run! Check your work, start the local server, and see what you get. It should look like this:

Not much is working yet, but you should be able to:

- Press the Edit Meals button and be taken to the meal list screen.

- Press the Back button on the meal list screen to return to the first screen.

- Use the Edit and Close buttons to show and hide the (future) restaurant-editing controls.

You should also be able to get at the meal-entry and meal-list pages through direct URLs—that is, `localhost:3000/meal-entry` should show you the main page and `localhost:3000/meal-list` should show you the meal list page.

If something isn't working right, go back and compare your work against the code we've provided and make sure you didn't make any mistakes. We can't walk you through the debugging because we can't predict all the ways things might go wrong. But since we know the code we've provided here works, usually any problems are simply typos—a missing comma or brace, a misspelled variable, and so on. At each "test your work" phase, you should be prepared for inevitable mistakes like that. We make them all the time.

> You may see warning messages in the web console from time to time that aren't fatal. If your app is running fine, it's usually safe to ignore them.

Reflect upon your success and take a break if you need it. In the next section, we go back to `MealEntryComponent` and its template and begin making it actually do things.

WE MUST KNOW OUR DATA TO MAKE OUR DATA SERVICES

We've reached a point where we can't proceed without defining what form our data will take.

UI/UX designers focus on the parts of apps that users see—not just the visual design but the flow of operations. To the back-end developer, these are seldom the main event. Most of the working code in this application will be about the underlying data: retrieving it, formatting it into a style the user wants to see, altering it, and saving it.

We have two distinct types of data we need to be *persistent* (remember, that means "we have to have a way to save it so it's still there even after the app is closed").

The first type is a meal. We hold four pieces of information about a single meal:

- where we ate it

- how much we spent on it

■ what day we ate it

■ which meal of the day it was

Three of those pieces of information are best stored as strings. The restaurant could be stored as a string, but we're going to store it as a number. What the meal data will actually hold is a restaurant ID—an internal number, never seen by anyone but us fools writing the app—which can then be used to look up a restaurant name.

Why do this? Well, suppose you actually stored the restaurant name (string) in the meals data. Now imagine you've recorded all the meals you've eaten over the course of many months at a restaurant called "Macbeth's." All is well until one day Macbeth's changes owners and renames itself to "Macduff's." You, liking continuity, want to change all your meals you've already entered for Macbeth's to say "Macduff's" instead so that all your meals there, before or after the name change, will appear in the same list.

To do this, in the system you've built, we have to search through all the meals ever entered, find the ones whose restaurant name matches "Macbeth's," and rename them all. If you have a lot of records, this is a slow process.

If all you had stored in the meals data is a restaurant ID number, then sure, every time you want to display information for that restaurant, you have to go look up restaurant 5 and learn that it's "Macbeth's"—but if you need to change the name, how many records do you have to actually change? *One.* All meals eaten in restaurant 5 are still in restaurant 5. All we have to do is change the name of whatever restaurant is 5 in the *restaurants* data—our other data type.

Create and save the file meal.ts as shown:

```
export class Meal {
  name: string; // BLDS
  date: string; // YYYYMMDD
  location: number; // restaurant ID
  amount: string;
}
```

Create and save the file restaurant.ts as shown:

```
export class Restaurant {
  id: number;
  name: string;
}
```

These could have both been in a single .ts file, but this way, it's clearer exactly what each little file does. We'll need to import from them every time we use one of these two *data structures*, which is what you have just created even if you didn't know it. A data structure, formally, is a data type which contains multiple other pieces of data. We see later how you refer to the individual parts within the structure.

These are also examples of classes that are data-only; no code. And, as usual, they're both exported so that the rest of our code can see them and refer to them.

The extra information on lines in the Meal definition, the parts that begin with //, are comments. Everything that comes *after* // on a line is a comment—comments work the same in TypeScript as they do in .js files you've already seen. (There is also another way of designating comments, which we'll come to.)

We've put in those comments as a reminder of what format the data in those fields will be. The meal name (which meal of the day) we'll store as a one-letter code—*B* is for breakfast, and so on. The date will be stored as a four-digit year, a two-digit month, and a two-digit day, with no spaces or other punctuation. There are reasons to do this, which will be shown later, but it does mean our *storage format* is probably not going to be our *display format*, since people who aren't programmers mostly have trouble parsing dates that look like 20171007 (aka October 7, 2017). That's fine. We can deal with that.

Structure data in a way that makes the data easiest to manipulate without losing any information. There's always a way to make it pretty for the user later.

A data structure isn't actual data—just a *format* for data. We have a long way to go in terms of figuring out where we'll store data and how we'll save and retrieve it. But most of that will be addressed in the next section, when we deal with the data services.

Meanwhile, let's go back to MealEntryComponent.

This component will need to use both the Meal and Restaurant data types, so add these two lines near the top of the file, after the import of Router:

```
import { Meal } from './meal';
import { Restaurant } from './restaurant';
```

After the line that initializes showRestDiv, add a few new variables to the component:

```
selectedRestaurant = '';
meal = new Meal;
restaurants: Restaurant[];
```

Making a new object of a class is somewhat flexible in TypeScript. Instead of meal = new Meal, we could have said meal: Meal and it would have also been okay; because we know we're declaring that meal is a variable of type Meal, the new-object instantiation is implied. Just remember that one is considered an initialization (equals sign) and the other is a type declaration (colon).

Similarly, instead of saying

```
restaurants: Restaurant[]
```

we could have said

```
restaurants: Array<Restaurant>.
```

Either way, it means that "restaurant is an array of data of type Restaurant." We don't like the Array<something> syntax; we find it ugly and confusing. (Nothing else in TypeScript works that way, and the capitalization makes Array look like a class when it isn't.) In general, we only use it when we need to explicitly initialize an array to something—even an empty something, e.g.,

```
restaurants: Array<Restaurant> = []
```

because the initialization looks even weirder in the other format:

```
restaurants: Restaurant[] = []
```

Inside the ngOnInit() function, add these lines:

```
this.meal.date = '20171007';
this.meal.name = 'B';
this.meal.location = 0;
this.restaurants = [ {id: 1, name: 'Macbeth\'s'},
                     {id: 2, name: 'World of Salad'},
                     {id: 3, name: 'All Night Taco'},
                     {id: 4, name: 'International House of Kreplach'} ];
```

Some of this is fake data—for temporary testing purposes. We don't really want to start the date field at some fixed date; we want it to fill in "today's date," so later we'll replace the value here with a method of obtaining that. The restaurant data is also a short, fixed list. Eventually, we'll replace this with a call to our (future) restaurant data service, which will get all the restaurants we've stored.

Notice how we refer to individual elements of a data structure. We defined meal as data of type Meal. A single item of Meal data has four fields within it. To get at the date field within our meal variable, we say meal.date (and we need a this, because it's data declared outside this function, in the component).

The initialization of restaurants shows how you handle multi-field data when initializing. We defined restaurants as an array, so we need outer [ ], and inside those are several lists { }. Each list is one item of Restaurant data, and we provide the names of the fields in addition to the values. This format should look familiar to you since we just wrangled it for the routes table!

Also to note: "Macbeth's" has an apostrophe in its name. If we left it alone, tsc would confuse it with the apostrophes we use as string delimiters. So we *escape* it by preceding it with a backslash. The backslash won't be stored or displayed; it's just so we can get that apostrophe into the contents of the string without error.

Now that we have some fake restaurants and some initial data for our meal, let's get them into the form. Save your changes to meal-entry.component.ts, but leave it lying around. We'll be right back to it in a moment.

Two-way binding

Open up the template file meal-entry.component.html.

The line that read

```
<input id="amount" value="" />
```

should now be changed to

```
<input id="mealAmount" [(ngModel)]="meal.amount" />
```

We realize that [(ngModel)] is probably the weirdest thing you've seen yet in this book. If it's any consolation, it raised our eyebrows the first time we encountered it, too. But there's a reason for it.

First off, delimiters here on the template side don't always mean the same things they do on the component side. Here, parentheses don't *always* enclose a list of parameters, for example.

Angular uses parentheses around a type of event in places where the component must take action when something happens in the template. Thus, statements like this:

```
(click)="onClick()"
```

mean "component must run the onClick() function when this HTML element gets clicked." Angular calls this an *event binding*.

Angular also uses the following syntax in places where the template must set a property based on some value from the component:

```
[status]="myStatus"
```

In this case, the statement sets a status property in that HTML element to the value of whatever's in the variable myStatus. Angular calls this a *property binding*.

Thus our notation with the special word ngModel goes both ways: it fills in the form element with the value of a component variable, and if the contents of the form element are changed by the user, the changes are sent *back* to the component variable. A change to the data on either side, component or template, is automatically reflected to the other. Angular calls this a *two-way binding*. So Angular has chosen to give it both parentheses *and* brackets. This is the only place you'll find that peculiar notation, and when you see it, it will always have the magic word ngModel inside it.

> Some programmers have described this syntax, and not always with love, as "banana in a box" notation.

It's hard to explain but easy to use: this form element stays synchronized with whatever's in meal.amount. If the code changes meal.amount, then the changes show up in the form; if the user changes the value in the form, then the changes are available to the code. This is *extremely convenient*. A little further down we'll have to keep component and template data in step a different way, and you'll see what we mean.

The ngModel selector does a number of different things relating to form controls, but we don't use it for anything except bindings, which link a form element's value to component data. (However, you'll see shortly that we don't always use it for *two-way* bindings.)

Because [(ngModel)] *expects* that an assignment from the component's data will follow, we don't have to use the interpolation syntax we've already learned. That is, we do *not* need to write

```
[(ngModel)] = "{{meal.amount}}"
```

. . . It's a given that we're looking for the name of some component variable inside those quotes. Elsewhere in the form, though, as you'll see, we do still have to use the interpolation markup.

There's another thing we have to discuss on this line, but let's add in some more new material first. Change the line

```
<select id="restaurantID">
```

to

```
<select id="restaurantID" #restaurantID [(ngModel)]="meal.location">
```

Next, *following* the line with option value="0", add this line:

```
<option *ngFor="let r of restaurants" value="{{r.id}}">{{r.name}}</option>
```

For and *ngFor

Several times in the course of writing this chapter, we stop to consider things we explain differently to programmers and to people who aren't programmers (yet!) To a programmer, we don't actually need to explain what *ngFor does; they'd look at the line you just added to the template and understand immediately that it's a way of embedding a for loop into HTML elements.

Non-programmers, however, may not know what a for loop is. Have no fear.

A for loop executes the same set of instructions as long as the conditions you set for the loop are met. There are two ways to build a for loop. In the first method, you declare three things: the existence of a local variable and the value it starts at, a condition which needs to be valid for the loop to keep executing, and how to change the loop variable each time you go through the loop.

```
for (let c = 0; c < 52; c++) {
    some instructions go here;
}
```

means "start c at zero; keep executing the instructions inside the loop over and over as long as c is less than 52; as the last thing you do each time you go through the loop, increase the value in c by 1" (++ as an operator means "increase by 1"). The first time through the loop, c is 0; the second time through the loop, c is 1; the last time through the loop, c is 51. At the end of that, it gets incremented to 52, and the condition at the top of the loop no longer passes.

You can use this syntax simply to perform the instructions inside the braces fifty-two times, but you can also inspect and use the value of c inside the loop. If the contents of the loop were alert(c); you'd get a loop that showed you a series of pop-up messages containing numbers from 0 to 51.

The other form of for loop requires a local variable and an array.

```
for (let c of someArray) {
    some instructions here;
}
```

will set c to the same value as each item in someArray: in the order they appear in the array. If someArray = [4, 5, 6] then c will be set to 4 on the first time through the loop, 5 the second time, and 6 the third time.

Beware! In most other languages we've worked with, the word in the loop following `let c` is **in**, not **of**. If you do this in TypeScript, you will probably not get what you want. Instead:

```
for (let c in someArray) {}
```

sets **c** to the *indices* of the array items—that is, even though **someArray =** [4, 5, 6], **c** will be set to 0, 1, and 2—the count of the array elements. (An array's internal numbering system begins at 0, not 1.) There are some cases where this is useful but not many. **of** is what you normally need.

The *ngFor directive is structured like this second kind of `for` loop. It says "make a local variable r and set it to the contents of each item in restaurants in turn" and will display the <option> tag pair and its contents for each item it iterates. Given the contents of our fake restaurant data and the interpolations of r.id and r.name, here's the HTML the *ngFor would actually generate when the component is loaded:

```
<option value="1">Macbeth's</option>
<option value="2">World of Salad</option>
<option value="3">All Night Taco</option>
<option value="4">International House of Kreplach</option>
```

The naming of names

Before we start on the restaurant editing controls, let's sync the other two form fields with their component data.

Change the line which reads

```
<select id="name">
```

to

```
<select id="mealName" [(ngModel)]="meal.name">
```

Change the line which reads

```
<input id="date" value="" />
```

to

```
<input id="mealDate" [(ngModel)]="meal.date" />
```

When working with CSS, you've likely grown accustomed to labeling HTML elements with an id attribute. Each ID should be unique within that HTML page, and if for some reason in CSS you need to style one particular element, you refer to that element by its ID. In JavaScript or TypeScript, which use a Document Object Model (DOM) to determine how to refer to any given element on the page, the ID is also a part of that reference.

Form fields, unlike other HTML elements, have also classically had a name attribute. This is used in HTTP–based form transactions, plus a few other form tasks, none of which we're using at present. So the name attribute is less important to us than the id attribute, and in fact, we haven't provided names for any of these form fields.

One of our form fields—restaurantID—has a different kind of identifier. Notice that it has #restaurantID in addition to its id attribute. The pound sign prefix shows that we're declaring what Angular calls a *template reference variable*, which is a variable defined in the HTML (the template) that always contains the same data as the element it's declared in. In this case, the value of #restaurantID will always be the value of the <select> element containing it; the pound sign allows us to refer to that <select> element as if it's a local variable. You'll need identifiers like these if you have an element whose contents need to be used in an Angular directive or will be passed to an Angular component function.

For example, we've done this for restaurantID because we'll shortly add some HTML that checks its value in an *ngIf directive, like this:

```
<div *ngIf="restaurantID.value > 0">
```

and later we'll also be passing it back to some component functions, like this:

```
<button (click)="update(restaurantID.value)">
```

and we wouldn't be able to do either of those things unless we'd used the #restaurantID declaration.

It's okay—in fact, it's probably best practice—to set this reference variable to exactly the same as the element's id attribute; it will help you keep track of what's what, and since you're already obliged to keep your IDs unique, it will help you keep these variables unique as well.

We haven't bothered with a template reference variable for the other form fields because we won't need to use them that way. We've just changed them to the two-way binding (making their value attribute unnecessary, because the binding will provide the field's value) and improved their ID attributes a little to better indicate their purpose.

*ngIf

We've got a section of the page which appears and disappears (or, if you prefer, expands and collapses) when the user wants to see it. That section is going to be devoted to adding and altering restaurants. We won't be able to make it fully functional until we set up real restaurant data, but even with our fake data, we can begin the basics.

TastyTracking area with restaurant-editing controls that appear/disappear inline based on whether the user clicks or taps the Edit button.

Here's how we're going to have it work:

- If the user doesn't have a restaurant selected in the main <select> field, the input box in the new section will be empty, and the controls will indicate that the form is ready to add a new restaurant.

- If the user has already selected a restaurant when they open the pop-in section, that restaurant's name will be prefilled in the text box, and the controls will indicate that the form is for making changes to that restaurant.

- Either way, if the user adds a new restaurant or changes an existing one, the main selection is then changed to reflect this—it will be set either to the new restaurant or the updated name of the changed one.

- There will also be a deletion control which removes the restaurant name. Since we can't then select that restaurant, we will set the main selection back to zero (no restaurant selected).

If you recall our UI design from previous chapters, you'll note this is a deviation from our original spec. Todd felt this was a good setup that supported the create, update, and delete operations while keeping the controls compact and intuitive. Unfortunately, it turned out to be less intuitive than he thought, but we're going to implement it this way for now because it teaches some important points of using *ngIf which would otherwise be far less obvious. In Chapter 8, we cover both the usability implications of the decision as well as how to modify the behavior of this part of the page to match the original specs.

The easiest way to do this is to have these new parts of the page actually be two separate chunks of HTML: one set to be displayed for an add operation, the other to be displayed for an update. The way we determine which to display is to use *ngIf.

*ngIf is a directive that says, "Display the contents of this tag only if the condition that follows is true." That's the only thing it does. You can't make it process multiple conditions ("do this if true, or do this if false"). If you have a multi-case situation ("do this if A, do this if B, do this if C . . ."), then you want the *ngSwitch directive instead (which we don't use in this app).

In this case, we do want two conditions. We want to do one thing if the value of the main <select> is zero (no restaurant selected) and a different thing if the value of that <select> is any non-zero value. So we'll use two *ngIf directives.

Replace the placeholder line

```
Restaurant editing stuff will go here
```

with the following:

```
<div *ngIf="restaurantID.value > 0">
 <input type="text" id="editRestaurantName" #editRestaurantName
    value="{{selectedRestaurant}}" size="30" />
 <button (click)="update(restaurantID.value, editRestaurantName.value)">
    Edit</button>
 <button (click)="delete(restaurantID.value)">Delete</button>
</div>

<div *ngIf="restaurantID.value == 0">
 <input type="text" id="newRestaurantName" #newRestaurantName size="30" />
 <button (click)="add(newRestaurantName.value)">Add</button>
</div>
```

The first of these divs gets displayed when we have selected a restaurant, i.e., the value of the <select> is greater than zero. It fills in the editing control with the selected restaurant's name and gives us Edit and Delete buttons, which call functions that we haven't written yet. But we know that for the hypothetical update() function, we'll want to pass in two parameters: the ID of the selected restaurant (so we know which restaurant to update in our data), and the altered name. For the future `delete()` function, all we need is the ID of the selected restaurant; whatever the user edited in the text box is irrelevant.

Notice that `.value` of an HTML element doesn't always mean the same thing; it depends on the context. `restaurantID.value` refers to the value of the outer `<select>`, so that's a restaurant ID number—what's actually chosen when you pick one of those options. `editRestaurantName.value` is the value of the input text box, so that's an actual *name* of a restaurant.

The second div will get displayed if the value of the `<select>` is equal to zero—nothing has been chosen. Notice that the equivalence test is *two* equals signs.[22] A single equals sign is used for *assignment*. If we made a mistake here and had written `restaurantID.value = 0`, we would be *setting it* to zero. Not what we want!

Equivalence versus assignment is one of those things that every language handles a little differently and that always throws novice programmers. (Sometimes experienced ones forget it, too, and then spend hours trying to debug the problem.) Human brains can tell from context whether you're assigning a value or testing it. Computers cannot, and they need a way of telling the two operations apart.

This div refers to a third function we haven't written yet, which will accept the restaurant name we want to add. We'll have to go back and at least write placeholder versions of these functions before long; our code won't get past `tsc` until we do, because it refers to a function that doesn't exist. But let's solve one more problem while we're looking at the template. Then we'll go back to the component file and fill in all the things we're making reference to here.

Why do `*ngIf` and `*ngFor` start with asterisks?

These directives, which show, hide, or repeat chunks of the HTML template, are considered by Angular to operate on inner templates—smaller templates within the main template. Where we would say

```
<div *ngIf="some condition">Contents here</div>
```

internally this would be translated to the more strict form

```
<template [ngIf]="some condition"><div>Contents here</div></template>
```

but no one bothers with this unless they have good reason to. The asterisk, in the first form, is shorthand for "Yeah, we know there's an implicit inner template here, let's save some typing."

---

[22] There is also an equivalence test which uses three equal signs. We explain it later in this chapter.

> This syntax affects only the three directives which conditionally display the contents of a template: *ngFor, *ngIf, and *ngSwitch (which we don't use in this app but could have, as already remarked). Since we only ever use these directives in their "shorthand" form, we always use the asterisk when we mention them, so you'll remember.
>
> ■

Not Angular's fault

Notice in the preceding section that, when we're updating, we fill in the contents of the input text box with

```
{{selectedRestaurant}}
```

What does that variable contain? Where does it get set? How does it get changed? In the component code, so far the only thing we've done with it is initialize it to an empty string.

What we *want* it to do is contain the restaurant name of the current restaurant selection. So whenever the user changes the selection they make for `restaurantID`, the contents of `selectedRestaurant` have to change as well. Okay, no problem. We've already done a two-way binding for `restaurantID`, so whenever the user changes the selection, it's updated in `meal`
`.location`, right?

Right, except `meal.location` holds a restaurant ID—a numeric ID. We want the restaurant *name* so we can edit it.

We know that each `<option>` for that `<select>` has the restaurant name as well as the ID. It's just a question of getting at it. Unfortunately, this is complex, and it's not complexity Angular has wished upon us—it's just a particular nastiness of the way HTML forms are handled.

The text within a particular `<option>`—that is, the text enclosed by `<option></option>` tags rather than the `value` specified in the `<option>` tag itself—has to be located by first asking the `<select>` "What is your current selection?" It will answer by returning an index number that has nothing to do with the values of the various options; it's the options numbered sequentially from zero, like array indices. You then have to say, "Okay, let me see the text of the `<option>` that the `<select>` says is currently chosen."

This is enough of a pain to get that it's worth passing back into `selectedRestaurant` every time the `<select>` changes, just so we'll have it at hand more easily. But to do that, we have to make a function that is called when the `<select>` changes. And if we do *that*, then we can't use the two-way binding to `meal.location` anymore, because it only ever does one thing when the selection changes: it updates `meal.location` and that's it.

Forge bravely ahead. Change the line that currently reads

```
<select id="restaurantID" #restaurantID [(ngModel)]="meal.location">
```

to (this is really all one line, but it should be okay broken into multiple lines like this)

```
<select id="restaurantID" #restaurantID
  [ngModel]="meal.location"
  (change)="onSelect($event.target.value,
      restaurantID.options[restaurantID.selectedIndex].text)">
```

Our banana-in-a-box has had the banana taken out of the box. Now we'll only use the one-way [ngModel] to set the initial selection to the value of meal.location. When the selection changes—provoking a (change) event—we'll call our (not yet written) onSelect() function. We'll pass it two parameters. The first, $event.target.value, means what it says: the value that's affected by this event, i.e. the value being changed. This will pass back the newly selected restaurant's ID.

The second parameter is the nasty one. The select control (restaurantID) stores its options in an array. We get the element of that array, whose index restaurantID says is its current selection (selectedIndex), and then refer to that element's text attribute. "From restaurantID's options array, get the text of the option whose index is the same as restaurantID.selectedIndex." This will (once our heads stop spinning) pass back the newly-selected restaurant's name.

We're on the hook for an onSelect() function that not only updates selectedRestaurant based on this data, but also updates meal.location, because we broke that automatic updating when we removed the two-way binding. We have to do it ourselves now.

Let's make one last small change to this file. Down near the bottom, after all of the form fields, where it says

```
<button>Save</button>
```

change that to

```
<button (click)="save()">Save</button>
```

That's all we're going to do to meal-entry.component.html for a while. At this point your file should look like the file on the following pages. (Your file may not look exactly the same. We may have broken some tags into multiple lines where you haven't or indented a little differently.)

```
<h2>TastyTracking</h2>
<div>
  <div><button (click)="gotoList()">Edit Meals</button></div>

  <div>
    <label>I spent $</label>
    <input id="mealAmount" [(ngModel)]="meal.amount" />
  </div>

  <div>
    <label>At</label>
    <select id="restaurantID" #restaurantID
      [ngModel]="meal.location"
      (change)="onSelect($event.target.value,
        restaurantID.options[restaurantID.selectedIndex].text)">
    <option value="0">-- select a restaurant --</option>
    <option *ngFor="let r of restaurants"
    value="{{r.id}}">{{r.name}}</option>
    </select><button *ngIf="!showRestDiv"
             (click)="showRestaurants()">Edit</button>

    <div *ngIf="showRestDiv">
      <div *ngIf="restaurantID.value > 0">
        <input type="text" id="editRestaurantName" #editRestaurantName
          value="{{selectedRestaurant}}" size="30" />
        <button (click)="update(restaurantID.value,
          editRestaurantName.value)">Edit</button>
        <button (click)="delete(restaurantID.value)">Delete</button>
      </div>

      <div *ngIf="restaurantID.value == 0">
        <input type="text" id="newRestaurantName"
          #newRestaurantName size="30" />
        <button (click)="add(newRestaurantName.value)">Add</button>
      </div>

      <button (click)="showRestaurants()">Close</button>
    </div>

  </div>

  <div>
    <label>On</label>
    <select id="mealName" [(ngModel)]="meal.name">
    <option value="B">Breakfast</option>
    <option value="L">Lunch</option>
```

```
    <option value="D">Dinner</option>
    <option value="S">Snack</option>
    </select>
  </div>

  <div>
    <label>On this date</label>
    <input id="mealDate" [(ngModel)]="meal.date" />
  </div>
  <button (click)="save()">Save</button>
</div>

<totals></totals>

<trends></trends>
```

There are five functions being called in that template that we haven't written yet: onSelect(), update(), delete(), add() and save(). In each case, we've been careful to note what parameters we're passing to the function. (The save() function has none.) It's not cheating to make a list or take notes so that, when you write the functions, you have a reminder of what you said they were going to accept as incoming data.

What is truth?

We can't actually write four of those functions for real until we have data services, but we can create placeholders, which will spell out the parameters we're accepting and remind us of what we need to do with them later. We can also set up some console output so we can see that they're actually doing something, even if we can't actually save any data yet.

Open meal-entry.component.ts. Let's start with the one function we *can* write completely. After the ngOnInit() function (although the functions can appear within the component in any order, we like that one to be listed first), insert the onSelect() function as shown:

```
onSelect(value: string, label: string): void {
  let numValue = parseInt(value);

  console.log('select', numValue, label);
  if (numValue > 0) {
    this.selectedRestaurant = label;
  }
  else {
    this.selectedRestaurant = '';
  }
  this.meal.location = numValue;
}
```

This function accepts a variable called value, which is a string, and a variable called label, also a string. It returns nothing. (The first parameter, if you've already forgotten, is the newly selected restaurant's ID; the second parameter is its name.)

We would prefer for value (the restaurant ID) to be a number. In fact, some parts of our code will require it to be a number. But the component code receives it as a string.[23] So we use the parseInt() function, which returns a numeric (integer) version of the string. We store that as numValue, and we'll work with that instead. We do the same in the upcoming update() and delete() functions.

We cover the console.log() statement shortly.

The if () else conditional means "if (condition is true), do the instructions in the first block; *else*—that is, if the condition is not true—do the instructions in the second block." We need this test because the user *could* be changing the value of the selection back to zero (no restaurant). If that's the case, we want to make selectedRestaurant empty, so that if the user pops in the restaurant-editing controls, the input box won't have anything in it. We have to have a separate case for this because, when the <select> is set to zero, the "restaurant name" contains "select a restaurant"—not what we want.

If the user did make a selection, we put the name of the restaurant in selectedRestaurant. Either way, whether that condition was true or false, we put the ID of the restaurant in meal .location.

Please note the use of this for all component-wide data.

Now some placeholders for the data-wrangling functions. Add the following:

```
update(id: string, name: string): void {
  let numID = parseInt(id);

  console.log('update', numID, name);
  // Need actual data update here
  this.meal.location = numID;
  this.selectedRestaurant = name;
  this.showRestDiv = false;
}


add(name: string): void {
  console.log('add', name);
  // Need actual data insert here
  // and push restaurant into component array
  // and select that restaurant
```

---

[23] This may be our fault, since we specified our options as <option value="0">, <option value="1">, etc., instead of <option value=0>, <option value=1>, etc. However, omitting those quotes is not good HTML and won't pass some strict validators.

```
    this.selectedRestaurant = name;
    this.showRestDiv = false;
}

delete(id: string): void {
  let numID = parseInt(id);

  console.log('delete', numID);
  // Need actual deletion here
  // Also need to delete all meals for this restaurant, a meal service call
  this.meal.location = 0;
  this.selectedRestaurant = '';
  this.showRestDiv = false;
}

// Need to replace console logging with user-visible error indications
save(): void {
  if (isNaN(parseFloat(this.meal.amount))) {
    console.log('amount is empty or not a number');
    return null;
  }
  else {
    if (parseFloat(this.meal.amount) <= 0) {
      console.log('amount must be positive/nonzero');
      return null;
    }
  }
  if (!this.meal.name) {
    console.log('invalid meal type');
    return null;
  }
  if (!this.meal.location) {
    console.log('invalid restaurant');
    return null;
  }
  if (!this.meal.date) {
    console.log('invalid date');
    return null;
  }

  // If here, then do actual stuff.
  console.log('save', this.meal.amount, this.meal.location,
              this.meal.name, this.meal.date);
  // Need actual data save here
```

```
    // Clear the amount for the next go - the rest of the fields can stay as is
    // this will also help prevent save button stutter
    this.meal.amount = '';
}
```

For these we have added some comment lines, some of which will be replaced by future work, some of which will stay as reminders of what's going on. The first three functions are pretty straightforward. The lines that will do actual data work will come from the future data service(s), and we can't add those yet.

The `selectedRestaurant` variable doesn't automatically get updated with the changed information, so we make `add()` and `update()` set that. For `update()` we also set `meal.location` to whatever restaurant we'd been altering. We'd do this for `add()`, too, and we would also select the new restaurant, but we can't—we don't know what to set it to. When we add a new restaurant, the data service is going to send us back the newly generated ID number. We don't have that yet. We could fake it, but it's not worth it; we'll be adding the data service soon. `add()` will also have to add the new restaurant to the component's `restaurants` array, which, again, we can't do without having an ID for the restaurant.

For `delete()` we set the selection to zero and we empty `selectedRestaurant`. For all three of these functions, we set `showRestDiv` to false to close the edit or add restaurants areas.

The `save()` function is a lot more complex, and it doesn't even actually save yet. All of the checking at the beginning is to make sure that there's valid data in every field of the meal structure. Mostly these tests are to prevent the user leaving any of the fields empty. This is more complicated than you might think because "empty" is nuanced in TypeScript. If someone doesn't fill in the date field, our code might receive it as an empty string, but it might also arrive as `null`—this depends on the way your browser handles form fields (and other circumstances; for example, if the user started to enter a date and then erased it).

An empty string (which we'd write as two single quotation marks with nothing between them) is different from `null` or `undefined`, just as zero is different from `null` or `undefined`. A variable that is `null` is not set to *any* kind of value, not even an empty value. A variable that is `undefined` was never initialized at all.

For example, if we wanted to spell out what we were trying to do for the date check, we might write

```
if (this.meal.date === '' || this.meal.date === null || this.meal.date ===
undefined)
```

where the two vertical bars || between conditions mean "or"—the combined test is "if this is true OR this is true OR this is true." A true evaluation for any one of the three parts is sufficient for the entire statement to evaluate as true.

But it's not necessary, because TypeScript will, when forced to treat non-Boolean data as if it were Boolean, make certain assumptions about what is "true" and what is "false." An empty string, a zero, a NaN result ("not a number"—more on that in a moment), a `null` value, or an `undefined` value will all evaluate as false. Any nonzero number or nonempty string evaluates as true.[24]

Since all three of the conditions we want to test are values that evaluate as false, we just say

```
if (!this.meal.date)
```

meaning "if not `this.meal.date`" or "if we got something false in `this.meal.date`."

The amount field needs some special handling. It's a string, not a number, but we need to test its contents *as if* it's a number. We also have more "bad data" conditions to test here than the others: it can't be empty, it can't be zero, it can't be negative, and it can't be a string that doesn't translate to a number (such as "Bob").

Complicating this is the fact that the *number* 0 evaluates as false, but the *string* '0' is considered a nonempty string and evaluates to true, which is not what we want.

First, we check to see if it's not a number (NaN). We can't compare directly against NaN status, which is special and quirky. This won't work:

```
if (this.meal.amount == NaN)
```

We have a `isNaN()` function available, which returns true if the parameter cannot be evaluated as a number. But we also can't say

```
if (isNaN(this.meal.amount))
```

because for some reason, even though you can run `isNaN()` on a literal string—`isNaN('hi there')` is legal—you can't use it on a variable of type string; the function wants a parameter that's been defined as a number. Yes, we realize that doesn't make sense. No worries:

```
if (isNaN(parseFloat(this.meal.amount)))
```

is what we want. That is, first we use `parseFloat()` to *try* to return a numeric equivalent of `meal.amount`. If it can't do so, it'll return NaN, and `isNaN()` will respond accordingly. (Watch those nested parentheses; it's easy to lose count and create a syntax error.)

We use `parseFloat()` here because the amounts may contain decimal portions (e.g., 10.33), and thus we want *floating-point* numbers. Using `parseInt()` wouldn't matter for this is-it-any-kind-of-number test, but it would truncate the decimal portion (`parseInt('10.33')` returns

---

[24] This is sometimes referred to as having "truthy" or "falsy" values. Warning: arrays, lists, and complex data structures automatically evaluate to true if they exist, even if they're empty.

10), so let's use the function that's appropriate to the data. (`parseInt()` is fine for restaurant IDs, which are always whole integers.)

The good news for us is that `null` and `undefined` also come out of `parseFloat()` as `NaN`, so we need no special cases for those possibilities.

We still need a second test, though. It goes inside the `else` block of the first test because if we have a not-a-number, there's no point in doing this second test. So this second test will happen only if the first one doesn't evaluate true. (When trying to follow nested statements, always pay close attention to your curly braces so you don't lose your place in the logic.) The second test performs the `parseFloat()` again, and checks to see if the result is less than or equal to zero. (We know it'll be a legal number of some kind, because if it weren't, we wouldn't have reached this test.)

This code is slightly inefficient. Can you see how/why?

It would be better to write it like this (and you should go ahead and do so):

```
save(): void {
  let amtAsNum = parseFloat(this.meal.amount);
  if (isNaN(amtAsNum)) {
    console.log('amount is empty or not a number');
    return null;
  }
  else {
    if (amtAsNum <= 0) {
      console.log('amount must be positive/nonzero');
      return null;
    }
  }
 [rest of function is unaltered]
```

For the cost of a local variable `amtAsNum`, we spare having to call `parseFloat()` twice for the same task. This also makes the logic clearer:

- Try to get a numeric value.

- If that value isn't a number, show an error and fall out of the function.

- If the value is a number, check to see if it's less than or equal to zero; if it is, show an error and fall out of the function.

"Fall out of the function" refers to those `return` statements throughout the data checks. `save()` returns type void—it's not supposed to return anything, and in fact `null` is the only thing it legally *can* return. But the `return` statement also means "stop executing this function right now, go no further, we're done," and that's what we're using it for here. The idea is that if any of these bad-data tests are triggered, the part of the function that begins at

```
// If here, then do actual stuff.
```

will never happen.

The `console.log()` function prints messages into the web console. You can give it parameters, which are literal values, variable names, or a combination of both (separated by commas), as seen in the message that prints when you "successfully" save. Right now, for testing, logging errors to console suffices. Later, as the comment at the top of the function notes, we'll need a way of showing bad-data errors to the user so they know what they did wrong.

Why did we make the amount field of the **meal** structure a string? It's always going to contain a numeric amount; why didn't we declare it to be a number?

There are two reasons. The first is that we knew in advance that we were going to be using a type of data storage that *only stores things as strings*, we were already going to have to sling around lots of **parseInt()** statements to deal with the restaurant ID, and we didn't want to have to do it for this field, too.

The second is that you don't always get to control the data structure you're reading from and writing to, and often data is in a format that doesn't work very well for your purposes. You have to be able to write code that adapts data to your needs, and we've done this on purpose to give you practice at it.

We're missing one piece of data checking. We need to add a test for the date field to determine whether it's a valid date. But that requires a date-handling library, which we're not quite ready for yet. For now, keep your input to YYYYDDMM format in your tests. Later, we go even further and add a date-picker control that minimizes the chances that the user will put something foolish in that field.

Any time you give the user a place to enter data, you must assume they will try to put bad data into it in any way possible. The beauty of the restaurant ID and the meal code being obtained from pulldown lists is there's no way the user can hand-enter bad data there; they can't type in a meal code that doesn't exist, for example. But you can't use picklists for everything.

When all the data is well-groomed, then we can pass it to our nonexistent data service. After that, the only other job in the `save()` function is to clear the amount. This makes the data invalid on purpose; if the user manages to click the Save button multiple times, then only the first of those will be performed and we won't store five copies of the same information. We leave all the other items as they are. This is a judgment call. If we thought the user were likely to enter a lot of disparate items at the same time, for example, we could argue that it made more sense to clear the restaurant back to "no selection" and the date back to today after each save. But we think it's slightly more likely that if the user is entering several meals at the same time, they'll be on the same date, and as for the restaurant, changing it from a previous selection is neither more nor less grueling than changing it from zero.

It's time for another test. Before we can do that, though, we have one more task. The ngModel directive is part of the forms-handling module of Angular, and though we don't need to note that explicitly in our components, the application module needs to know that we're using it.

Open app.module.ts and make the following two changes.

Just after the BrowserModule import line, add this line:

```
import { FormsModule }   from '@angular/forms';
```

Change the imports section of the @NgModule() parameters to look like this:

```
imports:     [ BrowserModule, FormsModule, routing ],
```

Now you should be ready for a test. Save any work you haven't saved. Make sure you open the web console after the app starts so you can see messages. Run the app and test the following functions:

- Restaurant list is properly filled with our fake data.

- Meal type list is filled, and Breakfast is the default selection.

- Date is properly prefilled with our test date 20171007.

- Console message when you add a restaurant showing what would have been added.

- Console message when you update a restaurant showing what the name would have changed to.

- Console message when deleting a restaurant, showing what would have been deleted.

- Console message when saving the form contents, showing what would have been saved.

- Console messages for various combinations of bad or missing data in the form when you try to save.

Take a deep breath after you finish testing. Stand up. Stretch. Possibly get a refreshing beverage.

THE DATA SERVICES

As already discussed, our app needs some place to store persistent data. It wouldn't be very useful if all your meal and restaurant entries vanished as soon as you closed the web browser. Given that this is a problem that pretty much every web application has to deal with, it may surprise you to know that solving it is a bit of a challenge.

Many web apps talk to a data service that's on a remote server somewhere. That data service probably has a real database and a library of documented functions for making requests. This is out of scope for an introductory book. If we wanted to do this, we'd have to show you how to find and set up database software, set up a web server, and write code on that server that provides the API—the data-accessor functions. We'd also have to teach you something about handling HTTP requests and asynchronous data. These are all useful things to know, but we can't cover them here. (We have, though, addressed it briefly in a supplemental file in your npm package should you one day find that you have a data service you need to talk to. See page 269 for more.)

Saving data in the local filesystem—that is, on your computer's hard drive—is also a problem because it's considered a security hazard. If the web app had the ability to write to a file, it would have the ability to write to *any* file on your computer, and then you'd get malicious apps that do things like embedding viruses in your operating system files. For this reason, it's not allowed by your browser or by any of the tools we're using.

What we're going to use instead is a feature of your web browser called *local storage*. It's a special space that the browser knows how to write data to and read from. It's considered safe in that the browser won't let the app write anywhere but into this protected space, where malicious things can't happen.

Using local storage means we operate under a few rules and restrictions:

- Local storage is local to that computer (or phone or tablet) and that web browser. Data you save on your work computer won't be available to your phone; data you save using Firefox on a given computer will not be visible to Chrome on that same computer. (It would be possible to write a tool that exported all your data in a suitable format for importing into a different browser—but that's also out of scope for us.)

- Local storage is shared by every other app that uses local storage (on that browser/computer), so we need to mark any data we save so it's clear that it's "ours" and won't accidentally be altered or erased by any other local-storage-using app.

- All data is kept in local storage as strings. So if we need a numeric value, we'll have to store it as a string and convert it to a number as needed.

- Clearing the browser cache doesn't clear local storage, but on some browsers, the "clear all cookies" option does. (Cookies, which web pages use to hold status and tracking information about you and are similar in many ways, are stored in the same data space as local storage, and some browsers simply nuke that entire space when the user selects "clear all.")

It's not perfect, but it's the best we have.

One benefit of using a data service is that the functions calling the data don't want or need to know what's going on under the hood. As long as you don't change what parameters those functions accept or the type of output they generate, you can change all the inner workings, and your callers wouldn't care. So if you wanted to replace these data services with ones that do talk to a remote database somewhere, you'd only need to change the services themselves, not any of the calling code.

To that end, it's usually good design to keep your accessor functions generic and follow the CRUD model:

- One function to create a new record (and, usually, return the ID of the record thus created)

- One function to retrieve a record or a set of records, depending on the parameters

- One function to update the contents of an existing record

- One function to delete a record

As already noted, we need two data services, one for restaurants and one for meals. We're going to do restaurants first because it's considerably simpler.

The restaurant service

Create a new file (in the app directory, of course) called `restaurant.service.ts`.

Let's start with an empty framework so we can review that, and we'll fill in the functions in a moment.

```
import { Injectable } from '@angular/core';

import { Restaurant } from './restaurant';

@Injectable()
export class RestaurantService {

  getList(): Restaurant[] {
  }

  create(name: string): Restaurant {
  }
```

```
    update(id: number, name: string): Restaurant {
    }

    delete(id: number): void {
    }
}
```

We need to import `Injectable` so that we can use the `@Injectable()` decorator, and we need to import our own `Restaurant` data class so we can use it.

Our service, called `RestaurantService`, is declared to also be an injectable (refer back to the discussion on injectables if you need to) by using the decorator. Unlike some of the others we've used, this decorator doesn't need any special parameters; we just need to say "it's an injectable" and that's that.

We don't need a "get a single restaurant" function, so we don't have one. The only retrieval we'll need to do is to fetch the entire list of restaurants. This function, `getList()`, accepts no parameters and returns an array of `Restaurant` data (notice the square brackets).

The `create()` function accepts the name of the new restaurant; it will return `Restaurant` data, sending back the name and the newly generated ID of the restaurant.

The `update()` function takes both the ID of the restaurant to change and the new name to give it. It could plausibly return nothing (void) but we've chosen to return the updated `Restaurant` data, just in case the caller wants it.

The `delete()` function takes the ID of the restaurant to remove and returns nothing.

We'll fill them in in that order.

The `getList()` function, in full:

```
getList(): Restaurant[] {
  let rests: Array<Restaurant> = [];

  for (let x = 0; x < localStorage.length; x++) {
    let rest = new Restaurant;
    let key = localStorage.key(x);
// Local storage keys for restaurants are named in the format
// TTR_N+, where N+ is the ID number of the restaurant.
    let re = /^TTR_(\d+)$/;
    let results: Array<string>;

    if ((results = re.exec(key)) !== null) {
      rest.id = parseInt(results[1]);
      rest.name = localStorage.getItem(key);
      rests.push(rest);
```

```
      }
    }
    return rests;
  }
```

We will often use a blank line to separate our variable declarations, which should be at the beginning of the block in which they occur, from the working code. We find this makes the function easier to read.

Let's pause for a moment to discuss variable scope. In JavaScript, the usual way of declaring a local variable is to use the keyword `var`. We use `let` instead (this is a JavaScript ES6 idea that TypeScript has adopted early) because `var` has "leaky" scope and `let` does not. With `let`, "local" is indeed local, which is always what we want when we use it. What does that mean?

The variable `rests` is declared within the main block of the function. It's visible to all inner blocks of the function—everything at a deeper level—but isn't visible outside the function (e.g., up at the component level). Once the function ends, the variable ceases to exist.

The variables `rest`, `key`, `re`, and `results` (and the loop variable `x`) are declared in an inner block, the block of the `for` loop. They're visible only within the `for` loop; the rest of the function outside the `for` loop's brackets can't see them. When we use `let`, this is strictly enforced; if we used `var`, in certain cases, the outer portion of the function *could* see those variables, and if you weren't expecting it to work that way, could cause problems.

Why declare some things in some places and not others? The four variables in the `for` loop are ones we want to start fresh every time the `for` loop iterates. Every time the `for` loop completes an iteration, those four variables expire, and they get redeclared (and reinitialized) when the loop starts over again at the top. That's the desired behavior. The `rests` variable, on the other hand, has to maintain persistent data throughout all the loop iterations—it's where we're holding any results we want to return at the end of the function, so we don't want to erase it each time we loop. It gets declared with whole-function scope.

As a general rule, declare variables only for the most minimal scope you need. Don't bother declaring something at the entire-function level if you only need it inside a single conditional block, unless there are other compelling reasons to do so.

Each local storage variable has a key (its name; how you find the value to do anything with it) and a value, and both must always be strings. As we already noted, and as the comments in the function remind us, we need some way of telling which items of local storage are ours. Here we do this by prefacing the item's key with TTR_ (TastyTracker Restaurant). The keys we want here will always be TTR_ followed by a number. We don't know in advance how many digits the number will be; we just know that part of the key name will always be translatable to a number (the restaurant ID).

Unfortunately, we have no better way to "get all our restaurants" than to iterate through *all* keys in local storage—not just ours, anybody's—and sift out the ones that match what we want. `localStorage.length` is a property of local storage[25] that tells us the total number of keys. Internally, they're indexed just like an array, and like arrays, the first item is item zero, so if local storage contains 20 items, we iterate from 0 to 19. The `for` loop says: declare local variable `x` and initialize it to zero; keep iterating as long as `x` is less than `localStorage.length`; at the end of each iteration add one to `x`.

Inside the loop, we use another property of local storage, `localStorage.key()`, which returns the key of the item at that index. We pass it `x`, and it gives us the key of item `x`. Now we have the key of a particular item, and we need to test it against a pattern to see if it's one of the keys we want. That pattern is a *regular expression*, and it's set in the variable `re`.

Full explanation of regular expressions would take more space than we have.[26] In brief, they're a way of specifying patterns using "wildcard" placeholders and other special symbols that can stand for different types of characters. In this regular expression (the slashes at front and back are the usual delimiters for a regular expression), the `^` means "start looking for a match at the very beginning of the string," the `TTR_` text is its literal self, `\d` means "any digit," and the `+` means "one or more of those"—so, one or more digits. The parentheses enclosing that part of the regular expression are a way of "holding" it so we can refer to just that part of the matched string later. The `$` means "this is the end of the string"; if we encountered a key like `TTR_55_somethingelse`, that wouldn't be a match, because we don't want there to be anything after the digits.

So we're looking for a key that begins with `TTR_` followed by at least one digit and has nothing else after the digit(s). To actually *use* this regular expression, we have to use the variable's `exec()` method (which we get automatically when TypeScript sees we're declaring a regular expression). `re.exec(key)` means "let's try to match this regular expression against `key` and see if it fits." It will return an array of results if it matches and `null` if it doesn't.

The `if` statement is a little tricky because it does both an assignment and an evaluation. We set `results` to whatever comes out of `re.exec(key)`, no matter what, but we also compare the result to `null`. (The extra parentheses are so neither we nor `tsc` will get confused about what order to do things in. Here it's assignment first, then evaluation.) `!==` is "not equal to," so the `if` block happens only if the results from the `re.exec()` aren't `null`—that is, if we got a match.

The `results` data is an array, as noted. The 0 item always contains the whole string that was matched. Items after that are the contents of any parentheses we used in the regular expression, going from left to right in the expression—whatever was in the first pair of parentheses is array item 1, and so on. We had only one, and it will contain the part of the key which is *just* the digits.

---

[25] Although local storage works in all browsers, not just in Firefox, we recommend the Mozilla Developer Network for more in-depth reading about local storage: developer.mozilla.org/en-US/docs/Web/API/Storage/LocalStorage and developer.mozilla.org/en-US/docs/Web/API/Web_Storage_API/Using_the_Web_Storage_API.

[26] Another case where we recommend the Mozilla Developer Network: developer.mozilla.org/en-US/docs/Web/JavaScript/Guide/Regular_Expressions.

This is our restaurant ID! So we store it in `rest.id`. (It's a string, and `rest.id` wants a number, so we have to use `parseInt()`.)

We then take the key and pass it to `localStorage.getItem()`, which gives us back the actual value referred to by that key. That's the restaurant name, and we store it in rest.name.

The next line's very important, because remember, `rest` is scoped to just the `for` loop. Next loop, we start over with a fresh value for `rest`. So we need to push that value onto our outer array, `rests`. "Push" means "add it to the end of the array." We get the `push()` method automatically when we declare something to be an array. Obviously, to push something onto an array, the data types must match: `rest` is a `Restaurant`; `rests` is an array of `Restaurant`. All good.

Once we've looped through all the local storage keys, `rests` will contain data for any keys that matched, and we return that to the caller as the last task of the function.

We have to do the same iterate-through-all-keys dance when we're creating a new restaurant. Can you think of the reason why?

```
create(name: string): Restaurant {
  let rest = new Restaurant;
  let key = 'TTR_';
  let newid = 0;

  for (let x = 0; x < localStorage.length; x++) {
    let pk = localStorage.key(x);
    let re = /^TTR_(\d+)$/;
    let results: Array<string>;

    if ((results = re.exec(pk)) !== null) {
      let oldid = parseInt(results[1]);
      if (oldid > newid) {
        newid = oldid;
      }
    }
  }
  newid = newid + 1;
  key = key + newid.toString();
  localStorage.setItem(key, name);

  rest.id = newid;
  rest.name = name;

  return rest;
}
```

The problem is that we need an ID for our new restaurant. There are other ways to do this. We could hold a special value somewhere in local storage that contained "last ID used," and we could read and update that instead. In this case, local storage is usually fast enough, and new restaurants will be added seldom enough, that we don't mind the extra work. If your data source were very slow, you might want to take a different approach.

When we get a restaurant key, we note its ID number (not neglecting to `parseInt()`). If that ID number is larger than `newid`, which we start at zero, set `newid` to that ID. At the end of the `for` loop, `newid` will contain the largest of the IDs we found. So once the loop is over, we add one to that (`newid++` would have worked, too). That's our new ID number. If the highest ID we had so far was 55, then our new one will be 56.

Can you see why `newid` has to be declared and initialized *outside* the `for` loop?

Notice that if someone deletes an earlier restaurant that isn't the last one, the ID of the earlier restaurant will never be reused. That is, if restaurant 33 is deleted, and we have fifty restaurants, then the next one will be 51; we won't reuse ID 33. For a demo app like TastyTracker, this isn't a problem; in some systems, it could be.

Once we have a new ID, we create a key by *concatenating* (gluing together in the order listed) the new ID onto the 'TTR_' we've already put in the key. The plus operator means "addition" when working with numbers but means "concatenate" when working with strings. Oh, except that we effectively declared `newid` as a number when we initialized it to zero. No problem. It has an implicit `toString()` method that we can use to get a string equivalent of its value.

> `parseInt()` and `parseFloat()` are standalone functions. `toString()` is a method of a numeric variable. This is why the syntax for calling it is different. Don't be confused.

Then we use the `localStorage.setItem()` method to store our new data. It accepts two strings, the key and the value, and does what you expect it to do. We then fill `rest` with our new data just so we can return it to the caller.

The `update()` function is much simpler, since we don't need to search for any keys; we're passed in everything we need. We glue together our key right in the variable initialization, call `localStorage.setItem()`, and return a `Restaurant`—and the last part of that is an optional nicety.

```
update(id: number, name: string): Restaurant {
  let rest = new Restaurant;
  let key = 'TTR_' + id.toString();

  localStorage.setItem(key, name);
```

```
    rest.id = id;
    rest.name = name;

    return rest;
}
```

Finally, the delete() function.

```
delete(id: number): void {
  let key = 'TTR_' + id.toString();

  localStorage.removeItem(key);
  return null;
}
```

The localStorage.removeItem() method accepts a key and does what it says it will do.

Having now seen the setItem(), getItem(), removeItem() and key() methods of localStorage, and its length property, you've seen everything you need to know about local storage. In fact, that's almost all there is to it. There are a couple of other methods we don't use, but local storage isn't very sophisticated. Neither is our restaurant data service, but it doesn't need to be. The other data service is considerably more complex.

Now that our restaurant data service is written, we need to go back and add it to calling code in order to use it. But let's tackle the meal data service first, then we'll put them both into use at the same time. (We'll make no further changes to restaurant.service.ts. After adding the functions above, make sure you save it before proceeding.)

The meal service

For the meal service, we don't need to generate IDs as we do for restaurants. We're able to create a unique key for each meal record based on the meal data itself. It's very unlikely that Donna would eat lunch twice in the same restaurant on the same date, so the combination of restaurant + meal type + date is unique . . . or at least sufficiently unique for our purposes.

(If users did try to enter the same meal type on the same day in the same restaurant, the new entry would replace the old one. For our app, this isn't a fatal flaw and could even be considered a desirable feature.)

This method does make our data keys complex, though. A typical meal might have the following key:

```
TTM_20171007_L_25
```

where 20171007 is the date of the meal, L is the code for the meal type (lunch), and 25 is the ID of the restaurant. (The value named by the key, of course, is the meal amount.) The TTM is text to help us sort out only the keys we want, just as TTR was for the restaurants.

Another complication is that the "get lists of meals" function must do multiple things— retrieving meals by date, retrieving them by meal type, and retrieving by either date or meal for statistical purposes—and decide, based on what information we pass it, which of those things to do.

Let's begin with the bare bones, as we did for the restaurant service. Open a new file called meal.service.ts and enter the following:

```
import { Injectable } from '@angular/core';

import { Meal } from './meal';

@Injectable()
export class MealService {

/* We need four different types of retrieval by parameter:
   by restaurant (for the listing page) by date, by meal, and/or
   by date AND meal (for the stats) */

/* The first three params are required but could be zero/empty.
   The fourth param is optional; if it's used, then the two date
   params together form a date range.
   If the second date is present but the first date is empty,
   it will be ignored. */

getList(restaurant: number, mealtype: string,
        date1: string, date2?: string): Meal[] {
}

create(date: string, name: string,
        location: number, amount: string): Meal {
}

delete(date: string, name: string, location: number): void {
}

deleteByRestaurant(id: number): void {
}

}
```

We haven't left out any functions. Once again, we don't need a "get a single meal" function, and there's no `update()` function for reasons that will be explained when we get there. On the other hand, we've added a placeholder for a `deleteByRestaurant()` function, which we won't fill in until considerably later.

The top matter is almost identical to the restaurant service, except that we're declaring `MealService` and we need to import the `Meal` data type, not `Restaurant`.

We've used the alternate comment format that TypeScript permits, which is more useful for multiline comments. Unlike `//`, these cannot share a line with non-comment code. Everything between `/*` and `*/` is considered a comment.

The second of those comment blocks is there to help you remember what the parameters to `getList()` do. The question mark in

```
date2?: string
```

isn't part of the variable name, but an indicator that `date2` is optional; we don't have to provide it to the function at all. We could certainly send the first three parameters as empty or zero, but we *would* have to send them. `date2` can be omitted entirely.

> If you use optional parameters, they must always be the last parameters; that is, they must always come after any required ones. Also, if you omit an optional parameter midway through the list, you need to pass in undefined as a placeholder. For example, if you had the function
>
> ```
> someFunction(name: string, prefix?: string, suffix?: string)
> ```
>
> and you wanted to provide suffix but not prefix, you'd have to call it as
>
> ```
> someFunction("John Doe", undefined, "Jr.");
> ```
>
> If you left off both prefix and suffix, then you wouldn't need to bother. The idea is, if a parameter is missing, tsc needs to always be able to determine *which* one is missing.

Here's the contents of `getList()`. Do not be alarmed.

```
getList(restaurant: number, mealtype: string,
        date1: string, date2?: string): Meal[] {
  let meals: Array<Meal> = [];
```

```
    for (var x = 0; x < localStorage.length; x++) {
      let key = localStorage.key(x);
      let re = /^TTM_/;

      let match_id = false;
      let match_type = false;
      let match_date = false;

      // What we're doing here is: if a parameter wasn't passed in,
      // set its match to true so that parameter is an automatic pass.
      // In other words, if ID is zero, then ANY ID is okay.
      if (restaurant === 0) {
        match_id = true;
      }
      if (mealtype === '') {
        match_type = true;
      }
      if (date1 === '') {
        match_date = true;
      }

// Local storage keys for meals are named in the format
// TTM_YYYYMMDD_C_NN
// where C is the meal code (BLDS) and NN is the restaurant ID.
// For this we're going to use both a re.exec (to get keys which start TTM_)
// AND a split on underscores.

      if (re.exec(key) !== null) {
        let parts = key.split('_');
        // parts[0] contains 'TTM', ignore it

        if (!match_id && (parseInt(parts[3]) === restaurant)) {
          match_id = true;
        }
        if (!match_type && (parts[2] === mealtype)) {
          match_type = true;
        }

        if (date2) { // we have a date range
          // This logic only works if all three dates are YYYYMMDD
          // and correctly zero-padded.
          if (!match_date && parts[1] >= date1 && parts[1] <= date2) {
            match_date = true;
          }
        }
      }
```

```
      else {
        if (!match_date && (parts[1] === date1)) {
          match_date = true;
        }
      }

      // If we passed all filters in play, push to array.
      if (match_id && match_type && match_date) {
        let meal = new Meal;

        meal.date = parts[1];
        meal.name = parts[2];
        meal.location = parseInt(parts[3]);
        meal.amount = localStorage.getItem(key);
        meals.push(meal);
      }
    } // if a TTM_ key
  } // for each key

  return meals;
}
```

Almost all of this function, except for declaring `meals` and returning it at the end, takes place inside a big "search through all keys in local storage" loop, whose mechanism you already know. Here our regular expression is set to just look for TTM_; we're going to fetch all the TTM_ keys and take them apart in a separate step. Since we only care about whether it matches, we're not going to bother retaining the results of the `re.exec()`.

All the complexity here is because we could be searching for several different things. We could be trying to find all meals that have a particular date; all meals of a particular meal type; all meals with a particular restaurant ID; or any combination of the three.

The three variables `match_id`, `match_type`, and `match_date` not only tell us what we're looking for, they tell us whether we found it. We start in each loop iteration by setting them to false, meaning "we haven't found a matching (ID, name, date) yet." But we may not be looking for all three of those things. If there's no restaurant ID passed to the function, we set `match_id` to true. Think of this as saying "*any* restaurant ID is an acceptable match"—in other words, saying that we're not searching for restaurant ID at all. Any we find will do. Same with the other two. If we didn't get a `date1` parameter, we set `match_date` to true so we bypass the date-matching search; if we didn't get a `mealtype`, we bypass the meal type search.

We then run our regular expression—you already know how that works. Assuming we have a TTM key, the next thing we do is split the key. The `split()` method, provided in any variable of string type, breaks it into pieces everywhere it finds the delimiter given and puts the pieces in the specified array. The delimiter itself is discarded. Here the delimiter is an underscore, so our key gets broken into four parts. With the example key we used earlier, `split()` would fill the `parts` array like this:

```
parts[0] = 'TTM'
parts[1] = '20171007'
parts[2] = 'L'
parts[3] = '25'
```

Now on to the tests.

```
if (!match_id && (parseInt(parts[3]) === restaurant))
```

If `match_id` is false—which means we're still looking for an ID match—and the integer version of `parts[3]` is the same as the restaurant ID passed into the function, then we have an ID match, and we set `match_id` to true.

```
if (!match_type && (parts[2] === mealtype))
```

If `match_type` is false (so we're searching for a meal type), and `parts[2]` is the same as the meal type passed in, we have a match, so set `match_type` to true.

Before we move on, let's consider some niceties. The `&&` operator is the counterpart to the `||` we've already encountered. `||` is "or," as in "this needs to be true or that needs to be true." `&&` is "and," as in "this needs to be true *and* that needs to be true." When conditions are separated by `||`, the overall statement evaluates as true if *any* of the conditions are true; when they are separated by `&&`, the overall statement evaluates as true only if *all* of the conditions are true. You can combine ands and ors in a single statement, but you'll need to use inner parentheses to force the order of operations into what you want.

The three-equals form of an equivalence test is more stringent than the two-equals form we've already seen. `==` will do some implicit type forcing. If you said `if (x == 0)` and `x` contained the string '0,' it would work; there would in effect be an invisible `parseInt()`. But `===` won't do that. For `===` to evaluate true, the items being compared must have the same value *and* be of the same type. We use it more often than `==` for clarity reasons, although it does mean we have to `parseInt()` our restaurant ID before we can test it for a match.

The date-matching portion is in two parts because we could be looking for either a single date or a range of dates. Date-range matching can be incredibly annoying; you know instinctively what "earlier than" and "later than" mean, but computers do not. We avoided the pain by storing our dates in YYYYMMDD format, which means that string comparison operators will work properly on them (and so would numeric operators, if we used `parseInt()` to treat them as numbers). This only works if the dates are always the same number of digits (eight), so you have to make sure that zeros are present for "padding" where appropriate—that is, October 7, 2017, is 20171007, not 2017107.

So if we have a date range, we have three dates: the start date of the range, the date we're checking from the key, and the end date of the range.

```
if (!match_date && parts[1] >= date1 && parts[1] <= date2)
```

means: if we're looking for a date match *and* our date from the key is greater than or equal to the start date of the range *and* the date from the key is less than or equal to the end date of the range. Or, in English, if the date we're checking is between the start and end dates, inclusive, then it's one we want.

If we didn't get a date2 parameter, then we're doing an exact date match, and that's just a test for equivalence:

```
if (!match_date && (parts[1] === date1))
```

Notice that test is inside the else portion of the if (date2) check.

Once we're done with all the individual matching tests, we check to see if all three of our match variables are true. (Remember, they'd also be set as true if we bypassed that particular kind of match.)

```
if (match_id && match_type && match_date)
```

We only store this particular key and its value if all three of them are true. If so, we fill in the four fields of our local meal variable (we use localStorage.getItem() to get the meal amount) and push it onto the meals array.

With many blocks and conditionals like this function, it's easy to forget to close blocks properly. The comments accompanying the closing braces on the two lines before return meals are there as a reminder to show you what they're closing, since the block is big enough for it to not be visually obvious. (And don't forget the closing brace for the function itself!)

You'll be relieved to know that the other two functions in this component are much simpler. (deleteByRestaurant(), which comes later, isn't very complex, either.)

```
create(date: string, name: string,
        location: number, amount: string): Meal {
  let meal = new Meal;
  let key = 'TTM';

  key = key + '_' + date + '_' + name + '_' + location.toString();
  localStorage.setItem(key, amount);
```

```
    meal.date = date;
    meal.name = name;
    meal.location = location;
    meal.amount = amount;

    return meal;
  }

  delete(date: string, name: string, location: number): void {
    let key = 'TTM';

    key = key + '_' + date + '_' + name + '_' + location.toString();
    localStorage.removeItem(key);

    return null;
  }
```

In both cases, we make a key by joining together our parameters with underscores between them (not neglecting to translate the numeric restaurant ID to a string), and use that key to do the appropriate thing in local storage. By this point, this logic should look familiar to you, since we've used it in the restaurant data service as well.

Why isn't there an update() function? Well, what would it look like? It would need a date, a meal type, and a restaurant ID so it could join them together to get the key of the item to update; and of course it would need an amount, because that's the actual data being updated. It would assemble the key, then it would call localStorage.setItem() to set the value of that key to the new amount. Then, to be polite to the caller, it would probably return a new Meal item containing the work it just did.

In other words, it would be *exactly the same* as the create() function! This is because local storage doesn't distinguish between an *insert* (new record) and an *update* the way databases do; it just stores whatever value you tell it in whatever key you tell it to use, and doesn't care (or need to care) if that key/value already existed.

The only reason the restaurant data service needed separate create() and update() functions is that create() had to go through the business of finding the next unused ID. Otherwise we'd have had only one function for both purposes there, too, and we could have easily written them both as a single function with a parameter check—"if an ID was passed in, it's an update; if not, it's a create."

Recall earlier when we said the keys we generate for meal data are "unique enough." It's not a fatal flaw in this app that, in the unlikely event that someone enters a second meal for the same meal type, date, and restaurant, it will overwrite the previous one. If we *did* consider that a fatal flaw, we could either try to generate a key with true uniqueness (we'd probably have to add some other identifier to it and make it even longer), or we could take the approach of having `create()` refuse to create a key that already existed. This would mean `create()` would have to iterate through all keys looking for a match to its parameters and give back an error if it found one. If we did that, then we *would* need separate `create()` and `update()` functions. But it would probably be overkill for our little app.

Once you've written these functions, save your work. We won't be back to `meal.service.ts` for a while. Now that we have our meal and restaurant services, we go back and teach `MealEntryComponent` how to use them.

Speaking to the services

The first job, once you have `meal-entry.component.ts` open and ready for work, is to import the two services we just created. Insert them just after the `Meal` and `Restaurant` imports:

```
import { MealService } from './meal.service';
import { RestaurantService } from './restaurant.service';
```

While you're up there, add one more import:

```
import * as moment from 'moment';
```

This is the `moment` date-handling library, which we're going to use in . . . a moment.

Remember that the two data services are injectables, so we declare a dependency on a private copy of them in the constructor, much as we did with the router way back at the beginning of this chapter. Change the constructor so it looks like this:

```
constructor(private router: Router,
            private restaurantService: RestaurantService,
            private mealService: MealService) {}
```

The lines in `ngOnInit()` where we set `this.restaurants` to our fake array of restaurants need to be removed and replaced by this line:

```
this.restaurants = this.restaurantService.getList();
```

From now on, we'll initialize that array of restaurants by reading them from the live data. Of course, for our first tests, there won't *be* any live data; we'll have to make some.

Now we'll change all the restaurant-handling functions to actually alter the restaurant data.

```
update(id: string, name: string): void {
  let numID = parseInt(id);
  let newrest = new Restaurant;

  console.log('update', numID, name);
  newrest = this.restaurantService.update(numID, name);
  this.restaurants = this.restaurantService.getList();
  this.meal.location = newrest.id;
  this.selectedRestaurant = name;
  this.showRestDiv = false;
}
```

We've added a variable that will hold the results returned from the restaurant service's update() function, and we set our component's meal.location to the ID we got back. This isn't strictly necessary—it should already be set to that ID anyway—but the line we've added that reloads the array of restaurants *is*. Otherwise, after the update, the list in the <select> element would still have the old name of whatever restaurant we edited.

```
add(name: string): void {
  let newrest = new Restaurant;

  console.log('add', name);
  newrest = this.restaurantService.create(name);
  this.restaurants.push(newrest);
  this.meal.location = newrest.id;
  this.selectedRestaurant = name;
  this.showRestDiv = false;
}
```

Here, setting meal.location to the new restaurant's ID *is* important. We want that restaurant selected after the user adds it; this matches the way they're likely to use the app. (If they're adding a restaurant, chances are it's because they want to enter a meal.) In order to do that properly, we must push the new restaurant onto the end of the array of restaurants so it's available to select. If we were doing something special to that array, like retrieving the restaurants in alphabetical order, we might have to completely reload the restaurant array after each alteration, like we did for update(), but this will do for now.

```
delete(id: string): void {
  let numID = parseInt(id);

  console.log('delete', numID);
  this.restaurantService.delete(numID);
```

```
    // Also need to delete all meals for this restaurant, a meal service call.
    this.restaurants = this.restaurantService.getList();
    this.meal.location = 0;
    this.selectedRestaurant = '';
    this.showRestDiv = false;
}
```

Here, too, we reload the entire restaurant array after the deletion, because a restaurant has been removed and we want to reflect that. (We deal with the matter mentioned in the comment later.)

That's it for our restaurant service needs. Now we need to modify the save() function to use the meal service. This function is a bit long to show you the whole thing again here, so just find the line that reads:

```
// Need actual data save here
```

and replace it with this:

```
this.mealService.create(this.meal.date, this.meal.name,
                        this.meal.location, this.meal.amount);
```

> If you omitted the comment we suggested, it goes after all the validity tests are done but before the line which resets this.meal.amount to an empty string.

That's the only change we need to make to save()—at least until we add better error reporting. Although . . .

We're not too happy about the date handling. No one but programmers ever enters a date as YYYYMMDD. If we prefill the date in a somewhat more normal format, then we provide a cue to the user to stick with that format. We can change it back to the YYYYMMDD format the data requires internally at save time. Let's go for the US standard of MM/DD/YYYY.

Inside ngOnInit(), replace the line

```
this.meal.date = '20171007';
```

with these two lines

```
let curdate = moment().format('MM/DD/YYYY');
this.meal.date = curdate; // Storing in WRONG FORMAT for display reasons
```

The moment library contains a lot of date manipulation functions. moment's internal data type is a date, but it's not stored in a format easily usable by our code (or anything else); you manipulate it and output it using methods like format(). What moment().format() says is "make a new (temporary) moment object, then use its format() method to provide a copy of its internal date in the specified format." curdate doesn't contain one of moment's internal date objects; it just contains a string *representation* of a date, in the format MM/DD/YYYY. What date? We didn't give moment() any parameters, so it defaults to today's date, "today" meaning whenever this component is loaded.

Notice the comment about "wrong format." We've initialized meal.date to today's date, and we've deliberately done it in the format we want to show the user, *not* the format we need for internal storage. We have to convert back before we save.

At the top of the save() function, either just before or just after the let amtAsNum ... line, add these two declarations:

```
let mydate = moment(this.meal.date, 'MM/DD/YYYY');
let newdate = '';
```

mydate is a moment object. Instead of setting it to today's date, we initialize it to the date the user provided in the form field. The MM/DD/YYYY specifier is to tell moment the format of the date string we're providing to it, so it knows how to read it.

Just after the // If here, then do actual stuff line, add:

```
newdate = mydate.format('YYYYMMDD');
```

We put a string copy of the date mydate is set to, in the format YYYYMMDD, into newdate. Now newdate has that date in the format we need.

There's no good reason to put it back in meal.date (which still has the date in the wrong format). That one's for display on the page, and we might as well just leave it that way. So change the line which calls the meal service:

```
this.mealService.create(newdate, this.meal.name,
                        this.meal.location, this.meal.amount);
```

There. One little problem solved.

Validating whether the user has entered a proper date is quite difficult, mostly because it's a pain to detect whether they entered the date month-first or day-first, especially for dates which could go either way such as 12/04/2017 (December 4 or April 12?). Adding a date-picker control later will help reduce the chance of this. But assuming the user behaves and sticks with the

MM/DD/YYYY format, we *can* ask moment to check for a valid date, e.g., make sure the user didn't put in 13 as the month or 32 as the day.

Change the validity test for the date field to this:

```
if (!this.meal.date || !mydate.isValid()) {
  console.log('invalid date');
  return null;
}
```

Since by then we've already tried to initialize mydate to the date from the form field, all we have to do is ask it whether it thinks it contains a valid date or not. The conditional now says "if there's no date or if that date isn't valid," then log the error and fall out.

It's time to do another test. But once again, there is a small task we need to do first. Can you guess what it is?

Open up app.module.ts. After the routing import, but before any of the component imports, add these:

```
import { MealService } from './meal.service';
import { RestaurantService } from './restaurant.service';
```

We have to import and declare these here because they're service providers. We must also add a new part to the @NgModule() parameters, between the declarations and bootstrap parameters:

```
providers:    [ MealService, RestaurantService ],
```

Save that and any other work you haven't saved, and run the application.

The restaurant list won't have any restaurants in it, so your first testing task is to add a few fake restaurants for testing. You should also make sure you can change their names after the fact and delete them. Make sure that after you add or edit a restaurant, the restaurant selection is automatically changed to the added or altered restaurant name; and if you delete a restaurant, the selection should be returned to zero ("select a restaurant").

If your browser has an area in which you can monitor what's in local storage (in Firefox it's called the Storage Inspector, and you'll see it in the same list of tools as the Web Console), it will be extremely helpful here. Note that local storage is handled as specific to a particular web domain, so you have to be at an localhost:3000/ page in order to see any items our app has put into local storage. Your browser may even offer you a way to remove those local storage items, which is handy for cleaning up mistakes. (In Firefox, right-click a listed stored item and you will be offered a deletion option.)

Once you're satisfied that you can create, alter, and delete restaurants properly, try saving some test meal entries. We don't yet have a way of displaying them in the app, so if you can't inspect local storage, you won't have any feedback that it's working properly . . . except `console.log()` messages, and you can add those in pretty much any place you like if you'd like to inspect what's going on.

Incidentally, we've left in all our `console.log()` messages we've used so far, but you can remove them at any time once you've decided there's no need for them anymore.

THE MEAL LIST

It's time to make the other page of the application. We've covered most of the concepts you'll need already, so we're going to concentrate on the two or three new things.

The template

We start with the template file, then alter the component to match. This file is different enough from the tiny placeholder version we had before that we'll just show you the whole thing. Edit `meal-list.component.html` and make it look like this:

```
<h2>Edit Meals</h2>
<div><button (click)="gotoMain()">Back</button></div>
<div>
  <select id="restaurantID" #restaurantID
    [ngModel]="selectedRestaurant"
    (change)="onSelect($event.target.value)">
  <option value="0">-- select a restaurant --</option>
  <option *ngFor="let r of restaurants" value="{{r.id}}">{{r.name}}</option>
  </select>

  <div *ngFor="let m of meals">
    $<input id="listMealValue" #listMealValue
       value="{{m.amount | number:'.2'}}" />
    <select id="listMealName" #listMealName >
      <option value="B" [attr.selected]="m.name==='B' ? true : null">
        Breakfast</option>
      <option value="L" [attr.selected]="m.name==='L' ? true : null">
        Lunch</option>
      <option value="D" [attr.selected]="m.name==='D' ? true : null">
        Dinner</option>
      <option value="S" [attr.selected]="m.name==='S' ? true : null">
```

```
        Snack</option>
    </select>
    <input id="listMealDate" #listMealDate
      value="{{m.date | dateDisplay}}" />
    <button (click)="save(listMealValue.value, listMealName.value,
      listMealDate.value)">Save</button>
    <button (click)="delete(m.name, m.date)">Delete</button>
  </div>
</div>
```

The first thing you should conclude is that we'll need some new functions: this component's versions of onSelect(), save(), and delete(). You may also notice some shenanigans in a couple of the interpolated variables, which will be explained in a moment. Less obvious, perhaps, is that the [(ngModel)] two-way binding doesn't appear anywhere here.

In MealEntryComponent, we chose to use the two-way binding so that when we changed anything in the form fields, the Meal data structure in the component was automatically updated. So when saving, all we had do to was save that component data, and save() needed no parameters. Here we take a different approach; we use one-way bindings to populate the listing, and if we want to save changes, we pass back all the altered data as parameters to the save() function. Similarly, with delete(), we pass back the data we need to determine which meal we're deleting.

This approach is the more sensible one to take on this page, where we're not dealing with changes to a single meal, but could potentially have a change to any item on a (possibly very long) list of meals.

If you're observant, you'll notice that each of those two functions seems to be missing a parameter. You need four pieces of data to save a meal: the restaurant, the meal type, the date, and the amount. We only pass three of those to save(). Similarly, you need three pieces of data to uniquely identify a meal so you can delete it—the restaurant, the meal type, and the date—and we only provide delete() with two. The answer in both cases is that these meals are listed *by restaurant*, so we already know what restaurant ID to use. It'll be the one that was selected at the top of the page. Only meals with that restaurant ID would have been listed and editable in the first place.

Notice also that for delete() we use the values we *populated* the meal entry with. That is, we use the original m.name and m.date that we had when we iterated through items with *ngFor. For save(), we use the form values—the ones the user might have altered. The effect of this is that delete() ignores any edits the user might have made to the same data. If we want to delete the Lunch meal for today for restaurant 10, we'll ignore the fact that the user was tinkering around and just changed it to Breakfast. Or, put another way, it's pointless to save/respect a user's changes to a particular meal if you're just going to delete it now anyway. .

The `<select>` options use a technique we haven't seen yet. In our other `<select>` lists so far, we haven't needed to initialize the selection to anything other than the default (first) choice when the page is first loaded. Here we must; each meal in the list should, obviously, have its own copy of this list set to the correct meal type.

Each `<option>` has a `selected` attribute, and a maximum of one option in the set should have that attribute set to `true`, to show which item is currently selected. We can alter that attribute by referring to `[attr.selected]`. The syntax with a `?` and a `:` is just a way of compressing "If condition is true, do the first response (the part following the `?`); if condition is false, do the second response instead (the part following the `:`)." So these say "If `m.name` is the same as the value of this option, set this option's `selected` attribute to `true`; otherwise, don't set it to anything."

The peculiar structure in two of the variable interpolations, which uses a | vertical bar, is a *pipe*. A pipe is something that alters data while it's in the process of being transmitted. Here "transmitted" isn't strictly correct, but the idea is the same: "Before we display this data, run it through this translator/modifier thingamajig to alter either its contents or its formatting." In Angular, there are several built-in pipes; you can also make your own. Here we have one of each.

```
{{m.amount | number:'.2'}}
```

means that before we display `m.amount` to the user, we run it through a "number pipe" that formats it to a certain number of digits to either side of the decimal point. In this case, the '.2' specifier means that we always want exactly two digits on the right of the decimal. This is so if the user enters a meal amount as just 20, we'll display it as 20.00. It doesn't change the actual data, just reformats it for display. (There is also a "currency pipe," but we didn't use that because we wanted more control over how and where we displayed the dollar sign, which is a literal in front of the `<input>` tag.)

```
{{m.date | dateDisplay}}
```

means to run the date through a pipe called `dateDisplay`, which doesn't exist yet because we have to write it! We do that shortly, after making changes to the component code, but you can probably guess what it will do—it will take our internal YYYYMMDD date data and display it as MM/DD/YYYY. We could preformat the data in the component code, of course, by iterating through every meal we fetched and using the `moment` functions to transform the date into MM/DD/YYYY. But we don't really need to do that; we don't have a reason to change the actual data, we just want it "pretty" for display. So a pipe is the right answer here. (Yes, we could have taken this approach in the meal-entry component as well. We didn't because we know the date-picker control we're going to add to it in Chapter 8 will complicate that.)

The component

Let's make the changes we need to `meal-list.component.ts`.

We need these five imports after the two that are already there:

```
import * as moment from 'moment';

import { Meal } from './meal';
import { Restaurant } from './restaurant';
import { MealService } from './meal.service';
import { RestaurantService } from './restaurant.service';
```

At the beginning of the component (just after the `export class` line), add the following variable declarations:

```
meals: Meal[];
selectedMeal: Meal;
restaurants: Restaurant[];
selectedRestaurant = 0;
```

Change the constructor to use the services as well as the router:

```
constructor(private router: Router,
            private mealService: MealService,
            private restaurantService: RestaurantService) {}
```

Change `ngOnInit()` to actually do something:

```
ngOnInit(): void {
  this.restaurants = this.restaurantService.getList();
}
```

Now let's add some new functions between `ngOnInit()` and `gotoMain()`. The first of these wasn't mentioned in the template.

```
getMeals(id: number): void {
  if (!id) {
    return null;
  }
  this.meals = this.mealService.getList(id, '', '');
}
```

If the provided restaurant ID is invalid or is zero, do nothing; otherwise, call the meal service's getList() function. Because the first three parameters to getList() are required but we only want to search for a particular restaurant ID, we are obliged to pass in empty strings for the other two parameters.

We separate out the getMeals() function because it will be used by both onSelect() and delete() and there's no point in having duplicate code in both of those functions.

Here's onSelect(), which is called when the user changes restaurant:

```
onSelect(value: string): void {
  let numValue = parseInt(value);

  if (numValue) {
    this.selectedRestaurant = numValue;
    this.getMeals(numValue);
  }
  else
  {
    this.selectedRestaurant = 0;
  }
}
```

Notice that we must parseInt() the value because, as we discussed back in MealEntryComponent, it comes to us as a string, even though we want and need it to be a number.

Assuming we got a valid, non-zero value, we set selectedRestaurant to that selection, retrieve the list of meals for that restaurant; if it's not a valid value, we set selectedRestaurant to zero just to be safe.

We keep selectedRestaurant updated with the current selection so the component always knows the current restaurant ID—as you'll see, we're about to need that for the save() and delete() functions.

```
save(amount: string, mealtype: string, mealdate: string) {
  let mydate = moment(mealdate, 'MM/DD/YYYY');
  let newdate = mydate.format('YYYYMMDD');
```

```
    console.log('save', amount, newdate, mealtype, this.selectedRestaurant);
    this.mealService.create(newdate, mealtype,
                            this.selectedRestaurant, amount);
  }

  delete(mealtype: string, mealdate: string) {
    console.log('delete', mealdate, mealtype, this.selectedRestaurant);
    this.mealService.delete(mealdate, mealtype, this.selectedRestaurant);
    this.getMeals(this.selectedRestaurant); // refresh list
  }
```

Why are we fooling around with the date format in the save() function? Because of the pipe in the template. We used the pipe to display the date nicely for the user, but that affected the value shown in the form, which is what we're using here. It arrives in MM/DD/YYYY format, so we have to change it back to YYYYMMDD before saving. In the delete() function, on the other hand, we use the original date data we populated the list with. It's still as YYYYMMDD because we never altered it, and so we can use it as is.

After deleting the meal, the delete() function calls getMeals(), which will reload "all meals for that restaurant" and thus refresh the list so the deleted meal is no longer displayed.

That's it for this component! But before we can test the list page, we have to create that date pipe, and we have to make the app module aware of it.

The date pipe

Create the new file date-display.pipe.ts as shown:

```
import { Pipe, PipeTransform } from '@angular/core';

@Pipe({ name: 'dateDisplay' })
export class DateDisplayPipe implements PipeTransform {
  transform(value: string): string {
    let re = /(\d\d\d\d)(\d\d)(\d\d)/;
    let results = re.exec(value);
    // If we wanted to, we could add a format specifier to this function
    // to return dates in various ways. But we're just going to stick with
    // US MM/DD/YYYY for now.
    return results[2] + '/' + results[3] + '/' + results[1];
  }
}
```

Pipes work a special way. They're an exported class, like pretty much everything else we've been working on, and they have the @Pipe() decorator in front to indicate that they're a pipe. But they *must* have a function called transform(), which is the entry point—that is, when you use this pipe, what you're really using is the pipe's transform() function. (There could be other functions in the class if the transform() function were complex enough to need them, but transform() is always where the work begins and ends.)

This particular transform() function accepts a string and returns a string. The actual work is just to run a regular expression match on the string. It uses parentheses to hold the various parts of a YYYYMMDD date, so results[1] holds the year, results[2] holds the month, and results[3] holds the day. It glues those parts back together with slashes between parts and returns that. Nothing to it.

Notice that although the class is called DateDisplayPipe, in the template we referred to it as dateDisplay. The template uses whatever's in the name parameter in the @Pipe() decorator. This parameter is required. Notice also the implements PipeTransform, which is also required, or your pipe wouldn't pipe.

Pipes are one of the things the app module needs to be made aware of, so go open app. module.ts. Add this line as the last of your imports, after the component imports:

```
import { DateDisplayPipe } from './date-display.pipe';
```

And change the declarations section of the @NgModule() parameters to read

```
declarations: [ AppComponent,
                MealEntryComponent,
                MealListComponent,
                TotalsComponent,
                TrendsComponent,
                DateDisplayPipe ],
```

A little problem

Save your work and run the app!

You'll need to add some meals, obviously, so you'll have something to look at on the meal list page. You'll probably want to create at least a couple of meals for each restaurant. Once you do, confirm on the meal list page that:

- When you change restaurants, the listing of meals changes accordingly.
- You can alter any of the three editable fields for a meal, press its **Save** button, and the changes will be saved. Note that save() does *not* reload the list; it doesn't need to, so if you want to

be sure changes were really saved, change to another restaurant and back to this one; that will reload and you can then check to see that the changes you made were kept.

▪ You can delete a meal by pressing its Delete button. The list of meals should refresh automatically.

One of the things listed above is not working the way it's supposed to. It may take you a couple of tests to find it.

If you change the amount of a meal and save that change, it works fine. But if you change either the meal type or the meal date and save, it makes a new meal entry. It doesn't replace the old one, and you end up with both the old and the new one. (You won't see it until you force the list to reload, as explained above.)

Remember that to the meal service there's absolutely no difference between inserting a new record and updating an existing one. It calls localStorage.setItem() with the data we provide, either way. If we change a meal's type or date, we're creating a new data key, and setItem() goes ahead and stores an amount in that new key . . . leaving the old one unaffected.

How do we solve this?

In this system, we can update the *value* of a key—the meal amount—without needing to change the key, but an "update" to the key itself is only accomplished by scrapping that key and making a new one. Suppose we want to change a meal from lunch to dinner. This changes the key—say, TTM_20171015_L_4 to TTM_20171015_D_4—and what we're really saying is "get rid of that old key, and save a new key with this value instead."

So let's do exactly that. Whenever we save changes here, we delete the old key and make a new one. If the only thing we're changing is the meal amount, that's not necessary, but the additional overhead is small enough that we won't make a special case just for that. We always delete the old key first; then maybe we'll be remaking the same key with a new amount, or a different key with the existing amount, or a different key with a different amount—but we won't need to care which.

However, this means we need to add more parameters to the save() function. Because not only do we need the new values, we also need some of the old ones . . . so we can find the original key to remove it.

Change the save() function in meal-list.component.ts to look like this:

```
save(amount: string, newtype: string, newdate: string,
    oldtype: string, olddate: string) {
  let mydate = moment(newdate, 'MM/DD/YYYY');

  newdate = mydate.format('YYYYMMDD');
  console.log('delete before save:', olddate, oldtype,
          this.selectedRestaurant);
  this.mealService.delete(olddate, oldtype, this.selectedRestaurant);
```

```
    console.log('save', amount, newdate, newtype,
              this.selectedRestaurant);
    this.mealService.create(newdate, newtype,
                         this.selectedRestaurant, amount);
}
```

Notice that we've removed a `let`. `newdate` now arrives as one of the function's parameters; when we do the date-format shuffle, we use `mydate` for the moment object, initialized based on `newdate`, and then we put the reformatted date string *back* into `newdate`.

We also need to change the function call in the template, to add the new parameters. Replace the part of `meal-list.component.html` that reads

```
save(listMealValue.value, listMealName.value, listMealDate.value)
```

with

```
save(listMealValue.value, listMealName.value, listMealDate.value,
    m.name, m.date)
```

Save these changes and test the app again. All should be well.

TOTALS AND TRENDS

These two components do a lot of behind-the-scenes work to get the statistics they need. The totals component is by far the less elaborate of the two, so let's start there.

The totals component

Open `totals.component.ts` and alter it by adding the following three import lines after the existing one:

```
import * as moment from 'moment';

import { Meal } from './meal';
import { MealService } from './meal.service';
```

Add the following variables to the component (after the `export class` line):

```
@Input() thumper: number;
totalToday: number = 0;
totalThisWeek: number = 0;
```

Yes, that format is something you haven't seen before; we explain the @Input() decorator in a moment.

Add a constructor after those, for our meal service:

```
constructor(private mealService: MealService) {}
```

Make ngOnChanges() actually do something:

```
ngOnChanges(): void {
    this.getTotals();
}
```

Although we haven't yet written the getTotals() function, which will actually generate new totals, in terms of operational flow, this is it for the component! Every time the component's data or other status changes, ngOnChanges() gets called and it updates running totals. Those get put into totalToday and totalThisWeek, which we'll make our totals template display. That's all we need.

ngOnChanges() also gets called as part of the component's initialization. It gets called after the class constructor but before ngOnInit(). So we don't actually *need* an ngOnInit() here. ngOnChanges() will happen not only on any change but also on first load, and that's as we like it.

The problem is, we also need to force this component to update itself when a meal is saved in the meal entry component. If the user enters a new meal, that affects our running totals; as soon as they save that new meal, we need to recalculate. How do we cue that?

The @Input() decorator says that this variable will be passed in as a property of the component. This will be clearer when we make some template alterations later, but think of it this way: it's saying, "yes, this is one of our component variables, we own it, but it gets set by whatever is loading this component." Its value is an input from outside the component.

We're going to use this variable (thumper) the following way: a different copy of thumper will be declared in MealEntryComponent. Whenever a meal is saved, we'll increment thumper. We don't care about the actual value of thumper; we just need something that we can "thump" every time we save a new meal. We pass that thumper into this component, where it changes our copy. (We'll also pass it into the trends component.) When it changes, it counts as a data change to this component, too, and triggers ngOnChanges().

Next we write the getTotals() function and its helper function, sumMeals(). Put them after ngOnChanges(), but make sure you keep them inside the closing brace of the component itself.

```
getTotals(): void {
  let workdate = moment();
  let curdate = workdate.format('YYYYMMDD');

  this.totalToday = this.sumMeals(curdate);

  this.totalThisWeek = this.totalToday;
  for (let i = 1; i < 7; i++) {
    let curDailySum: number = 0;
    workdate.subtract(1, 'days');
    curdate = workdate.format('YYYYMMDD');
    curDailySum = this.sumMeals(curdate);
    this.totalThisWeek = this.totalThisWeek + curDailySum;
  }
}

sumMeals(curdate: string): number {
  let meals: Array<Meal> = [];
  let curSum: number = 0;
  meals = this.mealService.getList(0, '', curdate);
  for (let m in meals) {
    curSum = curSum + parseFloat(meals[m].amount);
  }
  return curSum;
}
```

Starting at the top: We set workdate to today's date by default; curdate is a string copy of that date in YYYYMMDD format. We then get a sum of the costs of all meals for that date using sumMeals(). That's "today's total." We store that.

We think of a week here not as Sunday-to-Saturday but "seven days back, starting today." We already got today's sum, and we copy that into totalThisWeek. Now we must also get a sum for each of the preceding six days and add them all into totalThisWeek as well. We'll loop backward six times, temporarily put each day's sum in curDailySum and then add that into totalThisWeek at the end of each loop. We initialize curDailySum to zero each time the loop starts.

Among programming's many delights is realizing that what most people think of as "a week" or "a year" needs precise definition for a computer. Do you mean the last seven days, or a calendar week? Is a calendar week defined Sunday–Saturday, or Monday–Sunday? Is a year 365 days plus an occasional extra day, or January 1–December 31? The right answer varies and depends partially on how users expect time periods to work. For TastyTracker's calculations, we felt numeric tracking would provide more accurate, up-to-the-minute data than tying dates to the calendar, making it more valuable to Donna . . . but there's an exception to this rule that we get into later in the chapter.

Notice that we don't actually use the value of i; it's just a counter to loop six times, so it doesn't matter that i is counting *up* while we're moving backward through dates. To actually get each date we need, we use one of the moment methods to subtract a day from whatever date we had last. (We then need to get a YYYYMMDD copy of that new date, of course, for retrieval.)

sumMeals() accepts a YYYYMMDD date and uses the meal service to retrieve all meals for that date (notice we pass zero for restaurant ID and empty string for meal type). It then iterates through the array of meals found. No meals found on that date? No problem. It will iterate zero times, and curSum will stay at zero, where it was initialized. Inside the iteration, it takes the amount field of the meal data, uses parseFloat() (*not* parseInt()—this could have a decimal portion we don't want to lose), and adds that to curSum. It returns curSum to the caller when all's done.

Let's set up the template. Open totals.component.html and change it to the following:

```
<h2>TastyTotals</h2>
<div>
  <div><label>Today:</label> {{totalToday | currency:'USD':true:'.2'}}</div>
  <div><label>This week:</label>
      {{totalThisWeek | currency:'USD':true:'.2'}}</div>
</div>
```

Here we use that built-in currency pipe we mentioned earlier. The extra specifiers say that this is an amount in US dollars, that we want the appropriate currency indicator (i.e., the amounts will automatically get a $ in front), and that we demand two decimal places.

Before we can use this, we have to tinker with the meal entry component and its template to set up the thumper properly. But we do that after we handle the trends component. Save your work.

The trends component

This little component does a huge amount of retrieval and number-crunching. Do not be alarmed. We'll break it apart carefully.

First, the preliminaries, which will look familiar (but are not exactly the same, so be careful). Open trends.component.ts and make the following changes.

Add these three import lines after the existing one:

```
import * as moment from 'moment';

import { Meal } from './meal';
import { MealService } from './meal.service';
```

Add these variables to the component (after the export class line):

```
@Input() thumper: number;
totalThisWeek: number = 0;
totalLastWeek: number = 0;
averageInterval: string = 'D';
breakfastAverage: number = 0;
lunchAverage: number = 0;
dinnerAverage: number = 0;
snackAverage: number = 0;
```

Add a constructor so we can get at our meal service:

```
constructor(private mealService: MealService) {}
```

Make ngOnChanges() actually do something:

```
ngOnChanges(): void {
  this.getTotals();
  this.getAverages();
}
```

Follow ngOnChanges() with an onSelect() function, which will recalculate averages based on a user selection:

```
onSelect(interval: string): void {
  this.averageInterval = interval;
  this.getAverages();
}
```

The getTotals() function bears some similarities to the one in the totals component, but we use the date-range method here, because the version of sumMeals() in this component works on date ranges, for reasons that will become clear.

```
getTotals(): void {
    let workdate = moment();
    let date1: string;
    let date2: string;

    this.totalThisWeek = 0;
    this.totalLastWeek = 0;

    // Note that these are being assigned backward on purpose.
    // date1 is the EARLIER date of the two in the week range.
    date2 = workdate.format('YYYYMMDD');
    workdate.subtract(6, 'days');
    date1 = workdate.format('YYYYMMDD');
    this.totalThisWeek = this.sumMeals(date1, date2);

    workdate.subtract(1, 'days'); // so the ranges don't overlap

    date2 = workdate.format('YYYYMMDD');
    workdate.subtract(6, 'days');
    date1 = workdate.format('YYYYMMDD');
    this.totalLastWeek = this.sumMeals(date1, date2);
}
```

We use the workdate.subtract() method to obtain a range of dates. If today was 20171007, the first range would be obtained by subtracting six days, obtaining a range 20171001 to 20171007. We then subtract one more day, because we want the "week before that" range to end on 20170930; the ranges are inclusive and don't overlap. Then another six days back, so the previous-week range would be 20170924 to 20170930. You don't have to worry about "thirty days hath September" and such; moment knows all about that.

The rest is just calling sumMeals() and storing the sums it returns.

Now for the real work. getAverages() is long enough that we're going to give it to you in parts. Start with the local variables we need and initialization of component variables:

```
getAverages(): void {
    let bSums: Array<number> = [];
    let lSums: Array<number> = [];
    let dSums: Array<number> = [];
    let sSums: Array<number> = [];
```

```
let workdate = moment();
let date1: string;
let date2: string;
let curSum = 0;

this.breakfastAverage = 0;
this.lunchAverage = 0;
this.dinnerAverage = 0;
this.snackAverage = 0;
```

This function does three different things depending on the period of time we're evaluating. But no matter which of those things it's doing, we hold an array of sums for each meal type: bSums is the sums of breakfasts over the time period, lSums is the sum of lunches, and so on. The function's ultimate goal is to arrive at an average for each meal over the time period.

We begin with three separate blocks based on the selected time period (averageInterval).

```
// DAILY averages
if (this.averageInterval === 'D') {
  for (let c = 0; c < 365; c++) {
    date1 = workdate.format('YYYYMMDD');
    curSum = this.sumMeals(date1, null, 'B');
    if (curSum > 0) {
      bSums.push(curSum);
    }
    curSum = this.sumMeals(date1, null, 'L');
    if (curSum > 0) {
      lSums.push(curSum);
    }
    curSum = this.sumMeals(date1, null, 'D');
    if (curSum > 0) {
      dSums.push(curSum);
    }
    curSum = this.sumMeals(date1, null, 'S');
    if (curSum > 0) {
      sSums.push(curSum);
    }
    workdate.subtract(1, 'days');
  }
}
```

If we're doing daily averages, we start with today, then subtract one from the day at the end of the loop. The next loop acts on the previous day, and so on backward. We loop 365 times—we get a year's worth of days, in other words. (For these statistics, we're going to ignore the extra day in leap years.)

The way we're calling sumMeals() in this block, it will sum all meals on that day *of that type*. So first sumMeals() will get all the breakfasts on that day, sum them up, and push that into bSums. The second sumMeals() will sum up all the lunches for that day and push that in to lSums, and so on.

(Yes, this is overkill for daily averages, because normally there will only be one lunch on a given date, one breakfast, etc. But you *could* do it; you could enter one lunch in one restaurant and another lunch in a different restaurant on the same date. Our method also handles that unlikely circumstance. Also, doing it this way keeps to a consistent method that works the same as the next two blocks.)

```
// WEEKLY averages
if (this.averageInterval === 'W') {
  for (let c = 0; c < 52; c++) {
    date2 = workdate.format('YYYYMMDD');
    workdate.subtract(6, 'days');
    date1 = workdate.format('YYYYMMDD');
    curSum = this.sumMeals(date1, date2, 'B');
    if (curSum > 0) {
      bSums.push(curSum);
    }
    curSum = this.sumMeals(date1, date2, 'L');
    if (curSum > 0) {
      lSums.push(curSum);
    }
    curSum = this.sumMeals(date1, date2, 'D');
    if (curSum > 0) {
      dSums.push(curSum);
    }
    curSum = this.sumMeals(date1, date2, 'S');
    if (curSum > 0) {
      sSums.push(curSum);
    }
    workdate.subtract(1, 'days');
  }
}
```

For weekly averages, we create a date range for "today and six days before that," obtain the meals found within that date range, and get sums for each type of meal. We then offset one day, as we did for the "previous week" total in `getTotals()`, and go through the loop again and grab another "that date and six days before that." The `workdate` keeps moving steadily backward as we loop. We do this for fifty-two weeks.

```javascript
// MONTHLY averages
if (this.averageInterval === 'M') {
  for (let c = 0; c < 12; c++) {
    workdate.startOf('month');
    date1 = workdate.format('YYYYMMDD');
    workdate.endOf('month');
    date2 = workdate.format('YYYYMMDD');
    curSum = this.sumMeals(date1, date2, 'B');
    if (curSum > 0) {
      bSums.push(curSum);
    }
    curSum = this.sumMeals(date1, date2, 'L');
    if (curSum > 0) {
      lSums.push(curSum);
    }
    curSum = this.sumMeals(date1, date2, 'D');
    if (curSum > 0) {
      dSums.push(curSum);
    }
    curSum = this.sumMeals(date1, date2, 'S');
    if (curSum > 0) {
      sSums.push(curSum);
    }
    workdate.subtract(1, 'months');
  }
}
```

We handle months differently from the other two. For days and weeks, it makes sense to do a moving interval; that is, to consider a year's worth of days as "today and 364 days before that," as opposed to "anything in the calendar year 2017." If we did the daily averages by calendar year, you'd start with a clean slate every January and for the first few months of the year you'd have averages that were deceptively low. Same for weeks. If we defined a week as starting on a particular day of the week, you'd get a weekly average that was distorted by which day of the week you happened to be running the app.

But for months, we assume that when the user asks "show me the average for this month," they really do mean the calendar month—all breakfasts in October, for example—and if October is only half over at that point, the user will understand why the average is low.

If you disagree with this assumption, you can always make this section of code count backward in thirty-day moving intervals instead. But we'll use calendar months. We begin with the current month. The `workdate.startOf('month')` method returns the first day of the month (we specify YYYYMMDD format), so if it's currently October 2017, `date1` will be 20171001. `workdate.endOf('month')` does what you might expect, and `date2` will be 20171031.

Once we've summed the meals in that range, we subtract one from the month, and do it again. We do this for twelve months.[27]

Notice that all three of these blocks keep using `curSum` over and over, storing a temporary sum in it and testing to see if it's greater than zero. This is because we have chosen not to put "empty" days in our averages. Putting zero sums into our arrays of sums changes the number of items in the array, and that's what we'll divide by when we take the average, so it would lower the result.

For example, imagine you were just averaging a week's worth of breakfasts. (We don't actually take an average over that short a range in the code, but the real ones are too long to use as examples.) You spend five dollars every weekday for breakfast. You don't buy breakfast on weekends.

Breakfast average for the week with zero-amount meals included:

$(5 + 5 + 5 + 5 + 5 + 0 + 0) / 7 = \$3.57$

Breakfast average for the week without zero-amount meals included:

$(5 + 5 + 5 + 5 + 5) / 5 = \$5.00$

Since this is a *restaurant* meal tracker, we feel it makes more sense to say "you spent an average of $5.00 for breakfast that week on meals you ate outside the house" than "you spent an average of $3.57 on breakfast that week, but that doesn't count the two days you ate breakfast at home." This supports Donna's reason for using TastyTracker in the first place: she wants to reduce her spending, so we don't want to give her an artificially low picture of her expenses. But if you prefer a different approach, you can remove the `curSum` greater-than-zero checks.

At this point, no matter which time interval we chose, we have four arrays where each item in the array is the sum of all meals of that type for a single interval (one day, one week, or one month). We now average each of these arrays—but *only* if they have at least one item. The array could be completely empty; we could have bought no breakfasts that entire year, for example!

```
if (bSums.length > 0) {
  curSum = 0;
  for (let b of bSums) {
    curSum = curSum + b;
  }
  this.breakfastAverage = curSum / bSums.length;
}
```

---

[27] This is the last thing we'll use the moment library for in this code, but it has many more useful tricks. The full documentation can be found at momentjs.com/.

```
    if (lSums.length > 0) {
      curSum = 0;
      for (let l of lSums) {
        curSum = curSum + l;
      }
      this.lunchAverage = curSum / lSums.length;
    }
    if (dSums.length > 0) {
      curSum = 0;
      for (let d of dSums) {
        curSum = curSum + d;
      }
      this.dinnerAverage = curSum / dSums.length;
    }
    if (sSums.length > 0) {
      curSum = 0;
      for (let s of sSums) {
        curSum = curSum + s;
      }
      this.snackAverage = curSum / sSums.length;
    }
  }
```

The final curly brace, which doesn't seem to have a match, is the closing brace of the getAverages() function as a whole. Don't forget it.

The / operator is how programmers write division. The reason we check for a non-zero number of elements in each array is because we're dividing by the number of elements, and division by zero is illegal and will make your code very unhappy. If we really did buy no breakfasts that year, then breakfastAverage will stay at zero, where we initialized it.

The last thing we need is the sumMeals() function (which is doing most of the actual work).

```
sumMeals(date1: string, date2?: string, mealtype?: string): number {
  let meals: Array<Meal> = [];
  let curSum = 0;
  let mt = '';

  if (mealtype) {
    mt = mealtype;
  }
  meals = this.mealService.getList(0, mt, date1, date2);
  for (let m in meals) {
    curSum = curSum + parseFloat(meals[m].amount);
  }
```

```
      return curSum;
   }
```

The function requires a date parameter, optionally accepts a second date to specify a date range, and optionally accepts a meal type.

Note that although `mealtype` is optional to this function, it isn't optional to `mealService`
`.getList()`. We can't pass it a meal type of `undefined` (which is what would happen if we didn't provide one to `sumMeals()` and passed the parameter straight through). So we pass local variable `mt` to `getList()` instead. It's initialized as an empty string, and if we didn't get a `mealtype`, it stays that way. Sending an empty string for that parameter to `getList()` is acceptable.

Other than that little quirk, there should be nothing new to you here.

That's it for the trends component. We will, of course, also need to edit its template. Open `trends.component.html` and change it to read as follows:

```html
<h2>TastyTrends</h2>
<div>
  This week compared to last week:
  <div><label>This week:</label>
    {{totalThisWeek | currency:'USD':true:'.2'}}</div>
  <div><label>Last week:</label>
    {{totalLastWeek | currency:'USD':true:'.2'}}</div>
</div>

<div>
  On average, I spend this amount
  <select id="interval" #interval
    [ngModel]="averageInterval"
    (change)="onSelect($event.target.value)">
    <option value="D">Daily</option>
    <option value="W">Weekly</option>
    <option value="M">Monthly</option>
  </select>:<br/>
  <label>Breakfast</label>
    {{breakfastAverage | currency:'USD':true:'.2'}}<br/>
  <label>Lunch</label> {{lunchAverage | currency:'USD':true:'.2'}}<br/>
  <label>Dinner</label> {{dinnerAverage | currency:'USD':true:'.2'}}<br/>
  <label>Snacks</label> {{snackAverage | currency:'USD':true:'.2'}}
</div>
```

Again, at this point, there's nothing in here you haven't seen already, so let's move on to the last thing we need to do. Save your work.

The thumper

Open `meal-entry.component.ts`. At the end of the declarations of component variables, after

```
restaurants: Restaurant[];
```

add the line

```
thumper: number = 0;
```

At the end of the `save()` function, just after the line

```
this.meal.amount = '';
```

add these lines

```
// Thump the thumper
this.thumper++;
```

Open `meal-entry.component.html`. Change the `<totals>` and `<trends>` tag pairs at the end to look like this:

```
<totals [thumper]="thumper"></totals>
```

```
<trends [thumper]="thumper"></trends>
```

The property in square brackets is the `thumper` defined as an `@Input()` in the trends and totals components. The part in quotes means set it to the value of `MealEntryComponent`'s thumper, which we just created.

Save any work you haven't already saved, and run the app!

You may need to enter quite a few meals in various combinations to check that all the math in the totals and trends section is coming out right. Make sure the totals and trends sections update whenever you enter a new meal; that is, be sure to check that the thumper is working.

Don't forget to change averaging periods in the trends component to test what difference that makes. Keeping a list of what you've entered (or inspecting local storage, if you can do that in your browser) will be helpful for checking the math.

You've now finished what's called a *smoke test* version of the application. It's not beautiful yet, but it does everything that we need it to do.

Well, almost everything. In addition to incorporating the UI design, fixing the restaurant editing controls so they do what they were supposed to have done in the first place, and the two special controls (one for graphing the trends data, and one for helping the user select dates), there are a couple of things that don't work right and one thing which is fine as is but really should work better.

YOUR ASSIGNMENT

Your homework, before you begin the next chapter, is to find those three issues in the application. But you're still pretty new at diagnosing code, so we offer you two hints.

1. The restaurant add(), update() and delete() functions in MealEntryComponent each have an issue. One of them was mentioned somewhere in this chapter.

2. The improvement we really should make affects both the meal entry and meal list pages and was also alluded to somewhere in this chapter.

Is there anything else we're missing? Make your worklist for Chapter 8 before you proceed.

The "Chapter 7 files" area of our repository shows all the files that should be in your app directory at this point in the condition they should be in at the end of this chapter (that is, what they'd look like if you were following along in this chapter and the preceding one). These files change more in Chapter 8, but we kept this version so you can check your work so far against our examples.

8

PUTTING IT ALL TOGETHER

In this chapter, we take the visual styles and page layout from Chapter 5 and apply them to the components we wrote in Chapter 7.

We also make some improvements and a few bug fixes along the way. Here are some things we need to fix or improve (and this is where the answers to your homework from the previous chapter get checked, so if you haven't tried to make your own list of changes, stop and do that now):

- The lists of restaurants and meals should be sorted in some way. Right now, they appear in no particular order; the order in which keys are retrieved from local storage is essentially random. We'll sort the list of restaurants alphabetically on both pages where it appears. We'll also sort the list of meals by date and by meal type.

- It's possible to add a restaurant with an empty name or change the name of a restaurant so it becomes empty. This is a bad idea—although the data will handle it, it shows as a blank line in the restaurant list and causes confusion—so we'll need to change those functions to prevent it.

- When we delete a restaurant, we really should delete all the meals that were eaten in that restaurant. We'll discuss the full reasons why when we get to that change.

- We know we need to add some sort of date-picker control to make life easier for the user—and, by reducing the chances that they will enter a bad date, make life easier for us as well.

- We also know we need to add graphing for the trends component.

- Our restaurant editing controls need a slight redesign so they work more intuitively.

■ Finally, we need better visual response to user errors—specifically, when they omit required data when adding a meal, we need some way of indicating to them what they've left out.

We'll incorporate these changes component-by-component as we work our way through adding in the visual design.

BREAKING UP THE HTML

The pages we created in Chapter 5 are not going to be usable in their current form. We have to separate out the HTML applicable to each of our components and move that HTML to the component's template. The index.html file will contain only the outermost HTML—mostly script inclusions and other necessary setup. Next is the template for the root component, which is so small that it doesn't even have its own template file. Inside that is the template for either the meal-entry or meal-listing page (depending on what the router is set to at that time), and the former also includes the templates for the trends and totals component. Each of these components contributes its own chunk of HTML as it's called, in effect assembling an HTML page from parts each time the app is run or reloaded.

Open index.html in the project directory. This file won't change much, but its few changes are all very important. It's been two chapters since we looked at index.html, so we've repeated it here, along with the specific changes if you're having trouble picking them out by eye:

■ The viewport <meta> tag has had an attribute added.

■ A <meta> tag has been added to help with old versions of Internet Explorer.

■ Two <link> tags have been added for Bootstrap and Font Awesome CSS files.

■ Three <script> tags have been added for Bootstrap and its dependencies.

■ The <title> has been moved to the end of the <head> section for readability.

■ The <app-main> component has been put inside a <div> with a class of container-fluid.

Your index.html should look like this:

```html
<!DOCTYPE html>
<html lang="en">
  <head>
    <base href="/"/>
    <meta charset="UTF-8" />
    <meta name="viewport"
      content="width=device-width, initial-scale=1, shrink-to-fit=no" />
    <meta http-equiv="x-ua-compatible" content="ie=edge" />
```

```html
    <link rel="stylesheet"
      href="node_modules/bootstrap/dist/css/bootstrap.min.css" />
    <link rel="stylesheet"
      href="node_modules/font-awesome/css/font-awesome.min.css" />
    <link rel="stylesheet" href="styles.css" />

    <!-- 1. Load libraries -->
    <!-- The next line makes ES6 stuff work for older ES5-only browsers. -->
    <script src="node_modules/core-js/client/shim.min.js"></script>
    <!-- Angular needs the next line for bindings to work. -->
    <script src="node_modules/zone.js/dist/zone.js"></script>
    <!-- TypeScript's @() decorators need the following line. -->
    <script src="node_modules/reflect-metadata/Reflect.js"></script>
    <!-- And, of course, our module/path finder is last. -->
    <script src="node_modules/systemjs/dist/system.src.js"></script>
    <!-- 2. Configure SystemJS -->
    <script src="systemjs.config.js"></script>
    <script>
      System.import('app').catch(function(err){ console.error(err); });
    </script>

    <!-- 3. Bootstrap and its dependencies -->
    <script src="node_modules/jquery/dist/jquery.min.js"></script>
    <script src="node_modules/tether/dist/js/tether.min.js"></script>
    <script src="node_modules/bootstrap/dist/js/bootstrap.js"></script>

    <title>TastyTracker</title>

  </head>
  <body>
    <div class="container-fluid">
      <app-main>Loading...</app-main>
    </div>
  </body>
</html>
```

Before we move into the root component to check what adjustments we have to make there, we should also adjust `styles.css` in the project directory. Open that file and make the following changes:

As the very first style in the file, add

```css
a {
    cursor: pointer;
}
```

This is because we'll be using many clickable <a> tags, which don't happen to have a URL associated with them. The mouse cursor will remain an arrow when hovering over them unless we use this style to change it to a pointing hand.

Before the .edit-meals-width style, add a new style:

```
.disabled {
    color: #7FB9B5;
}
```

This color will be used when the "edit restaurant" control is unavailable, because no restaurant has been selected.

Change the .edit-meals-width style:

```
.edit-meals-width {
    width: 37rem;
}
```

We made it a bit wider to try to get the editing controls to align better on the page.

Add an !important attribute to the .red style:

```
.red {
    color: #9F0316 !important;
}
```

This is to force certain controls that should be shown in red to be that color even when the browser wants to use a different color for style inheritance reasons.

Save and close index.html and styles.css. We have some other styles to add later, but we'll add them to CSS files in the app directory specific to their components.

In the app directory, open app.component.ts. Its template should be changed to look like this:

```
template: `
        <section>
          <div class="row">
            <div class="col-xs-12 text-xs-center tealBG">
              <header role="banner">
                <h1>TastyTracker</h1>
              </header>
            </div>
```

```
        </div>
      </section>

      <router-outlet></router-outlet>
      `
```

All we've done here is take the full-width banner `<h1>` from the Chapter 5 `index.html` and made it part of this component's template. We could just as well have put the banner (everything but the `<router-outlet>` tag pair) into `index.html`, but we think it's cleaner to have `index.html` be nothing but setup and not start the "working" HTML until this point. You may prefer to do it differently.

Save `app.component.ts`.

Note the way the HTML will be assembled. It's important to keep this clear in your head so your `<div>` tags and so on all match up properly, the page is laid out the way you intend, et cetera. The lines in `index.html` that say

```
<div class="container-fluid">
  <app-main>Loading...</app-main>
</div>
```

will, when the app is loaded, behave as if you're replacing the `<app-main>` tag pair and its contents with the contents of the `<app-main>` template. So, the generated HTML will look like:

```
<div class="container-fluid">
  <section>
    <div class="row">
      <div class="col-xs-12 text-xs-center tealBG">
        <header role="banner">
          <h1>TastyTracker</h1>
        </header>
      </div>
    </div>
  </section>

  <router-outlet></router-outlet>
</div>
```

Notice the closing `</div>` from `index.html` stays outside of the dropped-in template, which is as we want it. When planning which HTML goes in which template, remember that you want to match tag pairs *within that template*; that is, every `<div>` in a template should have a closing `</div>` in that template as well. In other words, keep your tags well-closed within that level; don't assume a "lower" or "higher" chunk of the HTML will close them for you.

Next in the page assembly, there will be another substitution, replacing the `<router-outlet>` tag pair with whatever component template the router has chosen . . . and so on down. If it were just a matter of taking apart the two `.html` files from Chapter 5 and putting HTML snippets into the templates, we'd be nearly done already—but we also need to make a lot of other changes, so we'll discuss the work in detail as we go, file by file.

THE MEAL ENTRY COMPONENT

As we work on this component, we're going to change the behavior of the controls for adding, updating, and deleting restaurants to be closer to the original design. The one in Chapter 7 seemed like a good idea at the time but turned out to be confusing.

Although we won't say we've *never* made arbitrary, because-I-said-so UX decisions, it's always a good idea to test a design decision with actual users if you can. If you try to guess what users will want and prefer, even the most experienced UX designers will sometimes guess wrong. In this case, Debby planned one approach—the approach seen in Chapter 5—and Todd implemented an entirely different approach, one which made more sense to him, in Chapter 7. Each approach had merits. What to do next?

Testing the application

The further down the development road an application goes, the harder it is to change things later if you've made a bad user experience decision. Testing small portions of the application before they're built, or as their functionality is added during the development process, allows you to get answers quickly and retool parts of the app before development is complete. Pure functionality-focused quality assurance (QA) testing should also happen as parts of an application are built, and you've already done some of that in previous chapters to confirm your new code is working.

Using incremental tests to make decisions

In using Todd's "overloaded" "add restaurants" control, Debby found it confusing, and Todd agreed—but we didn't agree on the right alternate solution. It's very common for design and development teams (and management teams, and marketing teams . . .) to have different perspectives on the best way to solve a design or functionality problem; running a short test with actual users can provide answers quickly and affordably.

Because we were still knitting together Angular and Bootstrap files when the design disagreement arose, the simplest way to resolve this was *not* to use live code for our test but rather static screenshots. Remarkably, users can adapt very easily to tests based on images of software instead of working code. One approach is to place a few potential screens—even black and white wireframe pages—in front of users and ask them what they expect to be able to do on a screen, or how they expect to do it. Another approach is to use what's called a *first-click test* to gauge someone's response to a design or feature option.

A first-click test is exactly what it sounds like: place a screen in front of a user and ask them where they would click first to accomplish a task. Using Optimal Workshop's Chalkmark tool (optimalworkshop.com/chalkmark), we set up a two-question test with the following goal: determine which of our possible "add restaurant" options was the most intuitive. Chalkmark would track where people clicked and display results in a heatmap.

We created two versions of the TastyTracking section for people to review: one with our original design, and one with a plus symbol to represent the "add" concept. (Whether tapping this symbol would open a modal or display a new text field onscreen was up in the air; we simply needed to know whether people perceived the symbol as a way to add a restaurant.)

We then asked the following question twice: "In order to get a handle on how much you spend dining out, you've started using a new app on your phone to track what meals you buy, where you buy them, and when you spent the money. You go out to eat with your coworkers at a restaurant you've never been to before. Where would you tap to enter the new restaurant name?" This question provided a setting so participants would understand the situation of use, and it carefully did not use terminology like the word *add*, which could subtly cue the plus symbol and skew results.

Note that we were testing three possible solutions, but based on our assumptions about what each click meant, we only needed to ask the question twice.

- If participants clicked on the Select Restaurant drop-down, they could have been expecting an "enter new restaurant" option or tool in the drop-down.
- If they clicked on the pencil icon, they were expecting that to allow them to enter the new restaurant. (We wouldn't examine whether they also expected it to edit restaurants, because we were eliminating the "overloaded" behavior anyway.)
- If they clicked on the plus icon, they were expecting that to allow them to enter the new restaurant.

We also set Chalkmark to randomize the order in which participants would see the screen mockups. This would offset the influence seeing the first image had on the second.

Finally, we asked two followup questions:

- How easy or hard did you find it to complete the tasks?
- Was there a different way you expected to be able to complete the task, and if so, what was it?

Analyzing the results

This form of testing has a few advantages: it's easy to put together if you already have the mockups, which makes it faster to set up than a traditional talking-protocol usability test that requires recruiting and interviewing people individually. It was also run remotely; once we had Chalkmark set up, we tweeted a URL, and our followers were able to take the test on their own time, at their own computers. We had all our results within less than twenty-four hours.

There were also some disadvantages. We'd chosen this method because running a usability study, even a limited one, took more time than we had available, but the first-click test provided less insight into thought processes than we'd hoped. For example, it wasn't clear that participants understood that we'd literally been asking them to add a new restaurant name rather than selecting from a drop-down list of every nearby restaurant. Similarly, the size and text of the "select a restaurant" drop-down would automatically draw the eye, diminishing our ability to tell whether people would assume the pencil icon on its own suggested they could use it to add a restaurant.

Our results weren't what any designer or developer would call conclusive, other than that people found the tasks easy to perform, which was good news for application usability. Instead, what we found was that because results were so closely split between the drop-down and icons, *either* the "edit new restaurant" option in the drop-down or a plus symbol would work.

So, we had heatmaps that suggested either solution would work, and we had feedback in favor of the button as well as the Enter New Restaurant drop-down option. We also knew that no matter what choice we made, users like Donna would be relying on TastyTracker frequently, so they'd quickly learn and adjust to whatever behavior we chose. This made the deciding factor "what's easiest for the developer to implement?"—which was adding the plus symbol.

Heatmaps from image with edit icon only (left) and plus symbol and edit icon (right). The 40-percent text obscures the clicked area, but it's centered over the plus symbol.

QA testing

The test we just performed was focused purely on user experience, though obviously it had implications for application functionality. Once an application is complete, however—or complete enough to test with even if it lacks visual design, as with the smoke test version in Chapter 7—it can be fully tested. A software company may use professional QA tools to automate parts of the testing process, including simulating how the system behaves under heavy usage. For a demo app like TastyTracker, which will rarely have more than one user at a time once deployed, load testing isn't necessary, but you still need to walk through every feature of the software to make sure it's working as expected.

- Are all the CRUD operations being performed correctly? Run through each of them multiple times and make sure local storage is showing the results it should.

- What happens if you enter data the system isn't expecting—too many or too few numbers, an invalid date (e.g., 13/13/13), or letters in a numeric field?

- Are the calculations being performed correctly?

- Do the graphs show the results you expect both by default and when their filters are adjusted?

- From a design perspective, does everything look the way it should no matter what screen size you're using?

You may find a few bugs as you work through this suite of tests. (But hopefully not too many, since we've been testing as we go!) Log those bugs however you like—a spreadsheet, free or commercial bug-tracking software, or even just a scrap or two of paper—so you can prioritize which ones are most important to fix and keep track of their current status. As you fix a bug, test to confirm it's really fixed, then cross it off your list. Periodically, return to your complete suite of tests just to make sure you haven't broken anything that was previously working. (This is called *regression testing,* an essential part of professional QA; in the real world, a regression test won't always be run on a complete software package, but TastyTracker is small enough that you can and should go through your complete list of tests again at least once.)

We go over testing a little bit more at the end of this chapter, as part of your assignment.

Updating the restaurant edit code

The new approach to restaurant edits is:

- The ability to add a restaurant will always be available whether a restaurant is selected or not. Clicking the button for Add will open or close a text field where a new restaurant can be added, with a button to save the addition.

⬜ After a new restaurant is saved, it will automatically be selected, same as before.

⬜ The ability to update or delete a restaurant is only available when a restaurant is selected; otherwise, the Edit button will be disabled. When this button is clicked, a modal dialog containing editing and deletion options will be superimposed over the page.

⬜ Deletion will require a second action to confirm the deletion, especially since deleting a restaurant is somewhat more severe than the user may realize. (More on that later.)

Bootstrap is going to handle the modal dialog, and to minimize conflicts with other page elements, Bootstrap prefers that modal markup be the *first* thing in the page (or template) HTML. When we edit this HTML, in other words, we're going to have a section that is "out of sequence." The HTML of the dialog will appear well before the point in the page where it's actually used.

Open `meal-entry.component.html`. (We also have changes to make to the component file itself, but we'll do the template first.) This file has changed enough that we'll give you the whole thing from scratch; you can, if you prefer, try to edit the old contents into the new form, but you may find it easier to start from a clean slate as well.

The first part of the file is the modal contents:

```html
<!-- Bootstrap recommends that modals appear at the beginning of the template. -->
<div class="modal fade" id="editRestaurants" tabindex="-1"
     role="dialog" aria-labelledby="editRestaurantsLabel" aria-hidden="true">
  <div class="modal-dialog" role="document">
    <div class="modal-content">

      <div class="modal-header">
        <button type="button" class="close"
          data-dismiss="modal" aria-label="Close">
          <span aria-hidden="true"><i class="fa fa-times-circle"></i></span>
        </button>
        <h3 class="modal-title" id="editRestaurantsLabel">
          Edit Restaurants</h3>
      </div>

      <div class="modal-body">
        <form>
          <div class="form-group form-inline row">
              <!-- This label displays to screenreaders only. -->
              <label for="editRestaurantName" class="sr-only">
                Edit or delete restaurant name</label>
            <div class="col-xs-8">
              <input type="text" id="editRestaurantName" #editRestaurantName
```

```
                class="form-control" value="{{selectedRestaurant}}" />
          <a aria-label="Save changes"
           (click)="update(restaurantID.value, editRestaurantName.value)"
           data-dismiss="modal">
          <i class="fa fa-check large" aria-hidden="true"></i></a>
          <a aria-label="Delete restaurant" class="red"
           (click)="toggleConfirm()">
          <i class="fa fa-times large" aria-hidden="true"></i></a>
        </div>
      </div>

      <div *ngIf="showConfirmDiv"
        class="alert alert-warning row" role="alert">
        <div class="col-xs-1">
          <i class="fa fa-exclamation-circle large"
            aria-hidden="true"></i>
        </div>
        <div class="col-xs-11">
          <p>Deleting {{selectedRestaurant}} will also delete
            all meals eaten there.</p>
          <button type="button" class="btn btn-primary"
                  (click)="delete(restaurantID.value)"
                  data-dismiss="modal">OK, delete it</button>
          <button type="button" class="btn btn-secondary ml-1"
                  (click)="toggleConfirm()">Nope, keep it</button>
        </div>
      </div>
    </form>
  </div> <!-- modal-body -->

  </div> <!-- modal-content -->
  </div> <!-- modal-dialog -->
</div> <!-- modal -->
```

The overall id of the modal (editRestaurants) is important for HTML later in the template that will open and close it. After the outer <div> tags comes a section that draws the Close button in the upper-right corner of the dialog.

Inside the modal body, we have the editRestaurantName control, where the user actually types any changes to the restaurant name. We prefill it with the selectedRestaurant from the selection in the main part of the page. The Save Changes button, which will be a checkmark, calls our component's update() function with the restaurant's ID number and the edited name string. It also closes the modal dialog (the data-dismiss attribute). The Delete button, which will appear as an X, doesn't actually do a deletion but instead calls the toggleConfirm() function, which we write shortly and which makes the final section of the dialog visible.

The final section of the dialog—visible only when showConfirmDiv is true—explains to the user the perils of deletion and asks for confirmation. (Notice that the name of the selected restaurant is interpolated into the message.) If the user confirms deletion, *then* the delete() function is called. If they press the No button, the confirmation section of the dialog is collapsed. (We don't close the entire dialog because the user may then decide to edit the restaurant name.)

Why will deleting the restaurant also delete all meals eaten there? (At the moment, of course, it doesn't. We have to add extra code to the **delete()** function so it will do so.)

Imagine you've deleted a restaurant. Your data contains records of meals you ate there. What happens to those records? The restaurant ID that's in them is no longer valid. The user has no way of displaying those meals, because you can't select a nonexistent restaurant from the list.

Do we, upon deleting a restaurant, iterate through all those records and change their restaurant IDs to one that still exists? If so, which one? And how is the user expected to know what restaurant those records have been invisibly moved to?

Alternatively, we could make a "no restaurant" item and put all those orphaned meals there. But this goes against our logic that a restaurant is required data, and how would we allow the user to see those meals? We'd need a "meals with no restaurant" selection on the meal list page, at the very least.

One way or another, a restaurant deletion *must* take care of any orphaned meal data somehow. If you prefer one of the approaches above, you could always make your deletion function do that thing. We think the answer that makes sense is to delete any meals for a deleted restaurant.

Continuing with meal-entry.component.html, here's the next part of the file:

```html
<!-- Meal-entry component template actually 'begins' here. -->

<!-- This outer div isn't closed until OUTSIDE the totals component. -->
<div class="row">

  <div class="col-xs-12 col-md-6 mb-2 pl-0 pr-0">
    <section>
      <header><h2 class="text-xs-center">TastyTracking</h2></header>
      <form>

        <div class="row mb-2">
          <div class="col-xs-11 text-xs-right">
            <a (click)="gotoList()">
```

```
      <i class="fa fa-pencil" aria-hidden="true"></i> edit meals</a>
  </div>
</div>

<div class="form-group form-inline row">
  <label for="mealAmount"
    class="col-xs-4 col-form-label text-xs-right">I spent</label>
  <div class="col-xs-7">
    $ <input id="mealAmount" type="text" class="form-control"
            name="mealAmount" [(ngModel)]="meal.amount" />
  </div>
</div>

<div class="form-group form-inline row">
  <label for="restaurantID"
    class="col-xs-4 col-form-label text-xs-right">at</label>
  <div class="col-xs-7 ml-1">
    <select id="restaurantID" #restaurantID
      class="form-control custom-select"
      name="restaurantID" [ngModel]="meal.location"
     (change)="onSelect($event.target.value,
          restaurantID.options[restaurantID.selectedIndex].text)">
      <option value="0">-- select a restaurant --</option>
      <option *ngFor="let r of restaurants"
              value="{{r.id}}">{{r.name}}</option>
    </select>
    <a (click)="toggleAdd()" aria-label="Add restaurant">
      <i class="fa fa-plus" aria-hidden="true"></i></a>
    <a *ngIf="editingEnabled" data-toggle="modal"
      data-target="#editRestaurants" aria-label="Edit restaurants">
      <i class="fa fa-pencil large-less" aria-hidden="true"></i></a>
    <!-- This button is SUPPOSED to do nothing. -->
    <a *ngIf="!editingEnabled">
      <i class="fa fa-pencil large-less disabled"
        aria-hidden="true"></i></a>

    <div *ngIf="showAddDiv">
      <input id="newRestaurantName" #newRestaurantName
        name="newRestaurantName" type="text"
        class="form-control" />
      <a (click)="add(newRestaurantName.value)"
        aria-label="Save new restaurant">
        <i class="fa fa-check large-less"
          aria-hidden="true"></i></a>
    </div>
  </div>
```

```
        </div>

        <div class="form-group form-inline row">
          <label for="mealName"
            class="col-xs-4 col-form-label text-xs-right">on</label>
          <div class="col-xs-7 ml-1">
            <select id="mealName" class="form-control custom-select"
                    name="mealName" [(ngModel)]="meal.name">
              <option value="B">Breakfast</option>
              <option value="L">Lunch</option>
              <option value="D">Dinner</option>
              <option value="S">Snack</option>
            </select>
          </div>
        </div>
```

In Chapter 7, we discussed id= attributes versus name= attributes versus Angular's reference variables, the bare names beginning with #. We mentioned that we didn't use name= because that was mostly for form operations, and we didn't need them. We also didn't have explicit <form> tags at that point. Now we do have them, because some of the Bootstrap classes we're using, such as form-control, need to be applied to a tag within a form. And we've added name= attributes to several of these controls because they're now needed. (We just set them to be the same as the id=, which is legal and avoids confusion.)

Near the top of this portion, we see some lines that will draw a pencil icon at the top of the section, just below the <h2> header, and take us to the meal list page when clicked. Apart from layout and the icon, this hasn't changed.

The mealAmount and mealName controls also haven't changed, other than layout and being styled as form-control. The restaurant selection restaurantID hasn't itself changed much (although we will tinker internally with the onSelect() function). But the lines just *after* the select list have changed quite a bit.

A plus sign just to the right of the selection list will open and close the "add restaurant" section of the form when clicked, using toggleAdd(). This is followed by a pair of *ngIf tests that do two different things based on whether a restaurant is currently selected. (The onSelect() function will set or clear editingEnabled.) If one is, a pencil icon is displayed, which will open the modal dialog. If no restaurant is selected, a nonfunctional pencil icon will be displayed in the disabled style. As the comment notes, that pencil is *supposed* to do nothing.

Notice the specifier data-target="#editRestaurants" that says what modal to display. The # in this attribute is *not* one of Angular's reference variables; this is Bootstrap, which uses it for a different meaning: the div we identified as id="editRestaurants" up at the top of the file.

Next comes the "add restaurant" section, which is only displayed if showAddDiv is true. (toggleAdd() will change its value.) The checkmark icon beside the text field will call the add() function to save the new restaurant.

The last part of meal-entry.component.html is mostly the datepicker:

```
<div class="form-group form-inline row">
  <label for="mealDate"
   class="col-xs-4 col-form-label text-xs-right">on this date</label>
  <div class="col-xs-7 ml-1">
    <input id="mealDate" type="text" class="form-control"
           name="mealDate" [(ngModel)]="meal.date" />
    <a (click)="toggleDatepicker()" aria-label="Choose date">
      <i class="fa fa-calendar large-less"
        aria-hidden="true"></i></a>

    <div *ngIf="showDateDiv">
      <datepicker [curdate]="meal.date"
        (onDateChange)="setDate($event)">
      </datepicker>
    </div>
  </div>
</div>


<div class="row">
  <div class="col-xs-7 offset-xs-4">
    <button type="submit" class="btn btn-primary ml-1"
            (click)="save()">Save</button>
  </div>
</div>


    </form>
  </section>
</div>

<!-- totals and trends -->

<totals [thumper]="thumper"></totals>

</div>

<trends [thumper]="thumper"></trends>
```

Notice that the trends component is outside that closing </div>. This is deliberate. It's on a row of its own and will handle its own tags.

The gist of the date changes is that there will now be a calendar-page icon next to the date field, which, when clicked, shows or hides a `<div>` containing the datepicker component.

What datepicker component?

We have chosen to treat the datepicker component as if you're using someone else's library. That is, we're not going to explain its internals in detail; we're just going to tell you "take these three files and put them in your app directory." Yes, we wrote them, and yes, studying them may be useful to you, but reviewing *how* we wrote them is out of scope for this material. The three files are `datepicker.component.ts`, `datepicker.component.html`, and `datepicker.component.css`, and you'll find them in the `Final Files` folder installed as part of our npm `tastytracker-demo-pkg` package. Note that the CSS file doesn't go in the top project directory; it lives in app with the component and template files.

Go ahead and get those files and put them where they should be now.

The datepicker must be imported in the application module like all our other components. Might as well stop and do that. Open `app.module.ts` and add this line after all the other component imports:

```
import { DatepickerComponent } from './datepicker.component';
```

And don't forget to also add `DatepickerComponent` to the `declarations` array, between `TrendsComponent` and `DateDisplayPipe`.

The key concept of the datepicker component is that it is an *emitter*. We've already discussed the `@Input()` decorator as a way for a parent (outer) component to pass data to a child component (such as `thumper`). An emitter allows data to be passed in the opposite direction: The child component says, "I'm generating an event, so if this event is important to you, listen for it and respond to it."

In this case, the datepicker takes an input as well—it accepts the current `meal.date` and stores that inside its own component as `curdate`. When a user selects a new date in the datepicker, the datepicker emits an `onDateChange` event. It's allowed to pass back some data for that event, which comes back in `$event`, and this component must use that data to change the contents of this form's date field (via the `setDate()` function).

Save `meal-entry.component.html` if you haven't already, and make sure you've installed the three datepicker files. We now need to switch to the component side of things.

Open `meal-entry.component.ts`.

Among the component data declarations, replace the line

```
showRestDiv = false;
```

with these four lines:

```
showAddDiv = false;
editingEnabled = false;
showConfirmDiv = false;
showDateDiv = false;
```

We no longer have a "restaurant editing" div per se—that's the modal, and Bootstrap will handle it. But we now need specific markers to control (respectively) whether the "add restaurant" controls should be shown, whether a restaurant has been selected, whether the deletion confirmation section of the modal should be shown, and whether the datepicker should be shown.

The onSelect() function should be changed to:

```
onSelect(value: string, label: string): void {
  let numValue = parseInt(value);

  console.log('select', numValue, label);
  if (numValue > 0) {
    this.selectedRestaurant = label;
    this.editingEnabled = true;
  }
  else {
    this.selectedRestaurant = '';
    this.editingEnabled = false;
  }
  this.showConfirmDiv = false;
  this.meal.location = numValue;
}
```

Two of the added lines set or clear editingEnabled if a restaurant is selected, and the third hides the delete confirmation controls if the selected restaurant has changed, which is less confusing to the user. (We want the delete confirmation to not display by default when the modal dialog is opened.)

In the update() function, after the line

```
let newrest = new Restaurant;
```

add the following lines:

```
if (!name) {
  return null;
}
```

This will prevent an empty name from being saved.

Also, remove the line from the end of the function that says

```
this.showRestDiv = false;
```

Bootstrap will handle closing the modal for us.

In the add() function, after the line

```
let newrest = new Restaurant;
```

add the same check that you added to update():

```
if (!name) {
   return null;
}
```

Also, replace the line that says

```
this.showRestDiv = false;
```

with these two lines:

```
this.showAddDiv = false;
this.editingEnabled = true;
```

We close the "add restaurant" section once a new restaurant has been saved. Because that restaurant is now the selected one but the user hasn't actually triggered onSelect() again, we have to manually enable the editing control.

In the delete() function, there should be a comment about needing to delete all meals for a deleted restaurant. (If you didn't put in the comment, it would have been just after the line that calls restaurantService.delete().)

Replace the comment—or insert where the comment would have been—with this line:

```
this.mealService.deleteByRestaurant(numID);
```

That function is currently an empty placeholder, but we'll go back to the meal service to fill it in shortly.

Also, replace the line at the end of the function that says

```
this.showRestDiv = false;
```

with the line

```
this.editingEnabled = false;
```

This is the opposite of the problem we just fixed with add(). When a restaurant is deleted, there's no longer a restaurant selected—but onSelect() hasn't been used, so the editing control must be manually disabled.

Finally, the showRestaurants() function is defunct. Delete it and replace it with these four new functions.

```
toggleAdd(): void {
  this.showAddDiv = !this.showAddDiv;
}

toggleConfirm(): void {
  this.showConfirmDiv = !this.showConfirmDiv;
}

toggleDatepicker(): void {
  this.showDateDiv = !this.showDateDiv;
}

setDate(newdate: string): void {
  if (this.meal.date !== newdate) {
    this.meal.date = newdate;
    this.toggleDatepicker();
    // Use this slight runaround instead of just setting showDateDiv
    // or you'll get problems with a binding changed after page check.
  }
}
```

We'll come back to this file later to try to make the save() function a little more user-friendly, but this will do for now. Save your work.

THE TOTALS AND TRENDS COMPONENTS

The totals component itself needs no changes. Its template only needs new layout and styling.

Open `totals.component.html` and replace its existing five lines of content with the following:

```html
<div class="col-xs-12 col-md-6 mb-2 pl-0 pr-0">
  <section>
    <header class="mb-3"><h2 class="text-xs-center">TastyTotals</h2></header>
    <div class="row mx-auto" style="width:30rem;">

      <div class="col-xs-6 text-xs-center">
        <div class="circle">
          <span class="bigNumber">
            <strong>{{totalToday | currency:'USD':true:'.2'}}</strong>
          </span><br />spent on meals today
        </div>
      </div>

      <div class="col-xs-6 text-xs-center">
        <div class="circle">
          <span class="bigNumber">
            <strong>{{totalThisWeek | currency:'USD':true:'.2'}}</strong>
          </span><br />spent on meals this week
        </div>
      </div>

    </div>
  </section>
</div>
```

Save the file. That was the easy part. Now we have to deal with the trends component.

The trends component is, per the original design, supposed to have horizontal bar graphs in it. We tried for several days to work with various JavaScript graph libraries, including some that claimed to work with Angular 2 and did not. One library did but didn't support the kind of graph we wanted.

One issue with Angular's design is that although it's very good for doing its own things efficiently, it prevents splicing in other bits of JavaScript libraries at will. For example, the normal way of directly obtaining the ID of a given page element in JavaScript—`getElementById()`—just plain doesn't work in Angular. Furthermore, Angular strongly discourages direct access and manipulation of page elements by ID, for a number of reasons not worth going into here.

This meant that although there were any number of perfectly good JavaScript graph libraries, we couldn't get any of them properly "wrapped" in the Angular way of doing things. Others claim to have done so, but their documentation was so poor that we couldn't actually get any of their methods to work.

So we're going to make our own graphs using CSS. We'll write code in the component to determine the width of each bar in the graph, then draw that bar simply by styling a <div> appropriately.

Open trends.component.html and replace its contents with the following:

```html
<section>
  <header>
    <div class="row">
      <div class="col-xs-12 text-xs-center pl-0 pr-0">
        <h2>TastyTrends</h2>
      </div>
    </div>
  </header>

  <div class="row">
    <div class="col-xs-12">
      <p>TastyTracker keeps track of up to a year's worth of spending.</p>
    </div>
  </div>

  <div class="row">
    <div class="col-xs-12 col-md-6">
      <header><h3>This week compared to last week</h3></header>

      <div id="graphDiv1" #graphDiv1 class="mb-1">
        <div><h4 class="graphLabel">This week</h4>
            <div id="weekBar1" class="bar1"
              [ngStyle]="{'width': weekBar1}"></div>
            <span class="small" style="padding-left:0.25rem;">
              {{totalThisWeek | currency:'USD':true:'.2'}}</span>
        </div>
        <div><h4 class="graphLabel">Last week</h4>
            <div id="weekBar2" class="bar2"
              [ngStyle]="{'width': weekBar2}"></div>
            <span class="small" style="padding-left:0.25rem;">
              {{totalLastWeek | currency:'USD':true:'.2'}}</span>
        </div>
      </div>
    </div>
</div>
```

```
<div class="col-xs-12 col-md-6">
  <form class="form-inline">
  <!-- Both header and h3 tags need d-inline to force inline display. -->
    <header class="d-inline">
      <h3 class="d-inline">On average, I spend this amount</h3>
    </header>
    <div class="form-group">
      <label for="interval" class="sr-only">select time period</label>
      <select id="interval" #interval name="interval"
        class="form-control custom-select" [ngModel]="averageInterval"
            (change)="onSelect($event.target.value)">
      <option value="D">Daily</option>
      <option value="W">Weekly</option>
      <option value="M">Monthly</option>
      </select>
    </div>
  </form>

  <div id="graphDiv2" #graphDiv2>
    <div><h4 class="graphLabel">Breakfast</h4>
        <div id="mealBar1" class="bar1"
           [ngStyle]="{'width': mealBar1}"></div>
        <span class="small" style="padding-left:0.25rem;">
          {{breakfastAverage | currency:'USD':true:'.2'}}</span>
    </div>
    <div><h4 class="graphLabel">Lunch</h4>
        <div id="mealBar2" class="bar2"
           [ngStyle]="{'width': mealBar2}"></div>
        <span class="small" style="padding-left:0.25rem;">
          {{lunchAverage | currency:'USD':true:'.2'}}</span>
    </div>
    <div><h4 class="graphLabel">Dinner</h4>
        <div id="mealBar3" class="bar3"
           [ngStyle]="{'width': mealBar3}"></div>
        <span class="small" style="padding-left:0.25rem;">
          {{dinnerAverage | currency:'USD':true:'.2'}}</span>
    </div>
    <div><h4 class="graphLabel">Snacks</h4>
        <div id="mealBar4" class="bar4"
           [ngStyle]="{'width': mealBar4}"></div>
        <span class="small" style="padding-left:0.25rem;">
          {{snackAverage | currency:'USD':true:'.2'}}</span>
    </div>
  </div>
```

```
    </div>
  </div>
</section>
```

Note the lines in this file that use the new-to-us ngStyle keyword. These will allow us to dynamically set the styles of tags in which they appear.

There are a few CSS classes in this file that don't exist yet. Let's create them. Save that file and create the new file trends.component.css (it goes in the app directory with the other component files):

```css
.graphLabel {
    display:inline-block;
    padding-right:0.25rem;
    width:4rem;
}

.bar1, .bar2, .bar3, .bar4 {
    height:1rem;
    display:inline-block;
}

.bar1 {
    background-color:#B8A244;
}
.bar2 {
    background-color:#4F430F;
}
.bar3 {
    background-color:#7FB9B5;
}
.bar4 {
    background-color:#8B825D;
}
```

You'll notice that the four bar classes don't specify a width. As noted, we do that dynamically in the component code. The background-color styles of the four bar classes will determine the colors of the bars in the graph.

Save trends.component.css and open trends.component.ts. We have a fair bit of work to do here.

First, add the ViewChild object to the import statement at the top of the file, so the line reads:

```
import { Component, OnChanges, Input, ViewChild } from '@angular/core';
```

Inside the @Component() declarations, add a comma at the end of the templateUrl line (because it will no longer be the last item) and follow it with a styleUrls declaration, so that your @Component() block now looks like this:

```
@Component({
  selector: 'trends',
  templateUrl: 'app/trends.component.html',
  styleUrls: [ 'app/trends.component.css' ]
})
```

We haven't used the styleUrls declaration before, but each component can have one or more of its own CSS files. If there are classes in these local CSS files that are the same as ones in styles.css or any other outer CSS file, the local versions will be used. This enables us to not just declare but also override styles on a component-by-component basis. Notice that, unlike templateUrl, styleUrls is an array.

In the component data declarations, following the declaration of snackAverage, add these lines:

```
@ViewChild('graphDiv1') graphDiv1: any;
@ViewChild('graphDiv2') graphDiv2: any;
weekBar1: string;
weekBar2: string;
mealBar1: string;
mealBar2: string;
mealBar3: string;
mealBar4: string;
```

The @ViewChild() decorator is, of course, the reason we had to add ViewChild to the import line. It allows the component code to "see" a reference variable (the ones that start with #) from the template. For example, the first of those lines refers to a template reference variable called #graphDiv1, which will now be accessible via the component variable graphDiv1. In each case, we've given the component variable the same name to avoid confusion.

Both graphDiv1 and graphDiv2 refer to <div> tags and thus don't fit well into one of our standard variable types. (They aren't strings, they aren't numbers, etc.) We declare them as any, which essentially means "We don't know what it is, but we won't have to care, so it's okay." We can't assign values directly to them—saying something like graphDiv1 = 5 would be illegal—but we're only going to look at and set *properties* of these items.

At the end of the ngOnChanges() function, after

```
this.getAverages();
```

add these lines:

```
    this.initWeeklyGraph();
    this.initAverageGraph();
```

At the end of the onSelect() function, add this line:

```
    this.initAverageGraph();
```

Every time the component state changes, we must recalculate the widths of the bars in our two graphs, and when the user chooses a different averaging interval, we must recalculate the widths in the averages graph.

Now we need to actually write those two functions. At the bottom of the component (taking care that you're inside the closing brace of the component), add them:

```
initWeeklyGraph(): void {
  let maxWidth: number;
  let thisWeek: number = this.totalThisWeek;
  let lastWeek: number = this.totalLastWeek;
  let larger: number;
  let unit: number;
  let bar1width: number;
  let bar2width: number;

  maxWidth = this.graphDiv1.nativeElement.offsetWidth;
  maxWidth = maxWidth - 150; // to allow for legend and amount

  if (thisWeek >= lastWeek) {
    larger = thisWeek;
  }
  else {
    larger = lastWeek;
  }
  if (larger === 0) {
    larger = 1;
  }

  // If the larger amount is greater than the max width, we need to divide
  // both week's amounts by two and try again (rescaling the graph).
```

```
    // Ultimately we need 'unit' to be 1 or greater.
    while (larger > maxWidth) {
      thisWeek = Math.floor(thisWeek / 2);
      lastWeek = Math.floor(lastWeek / 2);
      larger = Math.floor(larger / 2);
    }
    unit = Math.floor(maxWidth / larger);

    bar1width = Math.floor(thisWeek * unit);
    this.weekBar1 = bar1width.toString() + "px";
    bar2width = Math.floor(lastWeek * unit);
    this.weekBar2 = bar2width.toString() + "px";
  }

  initAverageGraph(): void {
    let maxWidth: number;
    let breakfast: number = this.breakfastAverage;
    let lunch: number = this.lunchAverage;
    let dinner: number = this.dinnerAverage;
    let snacks: number = this.snackAverage;
    let largest: number;
    let unit: number;
    let bar1width: number;
    let bar2width: number;
    let bar3width: number;
    let bar4width: number;

    maxWidth = this.graphDiv2.nativeElement.offsetWidth;
    maxWidth = maxWidth - 150;

    if (breakfast >= lunch) {
      largest = breakfast;
    }
    else {
      largest = lunch;
    }
    if (largest < dinner) {
      largest = dinner;
    }
    if (largest < snacks) {
      largest = snacks;
    }
    if (largest === 0) {
      largest = 1;
    }
```

```
    while (largest > maxWidth) {
      breakfast = Math.floor(breakfast / 2);
      lunch = Math.floor(lunch / 2);
      dinner = Math.floor(dinner / 2);
      snacks = Math.floor(snacks / 2);
      largest = Math.floor(largest / 2);
    }

    unit = Math.floor(maxWidth / largest);
    bar1width = Math.floor(breakfast * unit);
    this.mealBar1 = bar1width.toString() + "px";
    bar2width = Math.floor(lunch * unit);
    this.mealBar2 = bar2width.toString() + "px";
    bar3width = Math.floor(dinner * unit);
    this.mealBar3 = bar3width.toString() + "px";
    bar4width = Math.floor(snacks * unit);
    this.mealBar4 = bar4width.toString() + "px";
  }
```

Let's take apart the logic of initWeeklyGraph().

The first step is to figure out what is the widest (longest) bar we can have in the chart that won't disrupt our page layout—how much space we have available to us. We inspect the offsetWidth property of graphDiv1.[28] Remember that graphDiv1 is the outer <div> that encloses all the bars of the chart. Its width is determined by the page layout, browser size, etc. The offsetWidth property will be a number—the width of the <div> in pixels.

We subtract 150 from it because this is a reasonable guess at how much space on each line of the chart will be taken up by the labels ("Last Week") and the display of the dollar amounts. We calculated this guess based on what our longest labels and numbers were likely to be and how much space they occupied in the font size that they'll appear in.

Now that we know the maximum width one of our bars can be, we have to figure out how big a single unit is—that is, how many pixels of bar equal one dollar of spending. We find the larger of the two amounts. It's possible that this could be zero (if both amounts are zero). If that happens, we set it to one; otherwise, we'd be dividing by zero in the next step, and that's not allowed.

If that larger amount is less than or equal to the total width we have available, great. But if it's more—for example, if our maxWidth is 300 and we spent $400 that week—we have to rescale; we cut both amounts in half (and also cut larger in half, just so we don't have to recalculate it). We will do this as many times as needed until we have a larger that isn't greater than maxWidth.

---

[28] The nativeElement portion of this reference is required by Angular. We have been unable to find a reason why anywhere in their documentation. We just know that if you're trying to get at properties of a template item you've accessed with @ViewChild(), you'll need it.

This is why we've copied our weekly totals into the local variables thisWeek and lastWeek—so we can operate on them without affecting the real values. The local copies are just used to figure out the widths of the bars and are not shown to the user.

> ■
>
> This is the first time we've used a while loop anywhere in our code. A while loop executes the statements inside the block as long as the condition in parentheses evaluates to true. If the condition starts out false, the statements in the loop are never executed. Obviously, something inside the loop should eventually make the condition false, or the while loop will never end!
>
> ■

Once we have a larger that isn't too large, we divide maxWidth by larger, and that gives us the size of our unit. The whole point of calculating larger is that the longest bar in the graph determines the scale for all of them.

You're probably wondering about Math.floor(). This is a standard JavaScript function, carried over to TypeScript, that returns the nearest whole number that is less than or equal to the parameter provided. These dollar amounts may have decimal portions, but we need integers. You may then wonder why we aren't using parseInt(). That's because parseInt() expects its parameter to be a string; here we're transforming numbers to numbers.

Now that we know our unit, the width of the bar is the dollar amount multiplied by the unit. So if our "this week" total was $200 and we determined that we had a scale where one dollar was two pixels wide, the width of the bar would be 400 pixels.

The last thing we have to do is pass our widths back to the <div> tags that make up the actual bars. Although there's a method of setting the style of a page element directly from component code using ViewChild, it doesn't work on all browsers and Angular discourages it. Instead, we declared in the template that the styles of our graph-bar <div> tags were bound to ngStyle, a special keyword that then allows us to change the style using component variables.

We know the width we want, but it's a number, and we have to translate it into a string that includes "px" after the digits, just as we'd write it if we were setting a "width" style by hand in HTML. We use the toString() method, and append "px" to that. This is what gets sent in the component variable(s).

The initAverageGraph() function operates exactly the same way. The only difference is that there are four amounts to compare instead of two, so the "get the largest value" portion is a little more complex.

Save your work.

THE MEAL LIST COMPONENT

We won't make any changes to the component itself right now, but we make a few as part of our error-checking improvements at the end of this chapter. The template must be restyled. Open `meal-list.component.html` and replace its contents with the following:

```
<div class="row">
  <section>
    <header>
      <div class="row">
        <div class="col-xs-12 text-xs-center pl-0 pr-0">
          <h2>Edit Meals</h2>
        </div>
      </div>
    </header>

    <div class="row">
      <div class="col-xs-6 offset-xs-4 text-xs-right mb-2">
        <a (click)="gotoMain()">return to main screen
          <i class="fa fa-arrow-right" aria-hidden="true"></i></a>
      </div>
    </div>

    <div class="edit-meals-width row mx-auto">
      <div class="col-xs-8">
        <form>
        <!-- Add edit-meals-width and mx-auto here again -->
        <!-- to force the restaurant selector to the same -->
        <!-- width as the content below it. -->
          <div class="form-group row edit-meals-width mx-auto">
            <label for="restaurantID" class="sr-only">
              select restaurant</label>
            <div class="col-xs-12">
              <select id="restaurantID" #restaurantID
                      name="restaurantID" class="form-control custom-select"
                      [ngModel]="selectedRestaurant"
                      (change)="onSelect($event.target.value)">
                <option value="0">-- select a restaurant --</option>
                <option *ngFor="let r of restaurants"
                  value="{{r.id}}">{{r.name}}</option>
              </select>
            </div>
          </div>
```

```html
<!-- Begin meal display, which shouldn't be inside the form, -->
<!-- but that's the way these classes are set up. -->

<div *ngFor="let m of meals"
  class="form-group row edit-meals-width mb-1 mx-auto">
  <div class="col-xs-3">
    <input id="listMealValue" #listMealValue
      type="text" class="form-control"
      value="{{m.amount | number:'.2'}}"
      aria-labelledby="Amount spent" />
  </div>
  <div class="col-xs-3">
    <select id="listMealName" #listMealName
            class="form-control custom-select"
            name="listMealName" aria-labelledby="Meal type">
      <option value="B"
       [attr.selected]="m.name==='B' ? true : null">
       Breakfast</option>
      <option value="L"
       [attr.selected]="m.name==='L' ? true : null">
       Lunch</option>
      <option value="D"
       [attr.selected]="m.name==='D' ? true : null">
       Dinner</option>
      <option value="S"
       [attr.selected]="m.name==='S' ? true : null">
       Snack</option>
    </select>
  </div>
  <div class="col-xs-3">
    <input id="listMealDate" #listMealDate
      type="text" class="form-control"
      value="{{m.date | dateDisplay}}"
      aria-labelledby="Meal date" />
  </div>
  <div class="col-xs-3">
    <a (click)="save(listMealValue.value, listMealName.value,
                    listMealDate.value, m.name, m.date)"
      aria-label="Save changes">
      <i class="fa fa-check large" aria-hidden="true"></i></a>
    <a (click)="delete(m.name, m.date)"
      aria-label="Delete restaurant" class="red">
      <i class="fa fa-times large" aria-hidden="true"></i></a>
  </div>
</div> <!-- *ngFor -->
```

```
          </form>
        </div>
      </div>
    </section>
  </div>
```

Save your work.

RESTAURANTS AND MEALS

At the beginning of this chapter, one of the changes we listed was to sort the restaurants and meals. The best place to put the code to do that is directly in the meal and restaurant services, so that when their respective "get the list" functions are called, the list is automatically delivered to the caller in order.

JavaScript (and, by extension, TypeScript) has a built-in sort() method that can be applied to virtually any data type, including complex ones. The catch is, if you apply it to data types it doesn't know how to sort, then you have to tell it how to do the sorting.

Open restaurant.service.ts.

Near the end of the getList() function, just *before* the line

```
return rests;
```

add this line:

```
    rests.sort(this.compare);
```

This says "sort whatever's in rests and use the compare function found elsewhere in this component to do so."

A compare function for a sort has to follow a rigid set of inputs and outputs. It accepts two items of the same type—call them A and B—that can be compared in any way you like. The function should return -1 if A is sorted before B; that is, if A should appear before B in sorted results. It should return 1 if A is to be sorted after B, and 0 if A and B are identical. The sort() method will call this function over and over as it works through the entire list of data.

In our case, we're going to be sorting based on the restaurant's name, and in TypeScript, the "greater than" and "less than" operators work perfectly fine for strings, so it's simple. Add this function to the component just after the getList() function:

```
compare(a: Restaurant, b: Restaurant): number {
  if (a.name < b.name) {
    return -1;
  }
  if (a.name > b.name) {
    return 1;
  }
  return 0;
}
```

Notice the `return 0` doesn't need an explicit test for equality, because the other two conditions exit the function when they return their respective values. If we got as far as the `return 0` line, then *A* isn't less than *B* and it isn't greater than *B*, so they *must* be equal.

Save the file. Now our list of restaurants will arrive in alphabetical order.

Open `meal.service.ts`.

Near the end of the `getList()` function, just *before*

```
return meals;
```

add this line:

```
meals.sort(this.compare);
```

The compare function in this component is going to sort by date. Depending on the date format, this could be quite hard, but since internally we hold dates as YYYYMMDD, we can sort them as if they're just large numbers (or string representations of large numbers; it'll work here either way). Add this function after the `getList()` function:

```
compare(a: Meal, b: Meal): number {
  if (a.date < b.date) {
    return -1;
  }
  if (a.date > b.date) {
    return 1;
  }
  return 0;
}
```

Simplicity itself.

While we're here, we also need to fill in the body of the placeholder `deleteByRestaurant()` function. It should look like this:

```
deleteByRestaurant(id: number): void {
  for (var x = 0; x < localStorage.length; x++) {
    let key = localStorage.key(x);
    let re = /^TTM_\d\d\d\d\d\d\d_\w_(\d+)/;
    let results: Array<string>;
    if ((results = re.exec(key)) !== null) {
      if (parseInt(results[1]) === id) {
        localStorage.removeItem(key);
      }
    }
  }
}
```

This function accepts a restaurant ID number, iterates through all the meal keys, and when it finds a meal that has that restaurant ID, removes it. You've seen everything in it already except the \w in the regular expression, which means "any alphanumeric character" and matches the one-letter meal type code.

Save your work.

At this point you should be able to run everything and see all the changes you've made!

> Depending on your browser and its version, you may see a lot of warnings in the web console about declarations in the Bootstrap .js file being ignored. You can safely disregard these messages as long as the app is looking and performing the way it should.

ERROR FEEDBACK

We have a number of places where the user can omit required data or supply bad data. Right now, those situations are set to "fail silently." For example, if you're adding a restaurant and you don't type in a restaurant name but click the checkmark anyway, it won't try to add an empty restaurant; it will do nothing.

Failing silently is fine for that control; it's obvious enough what's going on, especially since the response for a successful restaurant add is very different. (The restaurant would be added to the selection list and automatically become the current selection.) We also think it's acceptable for the app to silently refuse to update a restaurant name with an empty string—again, what's happening is pretty obvious.

But for the main meal entry form, having the Save button silently do nothing isn't good enough. There are four pieces of information on that form, and the save will fail if any of them are bad or missing. We need to give the user some feedback on what they left out or did wrong.

Angular has a built-in mechanism for responding to missing form data. It has certain advantages but, for our purposes, doesn't do what we want. We want to react to bad or missing data at the time the **Save** button is pressed, and we may choose to display different responses based on what specifically is wrong with the data. So we're going to handle it ourselves. But if you're curious about Angular's form-verification tools, see angular.io/docs/ts/latest/guide/forms.html.

Open `meal-entry.component.html`.

Immediately after these lines:

```
$ <input id="mealAmount" type="text" class="form-control"
         name="mealAmount" [(ngModel)]="meal.amount" />
```

add the line

```
<div *ngIf="invalidAmount"
    class="alert alert-danger">{{invalidAmtMessage}}</div>
```

We're going to be adding another Boolean value, `invalidAmount`, which our `save()` function will set, and if it's true, we'll display whatever is in `invalidAmtMessage` inside this `<div>`. The classes in the `<div>` will display it in red on a light-red background so it's nice and attention-getting.

Same for the restaurant selection. Immediately after the "add restaurant" `<div>`

```
<div *ngIf="showAddDiv">
  <input id="newRestaurantName" #newRestaurantName
    name="newRestaurantName" type="text" class="form-control" />
  <a (click)="add(newRestaurantName.value)"
    aria-label="Save new restaurant">
    <i class="fa fa-check large-less"
      aria-hidden="true"></i></a>
</div>
```

add this line:

```
<div *ngIf="invalidRestaurant" class="alert alert-danger">
  Please select a restaurant</div>
```

There's only one possible error message for that control, so we don't bother with an interpolated one.

We don't need any sort of error response for the meal type picker because it has no "empty" value; if the user doesn't bother to set it, the meal will be entered as breakfast, and they may have to go edit it later.

For the date control, immediately after

```
<a (click)="toggleDatepicker()" aria-label="Choose date">
  <i class="fa fa-calendar large-less"
    aria-hidden="true"></i></a>
```

add the line

```
<div *ngIf="invalidDate"
  class="alert alert-danger">{{invalidDateMessage}}</div>
```

Save the file.

Open `meal-entry.component.ts`.

Somewhere in the ever-growing list of component variable initializations, add the following lines:

```
invalidAmount = false;
invalidAmtMessage = '';
invalidRestaurant = false;
invalidDate = false;
invalidDateMessage = '';
```

All the rest of the work here is in the `save()` function. Change the function to look like this. We've removed some of the `console.log()` messages; with real error feedback, we don't need them anymore.

```
save(): void {
  let mydate = moment(this.meal.date, 'MM/DD/YYYY');
  let newdate = '';
  let amtAsNum = parseFloat(this.meal.amount);

  this.invalidAmount = false;
  this.invalidRestaurant = false;
  this.invalidDate = false;

  if (isNaN(amtAsNum)) {
    this.invalidAmount = true;
    this.invalidAmtMessage = 'Please enter an amount';
    return null;
```

```
    }
    else {
      if (amtAsNum <= 0) {
        this.invalidAmount = true;
        this.invalidAmtMessage = 'Please enter an amount greater than zero';
        return null;
      }
    }
    if (!this.meal.name) {
      return null;
    }
    if (!this.meal.location) {
      this.invalidRestaurant = true;
      return null;
    }
    if (!this.meal.date) {
      this.invalidDate = true;
      this.invalidDateMessage = 'Please enter a date (MM/DD/YYYY)';
      return null;
    }
    if (!mydate.isValid()) {
      this.invalidDate = true;
      this.invalidDateMessage = 'Please enter a valid date (MM/DD/YYYY)';
      return null;
    }

    // If here, then do actual stuff.
    newdate = mydate.format('YYYYMMDD');

    console.log('save', this.meal.amount, this.meal.location,
                this.meal.name, this.meal.date);
    this.mealService.create(newdate, this.meal.name,
                            this.meal.location, this.meal.amount);
    this.meal.amount = '';

    // Thump the thumper
    this.thumper++;
  }
```

Save the file.

This will only show one error at a time because of the return null exits. So if the user has left three of the required fields empty, then the first time they try to save, they'll only be shown the error about a missing amount; then, if they only fill that in and try to save again, they'll be pestered about a missing restaurant selection; then if they fill that in, too, on the next save they'll be told about the missing date. This is an annoyance, but it's one that usually only befalls software testers, who deliberately leave everything empty to see what happens. In practice, a user who leaves everything empty either really wasn't paying attention or pressed Save by accident, and seeing the first of the errors will hopefully cue them to notice and fix the others as well.

> If you prefer to take the approach of "show everything that's wrong with the form at the same time," then have a look at the badData Boolean approach we're about to use for the meal list, and adapt it to this save() function.

It may strike you as odd that we set all three of our new Booleans to false at the beginning of the save() function. This is to clear any previous errors. We're making a fresh attempt at saving and we're doing a fresh set of error checks. If we didn't do this, old error messages wouldn't disappear from the page even if their particular problem had been fixed.

While we're thinking about error handling, there's another part of this application where we haven't done any error handling *at all*, not even a "do nothing if bad data" fallback. Have you noticed it?

It's the meal list. Right now, you could save an edited meal with no amount (which would not be a huge problem) or no date (which would—the local storage key would be malformed and we wouldn't be able to retrieve it again to display or delete the meal).

Ideally, if the user has tried to provide empty or bad data for an amount or date field in this list, we'd highlight that particular field so the user knows exactly where the problem is. Unfortunately, that's impossible to do without completely redesigning the way we generate this output, and frankly, for this list, it would be overkill. We hope the user won't be editing meal data very often in the first place, and the nature of the list, with each meal having its own Save button, means they'll only be editing one meal at a time. So we can get away with displaying a single set of "bad data" messages at the top of the page if something is wrong, and presumably the user is aware of which item they were editing.

We do want to display all errors at the same time, though. If they have a bad amount *and* a bad date, we want to tell them about both problems at once. So we use a different method here than we did in the meal-entry component.

Open meal-list.component.ts.

Add three new component variable declarations:

```
badData = false;
badDataMessage1 = '';
badDataMessage2 = '';
```

Change the save() function so it reads like this:

```
save(amount: string, newtype: string, newdate: string,
     oldtype: string, olddate: string): void {
  let mydate = moment(newdate, 'MM/DD/YYYY');
  let amtAsNum = parseFloat(amount);

  this.badDataMessage1 = '';
  this.badDataMessage2 = '';
  this.badData = false;

  if (isNaN(amtAsNum)) {
    this.badDataMessage1 = "Please enter a numeric amount.";
    this.badData = true;
  }
  else {
    if (amtAsNum <= 0) {
      this.badDataMessage1 = "Please enter an amount greater than zero.";
      this.badData = true;
    }
  }
  if (!newdate) {
    this.badDataMessage2 = "Please enter a date.";
    this.badData = true;
  }
  else {
    if (!mydate.isValid()) {
      this.badDataMessage2 = "Please enter a valid date.";
      this.badData = true;
    }
  }

  if (!this.badData) {
    return null;
  }

  newdate = mydate.format('YYYYMMDD');

  console.log('delete before save:', olddate, oldtype,
              this.selectedRestaurant);
  this.mealService.delete(olddate, oldtype, this.selectedRestaurant);

  console.log('save', amount, newdate, newtype, this.selectedRestaurant);
  this.mealService.create(newdate, newtype,
                          this.selectedRestaurant, amount);
}
```

The idea here is that if any of our bad-or-missing-data conditions is hit, we set up a message for that particular kind of error, and we set the `badData` Boolean to true. Once all our checks are complete, if `badData` is still false (which is what we initialized it to before we started the checks), we can go ahead and save; if not, we exit without doing anything. The template will show all the error messages we set if `badData` is true. Of course, we have to actually add lines to the template to do that!

Save this file and open `meal-list.component.html`.

Just *before* the iterating `<div>`:

```
<div *ngFor="let m of meals"
  class="form-group row edit-meals-width mb-1 mx-auto">
```

add these lines:

```
<div *ngIf="badData" class="alert alert-danger">
  <p *ngIf="badDataMessage1">{{badDataMessage1}}</p>
  <p *ngIf="badDataMessage2">{{badDataMessage2}}</p>
</div>
```

Notice we've put each of the two possible messages in its own paragraph with its own `*ngIf`, so that the paragraph won't display or leave an empty line if the message is empty.

Save your work.

MOVING FORWARD

At this point, your application is as complete as it's going to be—at least as far as this book is concerned.

Certainly there is always room for improvement. For example, the meal-listing page, as noted in the previous section, is pretty minimal. There are new features, not in our scope, which could conceivably be planned and added. But those things are, as they say, left as an exercise for the student.

Although we hope that by now you've gotten a grasp of the basic techniques needed to write the underlying code for a web application, we don't pretend to have provided any more than that—the basics. There is much, much more to learn. At the end of this book, we provide some resources to learn more about the languages and frameworks you've begun to work with here.

YOUR ASSIGNMENT

Before proceeding to Chapter 9, your homework for this chapter is to test your application. Thoroughly. Better yet, ask someone who hasn't seen the application before to test it for you—new users almost always find bugs you'd never find yourself.

For a large application with many functions and pages, testing might require a full-scale *unit testing* plan, where each and every individual component or operation of the application is listed, and then all possible functions or malfunctions of that operation are listed, along with tests for each. That's probably too much for an app as small as ours, and yet there's more complexity here than you might think.

Let's consider a very simple component of our app, the control to add a new restaurant: the text field plus its checkmark button. (There would also be tests of whether it appears and disappears properly when the control to hide or show it is pressed, but that's a different component.) Confining ourselves to this one, we'd not only want to test that a restaurant name is saved properly, added to the selection list properly, and selected, but we'd also want to test failure modes. What happens when we press the checkmark without typing in a restaurant name? What happens if we just type spaces in the text field?[29] What happens if we paste some foreign-language or special characters into the text field?

Testing mostly doesn't involve checking the way things work when they go right. Instead, it's about trying to predict and prevent (or at least plan for) the ways things can go *wrong*. So far, we're guessing that you've tried a few bits of test data and then moved on. That's not good enough. The long-term averages in the trends functions require quite a lot of test data to determine whether they're working properly. You don't have a clear idea yet of whether the meal listing will be unwieldy when there are two hundred entries for a particular restaurant on the page. There's a function you probably haven't tested yet at all (the one we added in this chapter to delete all meals for a particular restaurant).

Try to put together a general overview of every operation this application performs, and then give some thought to testing the ways in which each might break. If you don't find the problems, someone using your application will.

---

[29] Bad things happen. Not fatally bad. A string of spaces defeats our "there's nothing in this field" test and will get saved as a restaurant with an empty name. We didn't go back and try to work around it because it didn't seem worth fixing; the user would almost have to be trying to do it deliberately. Besides, they can use and/or delete an empty-named restaurant; it's just confusing. Conversely, we tried several different sets of peculiar characters and they all worked fine. We had a lot of fun with the tests where all the restaurant names were phrases in Cyrillic and Japanese.

DEPLOYMENT

At this point, you have a fully operational and hopefully well-tested web application.

The only problem is that it's sitting on your local computer, only reachable via a temporary local web server, and it's in the middle of an installation of development tools and packages probably somewhere close to 200 MB in size, most of which you don't actually need to run the application.

One possibility for mobile devices is to use a tool such as Apache Cordova (cordova.apache.org) to "wrap" your web application as a free-standing mobile app. Cordova does this by, in essence, creating its own temporary local web server. When you launch a Cordova–wrapped app, invisibly it's doing more or less the same thing we've been doing when we run `npm start` and launch the `localhost:3000` web server. It's just not obvious to the user that this is happening. (See page 268 for more about Cordova and similar tools.)

But for most uses, a web application is launched from an external server. That means you have to decide on (and possibly pay for) a remote location where your application's files are stored and run. We can't pick a hosting provider for you, but options range from "cheap and not very helpful or reliable" to "bulletproof but expensive."

For now, let's behave as if you've picked a hosting provider somewhere. Minimally, what you have is an empty filespace and possibly nothing more than that. For the lowest-rent hosting providers, you don't have any control over the actual web server being run or its configuration—you're merely given a place to put files. That's all right. For our purposes, that suffices (as long as the site allows execution of JavaScript, and we don't presently know of any that don't).

We use *hosting provider* to mean some provider of remote filespace and possibly some web tools. The only tool they're required to provide is the web *server*, by which we mean the program that responds to requests from web browsers. When you go to a URL, you're really asking a server at that URL for a directory or a file. The web server must then know how to interpret the URL and send some sort of response—a web page or an error—back to you. Apache is a web server, as are NGINX and Microsoft's IIS. Remote-site providers like Amazon Web Services (aws.amazon.com) or Dreamhost® (dreamhost.com) are hosting providers. Bear in mind that not everyone makes this clear a distinction between the two.

This theoretical system at your hosting provider has an *htdocs root directory*—the topmost directory the web server can "see" and serve files from—and we're going to treat that directory as if it has a path of /, which is the way the web server thinks of it. We did this for the local server as well—our project directory may have been something like `D:\Angular Apps\TastyTracker`, but our local server treated the project directory as if it were /, the topmost directory.

When you go to an unqualified URL (no explicit directory or file names included in the URL) on a web domain somewhere, like this

    somedomain.com/

you're actually asking for the contents of the htdocs root directory from that domain, whatever it may be. Back in the early days of the web, the behavior if you didn't ask for a specific file was to literally list the contents of that directory: you'd be shown a list of the files in the `htdocs` root, and usually you could click on the name of any listed file to obtain it. This doesn't happen much anymore—it's not very secure and sites would rather control what they show you in any particular directory. However, there's still an implied rule; most web servers are configured so that if the user doesn't ask for a specific file, `index.html` will be shown by default.

So although this is obviously subject to the web server's configuration, it's usually a reasonable assumption that

    somedomain.com/

will try to show the user the contents of `index.html` from the `htdocs` root, whereas

    somedomain.com/somefile.html

will try to show somefile.html instead. Also,

    somedomain.com/some_directory/

will try to show the contents of an `index.html` file from the directory `some_directory` under the `htdocs` root, and

    somedomain.com/some_directory/somefile.html

will try to show `somefile.html` from `some_directory`.

In all cases, if the requested file doesn't exist or for some reason can't be shown, the web server will either display an appropriate error or fall back to displaying some other page, depending on how it was configured.

Knowing the paths on your (hypothetical) hosting provider's system is going to be very important later in this chapter. Depending on the system, you might be asked to upload your files into a directory that looks very different from the way the web server sees it. On one of our personal hosting providers, for example, the directory `/var/www/htdocs` is the *real* path of the htdocs root—but to the web server, that directory is the top, `/`. We're going to give remote paths from the web server's point of view; if we say to put a file into `/`, we mean put it into whatever directory your web server thinks is `/`.

DOWNSIZING THE APP

Most of the packages you've installed via npm contain a whole lot of stuff you don't actually need. They may contain the source files used to create the parts we *do* use or contain supporting tools that aren't needed once we have the final-form JavaScript libraries and CSS files we want.

Trying to figure out the only parts you need to run the app is a surprisingly tricky business. It may seem easy at the beginning—you know which JavaScript libraries you need, because between `index.html`, `systemjs.config.js`, and the application components themselves, they're all listed right there in the code. But those libraries can include other libraries, and *those* libraries can include other libraries. . . . To give just one example, our code doesn't directly refer to any parts of the RxJS (Reactive Extensions) toolkit—but we need many of them nonetheless, because the Angular libraries use them.

You could "walk through" all the files, searching for requirements and inclusions, and build a *dependency tree* yourself. This particular application is small enough that it's doable. (And it's what we did; it took an afternoon to do.) But some of the JavaScript involved doesn't make it easy—for example, the Angular libraries use a syntax for their required files that is hard for the novice to spot—and for a larger project, the task would be unmanageable.

At the time we went to press, the state of tools to help wrangle such things in an Angular 2 environment wasn't great. There are plenty of packages in JavaScript that do nothing but search out and display dependency trees—they look at the contents of the JavaScript files, try to figure out who needs what, and show you the results. But they don't do well with Angular components; they don't understand the syntax. (Yet. We fully expect that the tools will improve over time.)

These tools are called *bundlers,* and they grab the required files and create a *distribution* directory that has only those files in it. The bundler that Angular recommends using, Webpack (webpack.github.io), not only doesn't seem to work properly on our hybrid app of Angular using SystemJS plus Bootstrap and straight JavaScript libraries, but it's designed to create merged files— that is, it will create one enormous JavaScript file called something like `tastytracker.js` instead of preserving the identities of individual files. This seems counterproductive from a beginner's perspective.[30]

We're going to do it the hard way as a learning experience. But don't worry; we've done the trickiest bit, sorting out the minimal set of dependencies.

From our own files, we need our `index.html`, `styles.css`, and `systemjs.config.js` files from the project directory, and all `.js`, `.css`, and `.html` files from the app directory. We don't actually need to distribute the `.ts` files, which compile to JavaScript, nor the `.map` files, which are used to perform that compilation. It's the JavaScript that actually gets used. However, if you've made changes recently, you probably want to generate a fresh copy of the `.js` files, either by using the command `npm run tsc` or just starting the server with `npm start` and then stopping it again after it's finished loading.

Next, we have the list of dependencies outside our own files. For each of these we've included two filenames where possible. The second one, in parentheses, is the *minified* version of the file. This version has all of the extra spaces, line breaks, etc. removed and has other changes to reduce the size of the file. Unfortunately, the side effect of minification is to make the file nearly unreadable by humans. We'll be using the minified versions, but they don't save all that much space, and it's perfectly acceptable to choose to use the non-minified version instead.

Don't worry about moving these files around yet. When we distribute them, we'll be using a different directory setup. We'll get to that in the next section.

```
node_modules/@angular/common/bundles/common.umd.js (common.umd.min.js)
node_modules/@angular/compiler/bundles/compiler.umd.js (compiler.umd
.min.js)
node_modules/@angular/core/bundles/core.umd.js (core.umd.min.js)
node_modules/@angular/forms/bundles/forms.umd.js (forms.umd.min.js)
node_modules/@angular/platform-browser/bundles/platform-browser.umd.js
(platform-browser.umd.min.js)
node_modules/@angular/platform-browser-dynamic/bundles/platform-
browser-dynamic.umd.js (platform-browser-dynamic.umd.min.js)
```

---

[30] We reached a point in trying to deal with Webpack where we realized that we could get it to work, but only if we completely undid SystemJS's path handling, which is a vital part of the application as currently written. We didn't feel it was worth trying to do that—almost every file in the app would need to be altered—at this stage in the process. Webpack is probably going to be around for a while, though, and you may find it worthwhile to investigate. You may also want to search for resources on tools which try to use SystemJS's path handling to bundle applications; search for "SystemJS bundler." But beware: here be dragons.

```
node_modules/@angular/router/bundles/router.umd.js (router.umd.min.js)
node_modules/bootstrap/dist/css/bootstrap.min.css (bootstrap.min.css)
node_modules/bootstrap/dist/js/bootstrap.js (currently no minified
version)
node_modules/core-js/client/shim.js (shim.min.js)
node_modules/font-awesome/css/font-awesome.css (font-awesome.min.css)
node_modules/font-awesome/fonts/* (all files in this directory)
node_modules/jquery/dist/jquery.js (jquery.min.js)
node_modules/moment/locale/* (all files in this directory)
node_modules/moment/moment.js (minified is node_modules/moment/min/
moment.min.js)
node_modules/reflect-metadata/Reflect.js (no minified version)
node_modules/rxjs/ (see remarks following this list)
node_modules/systemjs/dist/system.js (system.src.js)
node_modules/tether/dist/js/tether.js (tether.min.js)
node_modules/zone.js/dist/zone.js (zone.min.js)
```

The RxJS libraries are the ones that have the most complicated set of dependencies. Many of them depend on each other, and several of the Angular libraries use them. The list of all forty-seven RxJS files we'll need appears in the next section, when we discuss the actual distribution structure.

This complicated list of files and directories brings up an issue we want to solve when posting files to our hosting provider.

SYSTEMJS AND RELATIVE PATHS

We need one Angular library out of each of seven deeply nested subdirectories. Do we really have to duplicate that whole directory tree just to use those files? That is, on our hosting provider, do we have to make node_modules, then @Angular, then common, then bundles, just to put a single file, common.umd.min.js, in it? None of the Angular libraries share the same filename (a *name collision*) with each other or any of the other libraries we need. In fact, there are no name collisions between any of our required files at all. (Lucky, lucky!) What's stopping us from just creating a libraries or js directory on our hosting provider and dropping all the .js files we need into it—flat, one-stop shopping without bothering with any of these subdirectories?

Well, as it happens, we *can* do that and mostly will. But as we do so, we have to respect the way the files want to find *each other*, which is beyond our control.

For example, the Angular common library, common.umd.min.js or its non-minified equivalent, requires the Angular core library. If the inclusion in common.umd.min.js looked like this

```
require('core.umd.min.js')
```

then it would be expecting to find `core.umd.min.js` in the same directory as itself. (Because there's no explicit path, "look in the same place as this" is assumed.) We could put the two files anywhere we like as long as they were both in the same place.

But those Angular files don't use actual `.js` file names in their requirements, and they don't use actual paths, either. What the `require` statement in `common.umd.js` actually says equates to[31] this:

```
require('@angular/core')
```

which has neither a real filename nor a real path in which to find it.

Angular depends on the SystemJS module loader to translate those non-paths and non-filenames into a real file location. Which is great for us, because it means when we move our libraries around, the only files we need to edit are `index.html` and `systemjs.config.js`. (We definitely do *not* want to have to edit any of the individual library files.) But we still have all these Angular libraries wanting to look for each other in `@angular`, whatever we set that to mean. In short, our Angular libraries can all live in the same directory, as long as we tell SystemJS that the fake paths starting with `@angular` all translate to that directory.

With RxJS, we can't flatten out the various subdirectories because of the way those libraries refer to one another. We tried to, using SystemJS trickery. It didn't work. There we must preserve the subdirectory structure.

Here's the structure we're going to set up on our hypothetical hosting provider:

- `/` [htdocs root] will contain `index.html`, `styles.css`, and `systemjs.config.js`

- `/app` will contain all the `.css`, `.html`, and `.js` files from our own `app` directory

- `/fonts` will contain Font Awesome's font files

- `/js` will contain all `.js` dependencies not in Angular or RxJS, plus two `.css` dependencies

- `/js/@angular` will contain all the Angular dependencies

- `/js/rxjs` will contain all the RxJS dependencies (some in subdirectories)

- `/js/locale` will contain moment's locale files

Font Awesome's font files don't go in a directory under `/js` because of the way Font Awesome looks for them, which is `../fonts` (meaning, "go up one level from wherever you are now and

---

[31] "Equates to" because there is no literal `require` statement anywhere in the Angular libraries that looks like our examples. They create the `require` statements dynamically, but the end result is the same.

then down into a fonts directory"). We'd rather treat it as a special case than edit the font-awesome.css file. (Again, we're trying to *not* change any files we didn't create ourselves.)

The full list of files needed, and the locations where they would be placed on your hypothetical web server, can be found in the file about_server_paths.txt in the tastytracker-demo-pkg directory.

Two of the files listed in about_server_paths.txt need to be modified before being put on the web server: index.html and systemjs.config.js. These both have to change because of the differences in paths between the development and production environments. Assuming that you couldn't modify the files directly in the production filesystem (some hosting providers don't equip you with file-editing tools), you'd want to make copies of those files and save modified versions of them in a different location locally, so as not to overwrite your original versions. The changes we'll make are to enable the app to run in our new directory organization, but these changes won't work with the directory setup we've been using in our development environment.

For index.html, every file path in a <script> or <link> tag that points somewhere in node_modules must now be altered to point into js, *without any of its previous subdirectories*. For example,

```
<script src="node_modules/core-js/client/shim.min.js"></script>
```

would now become

```
<script src="js/shim.min.js"></script>
```

Don't put a leading / on those paths. There are ten paths in this file that need alteration. The path to systemjs.config.js stays as it was, because it'll still be in the same directory as index.html.

This is also the point where you should update the filenames if you've decided to use a minified version where you previously weren't (or vice versa).

The other file that needs changes is systemjs.config.js. The primary change we're going to make is to the map portion. We're going to tell it to look for all Angular inclusions in the same place, and we'll also tinker with where to find moment.

```
map: {
  app: 'app', // Our stuff lives here.
  '@angular/common': 'npm:@angular/common.umd.min.js',
  '@angular/compiler': 'npm:@angular/compiler.umd.min.js',
  '@angular/core': 'npm:@angular/core.umd.min.js',
  '@angular/forms': 'npm:@angular/forms.umd.min.js',
  '@angular/platform-browser':
      'npm:@angular/platform-browser.umd.min.js',
  '@angular/platform-browser-dynamic':
      'npm:@angular/platform-browser-dynamic.umd.min.js',
  '@angular/router': 'npm:@angular/router.umd.min.js',
  'moment': 'npm:',
  'rxjs': 'npm:rxjs'
},
```

We kept the npm: prefix because it was easier than changing it in all these lines, but we need to change its meaning as well, up in the paths section:

```
paths: {
  'npm:': 'js/'
},
```

If you had a version of this file before that was using moment.min.js, then it used to be in a min subdirectory and now isn't. The moment: section of the packages area should now look like this:

```
moment: {
  main: './moment.min.js',
  defaultExtension: 'js'
},
```

Again, if you've chosen to use the minified versions of the various files where you previously weren't, or vice versa, make the appropriate name substitutions.

At this point, if you followed all the instructions above on your theoretical hosting provider, you have a running app. You would go to it via a URL to that site using whatever base web domain and so forth are given to you by your hosting provider. Since we're assuming your starting-point file is index.html and it's in the htdocs root, if the domain of your new hosting provider was mywebservice.com, you could direct your browser to mywebservice.com/ and your app would start.

But what if you couldn't do it that way?

VARIATIONS

Sometimes you'll be trying to run several different things on the same hosting provider. Sometimes you want the app to live in its own directory tree so that it doesn't interfere with other things you run from the same filesystem. Sometimes you'll want the starting point of the app to be a file that isn't index.html.

On one location we used for testing, the topmost directory of the app was /test_webapp, though all the subdirectories below that were the same. So index.html was in /test_webapp, moment.min.js was in /test_webapp/js, core.umd.min.js was in /test_webapp/js/@angular, and so on.

Accommodating this required only a single change.

At the top of index.html is a <base> tag:

```
<base href="/"/>
```

If the directory you're using as the "top" directory for your app (where index.html will live) is the same as the htdocs root directory, as it was in our prior example, you don't need to alter this tag. But in this new situation, where everything began at /test_webapp, we had to change the tag to

```
<base href="/test_webapp/"/>
```

to get everything to behave properly. (Both the leading and trailing slashes are important, so don't forget them.)

The <base> tag says, "Insert this path at the beginning of all relative paths provided elsewhere in this file." The path is from the point of view of the web server—it's telling the web server where relative paths found elsewhere in index.html will begin. (That's why the <base> tag has to come *before* any paths to other files.) Any paths that don't start with / are relative paths. So with a base of /, js/shim.min.js becomes /js/shim.min.js; with a base of /test_webapp/, js/shim.min.js becomes /test_webapp/js/shim.min.js, etc. This is very important for finding these dependencies correctly.

The <base> tag, in short, controls "where is the top directory" for your app. And, once again, all of this is from the web server's point of view! On the test server described, the *real* path was /var/www/htdocs/test_webapp, where /var/www/htdocs was what the web server considered to be its htdocs root /.

All of this path madness is designed to facilitate doing a lot of things in a single location. Big hosting providers could be storing thousands of people's sites in the same filespace; to prevent everyone's web pages from stepping on one another, each user is given their own web server configuration, which has its own "starting point." In effect, a single filespace is treated as if it's thousands of individual spaces, all neatly fenced off. As a user of a hosting provider, you hopefully won't have to notice this or care—but we're explaining it in case you do have to.

Now for a different variation. Put that `test_webapp` example aside and return to the previous setup, the file structure based in htdocs root. The `<base>` tag remains set to `/`. The difference now is, because you already have an `index.html` there that's doing something else important, you want the starting-point file to be called `tt.html` (for TastyTracker, of course). That's the only thing we want to change: the name of one file.

You might think that this just means a URL change; you can no longer start the app by just going to mywebservice.com/ but must go explicitly to mywebservice.com/tt.html instead.

It would be nice if that were all it took. Unfortunately, what will happen is you'll get a message in the web console about not being able to resolve `tt.html`. That message comes from the Angular router.

Actually, depending on your web server's configuration, you're likely to find that the router is refusing to behave properly even if your starting point is `index.html`. The navigational links between pages work fine; but if you try to load one of the page URLs directly—for example mywebservice.com/meal-entry—it won't work, and you'll get a "page not found" error.

FIXING THE ROUTER

The problem is that your web server is trying to do something with these URLs before Angular can get to them, and they're not real URLs. mywebservice.com/meal-entry is only meaningful to the router; it doesn't refer to an actual file anywhere in your production filesystem. But the only way we get the router to load is to come in through the starting-point file and load all our dependencies and components in the usual way.

What we need is to be able to load our starting-point file and all the other goodies no matter which of our URLs we go to, so the whole system can initialize properly—and yet still be aware of which of our two pages the user is requesting, so we can display the right thing.

To fix this, we need a special version of the app.routing.js file, one that we'll use only on the production filesystem and is separate from the version we used in development . . . and we need a little trickery.

You can either make the edits to app.routing.ts and recompile it into its .js version, or you could take a copy of app.routing.js and make edits to it directly. Unlike some of the other compiled .js files, this one is readable by mere mortals.

If you choose to edit and recompile app.routing.ts, change the appRoutes declaration to:

```
const appRoutes: Routes = [
  { path: '', redirectTo: '/meal-entry.html', pathMatch: 'full' },
  { path: 'meal-entry', redirectTo: '/meal-entry.html', pathMatch: 'full' },
  { path: 'meal-list', redirectTo: '/meal-list.html', pathMatch: 'full' },
  { path: 'meal-entry.html', component: MealEntryComponent },
  { path: 'meal-list.html', component: MealListComponent }
];
```

If you choose to edit app.routing.js directly, change the appRoutes declaration to:

```
var appRoutes = [
  { path: '', redirectTo: '/meal-entry.html', pathMatch: 'full' },
  { path: 'meal-entry', redirectTo: '/meal-entry.html', pathMatch: 'full' },
  { path: 'meal-list', redirectTo: '/meal-list.html', pathMatch: 'full' },
  { path: 'meal-entry.html',
    component: meal_entry_component_1.MealEntryComponent },
  { path: 'meal-list.html',
    component: meal_list_component_1.MealListComponent }
];
```

As always in the router, line order is important. What we're saying here is that, by default, we go to a URL of meal-entry.html, and the paths we use for the intra-page links (meal-entry and meal-list) also go to meal-entry.html and meal-list.html respectively. meal-entry.html and meal-list.html are now the URLs that actually load components; the others redirect to them.

Now comes the trickery. We need to make *real files* for meal-entry.html and meal-list.html. Otherwise the web server is still going to display a 404 error when you ask for them directly. There are two ways we can do this, and which one you use depends on what kind of access your hosting provider has given you. If you can get to a command line (and it will surely be a UNIX® command line), you can make *symbolic links*. These are similar to aliases on a Mac or shortcuts on a Windows computer. If you can't get to a command line to make symlinks, then there's a more wasteful way.

Assuming that you can get to a command prompt: go to the directory where your app's index.html file lives (we discuss the variation where you've named it tt.html or whatever in just a moment), and enter these two commands:

```
ln -s index.html meal-entry.html
ln -s index.html meal-list.html
```

What you've just done is create two imaginary files, meal-entry.html and meal-list .html, in the same directory as index.html. The web server can ask for them and display them, and treats them as real files; but they're really just "pointing to" index.html, and what's actually displayed and run is the contents of index.html.

This may not be possible. Even if you have a command line available to you, on some systems you need special permissions to make symlinks. No worries. There's another way: just make copies. Make one copy of index.html called meal-entry.html and another copy called meal-list .html and put all three on the hosting provider. As already noted, this is wasteful (three copies of the same file, all absolutely identical except for their names), and it's also bad programming practice, because if you make changes to one of them, you have to remember to change the other two as well. But it keeps both the web server and the router happy. The router sees which name is being asked for and will display the appropriate content, even though all three files are launching the application and initializing everything exactly the same way.

If you're in the situation where your starting-point file is called tt.html (or whatever file name you've chosen), then you'd still make symlinks or copies, just substituting the name of your file where the instructions above say index.html. But in that situation, you'll also need to make one more change to the router. The route that reads

```
{ path: '', redirectTo: '/meal-entry.html', pathMatch: 'full' },
```

should change to

```
{ path: 'tt.html', redirectTo: '/meal-entry.html', pathMatch: 'full' },
```

(Obviously, substitute whatever actual file name you've decided to use.) This is needed because a default empty path isn't useful to us in that situation; instead, the router needs to know what to do when tt.html is requested specifically.

Armed with all of this esoterica, you should be able to keep both the web server and the router happy in a wide variety of situations.

PRODUCTION MODE

There's one final change you may or may not wish to make to the version of the app you deploy on your hosting provider.

As you've tested various phases of this app, you've surely noticed the warning in the web console about how Angular is running in development mode, and you should `enableProdMode()` when you're ready to make a production version.

You do this by changing `main.ts` to read

```
import { platformBrowserDynamic } from '@angular/platform-browser-dynamic';
import { enableProdMode } from '@angular/core';
import { AppModule } from './app.module';
const platform = platformBrowserDynamic();
enableProdMode();
platform.bootstrapModule(AppModule);
```

and recompiling it and using the new `main.js` file so obtained.

Frankly, the biggest difference we noticed was how that warning disappeared. It's possible that the application started a *tiny* bit faster in production mode. The Angular reference pages say very little about what this change actually does internally. Still, it's harmless, so try it and see. (However, when changing code, make and test those changes in development mode first; production mode may conceal errors that you'd want to be aware of.)

TAKING IT FURTHER

With the application complete, ready for you or a Donna you know to start using it, it's time to look further ahead.

REPOSITORIES

If you've written software you'd like to share with others, either because you want their contributions to your code or because you simply want to show off what you've done, you could post it to a public *repository* online. Repositories are simply codebase storage areas that allow people to download code, *check out* some or all of it to make changes, *check in* their changes, and see previous versions of the code. These check out/check in features are especially important when multiple developers are working on the same large codebase, because they allow the system to keep track of who's doing what, which can prevent or resolve *conflicts*: those cases when different developers make changes to the same part of the code. When that happens, the system requires the developer to look at the conflicting changes and make a decision about which updates should be included.

Version control like this has been available for many years through commercial and open-source software, usually hosted by the organization building the software. However, development teams are now often turning to cloud-based solutions to handle this. The most well-known of these cloud-based version control systems is GitHub.

Because GitHub is so widely used, other sites and tools, such as npm's package listing (npmjs .com) and Adobe PhoneGap™'s cloud-based hybrid mobile app tool (discussed later in this chapter), integrate with GitHub repositories. For example, if you've already decided to store your code at GitHub to let other people contribute to it, you can also distribute your code as an npm package simply by creating an account on npmjs.com and supplying your GitHub repository URL as the package source.

You can use either GitHub's website or its Mac and Windows desktop clients to create a repository. Refer to GitHub's documentation (help.github.com) for help setting up and configuring your first repository.

HYBRID MOBILE APPS

As we mentioned in the introduction to this book, hybrid mobile apps run as individual software items on your phone but are initially constructed as web apps. You can build these apps in Bootstrap or other frameworks, although Ionic is an especially popular option. (Ionic is now built to use Angular 2, which you learned in this book, so you may find it easier to pick up than other frameworks.)

But in order to get what you've built into a form your phone can use, you need special software to wrap your web app in phone-friendly code. Two common choices for this are Apache Cordova, which is free and open-source, and Adobe PhoneGap, which is free for most projects, depending on how you use it. Ionic also has a cloud-based app development and deployment system called Ionic Cloud, but it's geared more toward native mobile apps than hybrid ones.

Both Cordova and PhoneGap work similarly, which isn't surprising when you realize that PhoneGap is based on Cordova. The primary difference is that Cordova works purely on the command line, whereas PhoneGap has been extended beyond that to work with Mac and Windows clients or a cloud-based option, PhoneGap Build.

Because Cordova requires command-line access, using it is a little more cumbersome than using Adobe's downloadable or cloud-based PhoneGap clients. However, you should be familiar with the command line by now, so if you want to use Cordova, download it with npm and follow the basic instructions at cordova.apache.org/docs/en/latest/guide/cli/index.html for creating, testing, and deploying an app. You may need to download special *SDKs* (software development kits) to ensure Cordova has the tools it needs to wrap your application appropriately; software emulators with the SDKs can help you test what your app looks like on a phone or tablet before you release it.

Both PhoneGap and Cordova require an XML configuration file describing the application and the platforms you're targeting. This config.xml file outlines basic app metadata, such as the author name and app version number, and optionally can include information about which platforms you're targeting, the plugins you're using, and so on.[32]

PhoneGap includes command-line tools similar to Cordova's. However, its desktop clients and cloud-based options are friendlier to people with limited technical experience. The desktop client allows you to create a project based on standard templates and runs its own internal server (much like npm) so that you can see how your app works in a browser—and better yet, on your phone—simply by pointing PhoneGap's free Android or iOS clients to the desktop client's server URL. The cloud-based option is even more straightforward, providing you've already packaged your app or posted code to GitHub; it will read directly from an uploaded ZIP file of your app or a GitHub URL to create the hybrid mobile app automatically.

ASYNCHRONOUS SERVICES

Although it wasn't within the scope of this book to set up an actual web-based data service, many web applications use them. This involves interacting with the data in an asynchronous way, when you're not sure how long it will take the data service to respond and you want to allow the app to continue working while you wait. You'll find a discussion of the basics of asynchronous operations in the about_asynchronous_data.txt file in the tastytracker-demo-pkg directory.

YOUR ASSIGNMENT

We'd like to say that your homework for this chapter is to find a hosting provider and deploy this app as described. We recognize that may not be a reasonable thing to ask; still, we encourage you to do so if it's at all possible. Sometimes it's impossible to tell how an application will behave in production until it's actually deployed. We would never have known about the router issues described in this chapter, for example, until we deployed to a remote filesystem; they don't happen when using the app on the local test server.

When putting an app in production for the first time, it's a good idea to allow yourself time to check the app and test it before letting others know it exists. Although "testing in production" is something you want to avoid, problems do happen; better for you to find them before you open

---

[32] For the complete list of config.xml options, see the Cordova documentation at cordova.apache.org/docs/en/6.x/config_ref/index.html. Also, the free ConfiGAP tool (configap.com), available for Mac and Windows, simplifies the process of creating a config.xml file for PhoneGap Build.

the doors to users. The worst bug is the one you learn about only after *hundreds* of users have already found it.

We also have one final assignment for you: figure out where you want to go next. You could decide to pursue programming in depth by attending classes at school, college, or a programming boot camp. You could decide to keep plugging away on your own; as you've seen, there are plenty of resources, though they require dedication and patience to wade through. (If you've made it this far in the book, you've got dedication and patience to spare.) You could decide you're only interested in the UX side of things or the programming side instead of the design side and seek out more resources for only the pieces you care about. Or you could decide that none of this is for you, and that's okay, too. The important thing is that you gave it a fair shot.

We wrote this book because we wanted to teach people that anyone can get a real web app off the ground. If you've followed through to the end, you've done that, and you have our heartfelt thanks and congratulations. (You get those even if you didn't finish, but those who *did* get extra congrats.) Design and programming take imagination, but, most of all, they take perseverance.

If you're ready, we want you to take that next step.

RESOURCES

USER RESEARCH AND USER EXPERIENCE DESIGN

There are more books and online resources in this category than we could possibly hope to list, so here are a few favorites:

- Jesse James Garrett, *The Elements of User Experience: User-Centered Design for the Web and Beyond* (2nd Edition) (New Riders, 2010)
- Steve Krug, *Don't Make Me Think, Revisited: A Common Sense Approach to Web Usability* (3rd Edition) (New Riders, 2014)
- The Mozilla Firefox team's detailed analysis of how they researched and developed user types for the browser: blog.mozilla.org/ux/2013/08/firefox-user-types-in-north-america/

RESPONSIVE WEB DESIGN

Our favorite books in this category come from A Book Apart, a small press spun off from the popular A List Apart website that offers web design and front-end programming resources. A List Apart also hosts a conference, An Event Apart, that takes place several times a year at cities across the United States and is well worth your time if you're serious about learning the latest tools and techniques in the field. (However, it's not cheap; though educational discounts are available, at the time we write this, regular registration fees range from $599–$1,390.)

A List Apart is where designer/developer Ethan Marcotte, who coined the term "responsive web design," first discussed the topic. Both the site and Marcotte's books remain excellent resources.

- Ethan Marcotte, *Responsive Web Design* (A Book Apart, 2011)
- Ethan Marcotte, *Responsive Design: Patterns & Principles* (A Book Apart, 2015)

VISUAL DESIGN AND INTERFACE DESIGN

As with user research and user experience design, there are vastly more books in this category than we could hope to list. However, a few we recommend are:

- Very much for typography nerds, but a classic in the genre: Robert Bringhurst's *The Elements of Typographic Style* (Hartley and Marks, 2013)
- Theresa Neil, *Mobile Design Pattern Gallery* (2nd edition) (O'Reilly Media, 2014)

- Tania Schlatter and Deborah A. Levinson, *Visual Usability: Principles and Practices for Designing Digital Applications* (Morgan Kaufmann, 2014)

- Jennifer Tidwell, *Designing Interfaces* (2nd edition) (O'Reilly Media, 2011)

BOOTSTRAP

With Bootstrap 4 still in alpha as we write this book, we're reluctant to point you to any resources beyond the Bootstrap 4 documentation. However, the basic principles of Bootstrap's grid still apply, as do its class names, so Bootstrap 3 resources that concentrate on grid work remain accurate (barring changes to breakpoint pixel widths).

- Bootstrap 4 : v4-alpha.getbootstrap.com

- Bootstrap 3 : getbootstrap.com

JAVASCRIPT

We're partial to the Mozilla Developer Network's pages. In addition to the language reference, they offer a set of excellent tutorial pages. We've also been known to look things up in the W3Schools' JavaScript documentation; though we don't consider them absolutely reliable, they're organized more toward a view of "I'm trying to do this thing to this particular HTML page element—what's its syntax?" which is often convenient.

- developer.mozilla.org/en-US/docs/Web/JavaScript/Reference

- w3schools.com/jsref/

ANGULAR 2

Online resources are still unfortunately sparse and not very good. Perhaps by the time this book is in your hands, that will have changed, but when we wrote this, we had the Angular 2 site to work from and very little else. We found a vast amount of helpful information on the web—for Angular 1. Angular 2's syntax, unfortunately, is significantly different, and the help for one cannot easily be applied to the other.

- angular.io/

TYPESCRIPT

The best resource is TypeScript's own website . . . but if you don't know JavaScript, you'll be disappointed. The TypeScript documentation concentrates on what it does differently from

JavaScript and leaves other things unsaid, assuming you already know them. So, for example, you won't find the basic syntax of a `where` loop anywhere in the TypeScript documentation, since it's exactly the same as in JavaScript.

- typescriptlang.org/

WEB HOSTING

Web hosting providers come and go. Right now, Amazon Web Services (AWS) seems poised to take over the world, but that could change at any moment. Google seems to be interested in competing for that market, as are smaller operations, like Heroku®. And, of course, there are still plenty of independent hosting companies, sometimes serving only a particular area. The best way to find a hosting provider is to search, compare prices and services, and read user reviews of their service if possible.

That said, sometimes it's difficult to sort through the jargon. The most important point for the relative novice is being sure of what you'll get for your money. In order to run your app, you'll need what is sometimes called a "stack"—an operating system, a web server, possibly a language interpreter (if you're writing code in a language that needs one), and possibly a database. You'll see people refer to a "LAMP stack," for example. This means Linux (the operating system), Apache (the web server), MySQL® (the database), and a Perl® or PHP interpreter (two languages frequently used for the underlying code below web apps).

Heroku is an example of a provider that supplies prebuilt stacks. You choose which of many possible stacks you want, and you don't control their setup; you merely put your app files onto the remote filesystem and hope they work. Other providers do some of the work of setting up the stack for you but not all, and you may be left with configuration tasks, which can be a rude surprise if you don't know how to do them. And some providers simply give you an empty box—no stack at all; that's your job. Know what you're buying.

There is simply no way to make a comprehensive list. Shop around.

ACKNOWLEDGMENTS

Although we're the only two authors of this book, it could never have been written without the patient and invaluable assistance of our friends, family, and colleagues. We'd like to thank Francis Heaney for first bringing this writing opportunity to us; Hilary Hall for reading every single chapter and confirming that a design and programming newbie could follow along; our far-flung Internet friends in public and private online forums who cheered us on and sympathized with our frustrations; Tania Schlatter, without whom *Visual Usability* and therefore Chapter 3 would not exist; our anonymous research participants, especially Amy, Clara, Martha, and Rose, as well as Mickey, who couldn't take part in the research but egged us on with obscure *Doctor Who* references instead; and everyone at Sterling Publishing for taking this book from hastily scribbled proposal to a printed work. We're grateful to you all.

ABOUT THE AUTHORS

Deborah A. Levinson has worked for more than twenty years providing expert user experience design and consultation, usability testing, and content assessment to software companies, higher education, and nonprofit institutions, including MIT, Furman University, the American Academy of Arts & Sciences, and the Mind and Life Institute. She has also taught introductory responsive web coding and jQuery to design students at Northeastern University. Debby is an MIT graduate and the co-author of *Visual Usability: Principles and Practices for Designing Digital Applications* and *The MIT Guide to Teaching Web Site Design*.

Todd Belton started programming computers in elementary school. Today, he primarily writes middleware to glue large databases to web applications. In his spare time he writes things that are not code and plays more computer games than he cares to admit.

INDEX